CampusCareerCenter's
The Job Hunting Guide

By Ron and Caryl Krannich, Ph.Ds

CAREER AND BUSINESS BOOKS AND SOFTWARE

101 Dynamite Answers to Interview Questions
101 Secrets of Highly Effective Speakers
201 Dynamite Job Search Letters
America's Top Internet Job Sites
Best Jobs for the 21st Century
Change Your Job, Change Your Life
The Complete Guide to Public Employment
The Directory of Federal Jobs and Employers
Discover the Best Jobs for You!
Dynamite Cover Letters
Dynamite Networking for Dynamite Jobs
Dynamite Resumes
Dynamite Salary Negotiations
Dynamite Tele-Search
The Educator's Guide to Alternative Jobs and Careers
Find a Federal Job Fast!
From Air Force Blue to Corporate Gray
From Army Green to Corporate Gray
From Navy Blue to Corporate Gray
Get a Raise in 7 Days
High Impact Resumes and Letters
Interview for Success
Job-Power Source and *Ultimate Job Source* (software)
Jobs and Careers With Nonprofit Organizations
The Job Hunting Guide
Military Resumes and Cover Letters
Moving Out of Education
Moving Out of Government
No One Will Hire Me!
Re-Careering in Turbulent Times
Resumes & Job Search Letters for Transitioning Military Personnel
Savvy Interviewing
Savvy Networker
Savvy Resume Writer

INTERNATIONAL AND TRAVEL BOOKS

Best Resumes and CVs for International Jobs
The Complete Guide to International Jobs and Careers
The Directory of Websites for International Jobs
International Jobs Directory
Jobs for Travel Lovers
Mayors and Managers in Thailand
Politics of Family Planning Policy in Thailand
Shopping and Traveling in Exotic Asia
Shopping in Exotic Places
Shopping the Exotic South Pacific
Travel Planning On the Internet
Treasures and Pleasures of Australia
Treasures and Pleasures of China
Treasures and Pleasures of Egypt
Treasures and Pleasures of Hong Kong
Treasures and Pleasures of India
Treasures and Pleasures of Indonesia
Treasures and Pleasures of Italy
Treasures and Pleasures of Mexico
Treasures and Pleasures of Morocco
Treasures and Pleasures of Paris and the French Riviera
Treasures and Pleasures of the Philippines
Treasures and Pleasures of Rio and São Paulo
Treasures and Pleasures of Singapore and Bali
Treasures and Pleasures of Singapore and Malaysia
Treasures and Pleasures of Southern Africa
Treasures and Pleasures of Thailand and Myanmar
Treasures and Pleasures of Vietnam and Cambodia

The
Job Hunting
Guide

TRANSITIONING FROM COLLEGE TO CAREER

Ronald L. Krannich, Ph.D.
Caryl Rae Krannich, Ph.D.

IMPACT PUBLICATIONS
Manassas Park, Virginia

Warning/Liability/Warranty: The authors and publisher have made every attempt to provide the reader with accurate, timely, and useful information. However, given the rapid changes taking place in today's economy and job market, change are inevitable, especially when we refer to specific websites which often change names or go out of business. The information presented here is for reference purposes only. The authors and publisher make no claims that using this information will guarantee the reader a job. The authors and publisher shall not be liable for any losses or damages incurred in the process of following the advice in this book.

Library of Congress Cataloguing-in-Publication Data

Krannich, Ronald L.
    The job hunting guide: transitioning from college to career / Ronald
L. Krannich and Caryl Rae Krannich
        p. cm.
    Includes bibliographical references and index.
    ISBN 1-57023-188-5   2002115035

Publisher: For information on Impact Publications, including current and forthcoming publications, authors, press kits, online bookstore, and submission requirements, visit our website: www.impactpublications.com.

Publicity/Rights: For information on publicity, author interviews, and subsidiary rights, contact the Media Relations Department: Tel. 703-361-7300, Fax 703-335-9486, or email: info@impactpublications.com.

Sales/Distribution: All bookstore sales are handled through Impact's trade distributor: National Book Network, 15200 NBN Way, Blue Ridge Summit, PA 17214, Tel. 1-800-462-6420. All other sales and distribution inquiries should be directed to the publisher: Sales Department, IMPACT PUBLICATIONS, 9104 Manassas Drive, Suite N, Manassas Park, VA 20111-5211, Tel. 703-361-7300, Fax 703-335-9486, or email: info@impactpublications.com.

Contents

Preface . . . . **x**

1 A Season for Everything **1**

- An Important Transition   1
- New Skills for Success   2
- No One to Help You   3
- The Great Disconnect   4
- 90 Days and You're Out!   4
- 12 Months and You May Be History   5
- Your Crash Course to Success   5
- What's Your Hiring I.Q.?   6
- Resources for Organizing Your Future   8
- Cramming for Success   9

2 Do First Things First **10**

- Forget the Trendy Generation Talk   10
- Find the Right Job Proactively   11
- 15 Mistakes Job Seekers Make   13
- Seven Steps to Job Search Success   14
- Organize a 90-Day Plan for Success   17
- Seek Assistance   18
- Alternative Career Services   21
- *Meet the New Career Advisor*   22
- Locate a Certified Career Professional   27

- Consider an Internship   27
- Your CampusCareerCenter Connection   29
- Important Prerequisites for Success   30

3   Specify Your Motivated Abilities and Skills (MAS) 34

- What Can This Stranger Do for Me?   34
- Show Me the Evidence   36
- Identify Your Skills   37
- More Self-Assessment Techniques   47
- Computerized Assessment Systems   48
- Online Assessment Options   48
- Recommended Self-Assessment Books   49
- Make Discovering Your MAS a Top Priority   51

4   Discover Your Interests and Values   53

- Vocational Interests   53
- Work Values   57
- Computerized Programs and Online Services   62
- Your Future as Objectives   62

5   Formulate an Employer-Oriented Objective 63

- The Next Step   63
- Goals and Objectives   64
- Analyze Your Past, View Your Future   64
- *So What Should a New Grad Do?*   65
- Focus on Employers' Needs   66
- Be Purposeful and Realistic   67
- State Manageable Goals   67
- Incorporate Your Dreams   69
- Talk the Language of Employers   69
- Three Steps to Setting Realistic Goals   70
- State an Employer-Oriented Objective   82
- Gurus and Goal Setting Resources   84

6   Conduct Research   87

- Investigate Job and Career Alternatives   87
- Target Organizations   89
- *Be an Opportunist – Find a Company That's Right for You*   90

- Contact Individuals 91
- Ask the Right Questions 92
- Identify the Right Community 94
- Know What's Really Important 97

7 Create Winning Resumes and Letters 99

- Communicate Positive Images 99
- A Love-Hate Relationship 100
- Missing the Point 100
- Myths and Promising Realities 101
- Resume Writing Mistakes 111
- Production, Distribution, and Follow-Up Errors 113
- Types of Resumes 114
- Structuring Resume Content 116
- Producing Drafts 117
- Evaluating the Final Product 118
- Final Production 118
- Job Search Letters 119
- Basic Preparation Rules 120
- Types of Letters 121
- Distribution and Management 123
- Responding to Classified Ads 123
- *Effective Job Seekers Follow Through* 124
- Self-Initiated Methods 125
- Useful Books and Software 126
- Online Writing Assistance and Services 129
- Resume Blasting Services 130
- Tooting Your Horn With Focus 131
- Resume Examples 132
- Letter Examples 136

8 Network Your Way to a Great Job 145

- Advertised and Hidden Job Markets 145
- Are You a Savvy Networker? 146
- Focus on Getting Interviews 149
- Prospecting and Networking 150
- Communicate Your Qualifications 150
- Develop Networks 152
- Prospect for Leads 154
- Handle and Minimize Rejections 156
- Be Honest and Sincere 157
- Practice the 5R's of Informational Interviewing 158

- Approach Key People   158
- Conduct the Interview Well   160
- Telephone for Job Leads   163
- Key Networking Books   164
- Internet Resources for Networking   165
- Network Your Way to Job Success   168

9   Interview for Jobs and Offers 169

- Stressful Times   169
- What's Your Interview Quotient (I.Q.)?   170
- Interview Sins and Knockouts   173
- Behavioral and Internet Trends   181
- Interview for the Job   182
- A Communication Focus   183
- Answer Questions   184
- *Take Your Briefcase With You to the Interview*   186
- Prepare for Objections and Negatives   187
- Encounter Behavior-Based Questions   191
- Develop Strong Storytelling Skills   193
- Face Illegal Questions   193
- Ask Questions   194
- Appear Likable   194
- Close the Interview   195
- Always Remember to Follow Up   196
- *References: What You Need to Know*   197
- Useful Interviewing Resources   198
- The Face-to-Face Encounter   199

10   Negotiate Your Best Salary and Benefits . . 200

- Most Salaries Are Negotiable   200
- Consider Your Financial Future   201
- Prepare for the Salary Question   201
- Time the Salary Question Well   202
- Handle the Salary Question With Tact   203
- Reach Common Ground and Agreement   204
- Consider Benefits With Care   206
- Offer a Renegotiation Option   206
- Take Time Before Accepting   207
- Know and Stress Your Value   208
- Use the Right Resources   209

11   Turn Your Job Into a Great Career 211

- Neither a Student Nor a Professional   211
- Take More Positive Actions   211
- Tales and Lessons From the Working World   213
- Be Alert to Changing Job Requirements   220
- Beware of Office Politics   221
- Conduct an Annual Career Check-Up   221
- Use Job-Keeping and Advancement Strategies   222
- Assess and Change When Necessary   225
- Revitalize Your Job   225

12   Government, Nonprofit, and International Jobs 227

- Public and International Arenas   227
- Government and Law Enforcement Jobs   228
- Nonprofit Opportunities   233
- International Jobs and Careers   239

13   CampusCareerCenter's Employer Network 249

Indexes 260

- Employers   260
- Subjects   260

The Authors 264

Career Resources 266

Preface

LIFE IS FULL OF IMPORTANT TRANSITIONS. WHEN YOU graduated from high school, you may have left home for the first time. Like many students, that transition was probably filled with uncertainty. But four or more years later the end result has been very rewarding. During your time in college, you acquired new knowledge, skills, and interests as well as expanded your circle of friends and developed professional relationships. Those experiences and relationships will serve you well as you launch your career and move ahead in the years to come.

You'll often look back at your college years as one of the best periods of your life. As you face your transition from college to career, you once again approach it with a combination of optimism, anxiety, and uncertainty. While you may have a picture in your mind of what you would like your life to look like over the next few years, chances are the reality may be very different. Welcome to the world of transitions! This will all play out in a few months and you'll get on with a new life.

For over 20 years we have worked with thousands of individuals making career transitions – students, teachers, military personnel, government employees, Peace Corps Volunteers, women, downsized workers, executives, and ex-offenders. Many of them share these common experiences:

- Highly motivated to make the right change
- Anxious about their future
- Uncertain about the best course of action
- Emotional highs and lows attendant with a roller coaster job search
- Sensitive and fragile self-esteem when faced with rejections

Most important of all, how they managed their transitions has significant consequences for their future. Indeed, they wanted to get it right from the very start by doing first things first, as we outline in Chapter 2.

Most people discover job finding to be both an exhilarating and humbling experience, depending on how their job search unfolds. In many cases, job seekers encounter numerous rejections which can result in losing their two most important assets – their positive attitude and self-esteem. When faced with a few rejections, some people have difficulty maintaining an upbeat and proactive job search. Instead, they retreat into the conventional by resorting to relatively passive and ineffective job search activities, such as sending resumes and letters in response to classified ads and job postings, or they accept the first job offer that comes along, even though it's not what they really want.

The Job Hunting Guide is designed to take you step-by-step through the process of finding a job. It's all about being a proactive job seeker, as we outline in summary form on page 12. We've attempted to make this guide as complete as possible by covering all of the essentials in a sequential manner – assessment, goal setting, research, resume and letter writing, networking, interviewing, and salary negotiations – as outlined in the illustrations on pages 15 and 19. In addition, we've included numerous real-life examples as well as linked the key job search steps to websites and employers and to the wise advice of career professionals on many college campuses. The result is one of the most complete and integrated job search guides designed for college students and recent graduates in search of the right job and career.

At the same time, this guide should serve you well in the future. Like most people, you will probably change jobs and careers several times during your worklife. When it comes time to do so, remember *The Job Hunting Guide* and your online friend, CampusCareerCenter.com. Incorporating many timeless principles and processes, this book may well become your passport to several job and career transitions – whether on the job (Chapter 12) or changing employers – in the years ahead.

A key linkage for this book and you is one of the most student-friendly communities you will encounter as you make your transition from college to career, CampusCareerCenter.com:

www.campuscareercenter.com

Representing a very talented community of students, employers, and college administrators, CampusCareerCenter.com offers a wealth of information and advice on internships and part-time and full-time jobs relevant to students and recent graduates. As we note on pages 29-30, CampusCareerCenter.com should become your best friend as you navigate your job search. It can quickly put you into contact with many employers who are interested in hiring students and recent graduates. These employers represent some of the best companies to work for as a student or recent graduate. They are looking for highly motivated and talented individuals who want to start a great career.

We wish to thank the many students, employers, college administrators, and CampusCareerCenter.com staff members who contributed to this book. This is a dedicated community that truly has your best interests in mind. Like us, they want you to make a great transition from college to career. We and they measure success in very simple terms – how successful you are in landing a great job and launching a terrific career.

We especially wish to thank four individuals at CampusCareerCenter.com for encouraging us to take on this project and providing us with access to their rich database of students, employers, and college administrators: Matt Casey, Brian Peddle, Debbie Ivey, and Pram Ekaputra. They and their talented staff are the nuts-and-bolts behind what you see on your computer screen when you visit CampusCareerCenter.com. Please feel confident that they are trying to provide you with the very best career information, advice, and employment contacts.

We also wish to thank several career professionals who contributed a series of insightful articles on conducting a college-to-career job search. Their work is well represented and attributed on pages 22, 65, 90, 124, and 197. Such contributions should give you a "heads up" on what you should be doing on your campus – visiting the career center and using its many useful resources and services, from one-on-one career counseling and job postings to scheduling on-campus interviews and sponsoring career fairs where you will have an opportunity to meet a variety of potential employers!

The book would not be complete without the contributions from many students who are part of the CampusCareerCenter.com community. In Chapter 2 and 11, they provide numerous insights into real-world workplace realities. They confirm what we and others have long known – the first few months on the job are critical to one's future career development. You can learn a great deal about workplace do's and don'ts by reviewing the observations and lessons of new employees in Chapter 12. Based on an analysis of their experiences, we identify on page 213 what we believe are important "rules for success" in this new world of post-college work.

We wish you the very best as you make this important transition from college to career. If you follow our job search advice in Chapters 2 through 10 and connect with the right employers in Chapters 11 through 13, you should be off and running in a career that is right for both you and the employer.

But do us and CampusCareerCenter a favor: let us know if we've made a contribution to your transition. We would love to hear about your job search experiences. In so doing, your observations and analyses might help other students who are embarking on a similar path into an unknown, but hopefully exciting, future in the world of work!

Ron and Caryl Krannich
krannich@impactpublications.com

CampusCareerCenter's
The Job Hunting Guide

1

A Season for Everything

CONGRATULATIONS! YOU'RE ABOUT TO GRADUATE AND go on to a rewarding job and career that truly reflects your interests, skills, and abilities – one that is "fit" for you. College has been a great life-changing experience – you have grown both personally and professionally. While you and your parents may be poorer for the experience, the future looks much richer. You will all be proud on two upcoming days – the day you graduate and the day you start your new job. You will also enjoy getting your first post-degree paycheck that serves as evidence that you probably made the right choices for both college and career! At least you hope this is the case as your final days in college unfold with great expectations.

An Important Transition

You are most likely not the same person you were four years ago. Perhaps your interests and goals have changed, your outlook on life is refreshingly new, your circle of friends and acquaintances has expanded, and you feel more confident about yourself and your ability to shape the future. While you may think you are part of the "lucky" or "cool" generation, you have more in common with other people than you may think. Indeed, what you are going through is typical of most generations that have passed through your college. Like millions of other people – be they military, Peace Corps Volunteers, retirees, laid-off employees, or workers searching for more meaningful employment – you are **in transition**, soon to be neither a student nor a professional. You've made many new friends, expanded your networks, acquired a great deal of knowledge and experience both inside and outside the classroom, and have developed new material needs and dreams. It's time to find a great job that also pays good money. You're a savvy student because you survived the many challenges of being a successful student. All you have to do is climb that next big hurdle – land a job you may have been dreaming about for the last couple of years. This new post-college job may take your life in many new and exciting directions. Hopefully, it's the right job for you. It's very important that you connect with key people who have the power to hire you. Accordingly, it's time to launch a new career and make money.

New Skills for Success

You're bright, self-confident, and eager to take on the world. But let's speak truth about where you may or may not be going and just how fast may be your journey. You need a job, especially one that appropriately reflects your education, skills, experience, interests, and salary expectations. It will probably be an entry-level job given your level of experience. It may be in business or government or with a nonprofit organization or even take you abroad with an international employer (see Chapter 12).

> *The same skills you used to succeed in college may not be the ones you need to land a good job and start a rewarding career.*

As many students quickly discover, finding a job requires certain knowledge and skills that are not well developed in college. The same skills you used to succeed in college – creativity, subject matter knowledge, and test taking – may not be the ones you need to land a good job and start a rewarding career. Indeed, many students discover in their senior year that they really aren't well prepared for making the transition from college to career. Here's the likely scenario facing most students:

- They think they may quickly get a job offer.

- They've heard it's a tough job market for students and now it's time to see just how tough it is for them.

- Lacking specific goals, they are not sure what they want to do tomorrow, much less five or 10 years from now.

- Faced with writing a resume, they seem confused about how long it should be or what type of information to include on it.

- Now that they have a resume, they are not sure what to do with it – mail, fax, or email it to whom?

- While they may have some work-related experience, they are uncertain how to communicate that experience to prospective employers.

- They've heard about networking but they are unclear exactly what it's all about when looking for a job.

- Knowing the Internet may be important to finding a job, they are uncertain which employment sites are the best or most useful for college graduates.

- Although their campus has a career center, they are not sure what it does or how they can best use it for finding a job.

- They ask fellow students job-related questions and get a little advice here and there from individuals who seem equally clueless about what to do next.

- They now realize this whole process could take longer than they initially expected. They wished they had started earlier than March!

- Busy with school work and social commitments in their final semester, they have difficulty focusing on themselves, employers, and what's really important to achieving a successful job search.

No One to Help You

Good students don't necessarily make good job seekers. They may have a great grade point average, completed many reports and presentations, met their college standards, participated in college activities, and held a part-time job. Their education and experience for an entry-level candidate look good on transcripts and in letters of recommendation. But when it comes time to prepare for the next step in their lives – selling themselves to potential employers – they need professional help that may or may not be available on campus. Ironically, most of that help is not found where they might expect to find assistance – from their academic department or professors. After all, their job is done – they educated you for a degree. You are no longer their responsibility, especially when it comes to the delicate issues of finding jobs and promoting oneself to employers. Those usually aren't viewed as legitimate academic activities. In fact, your department and professors may be equally clueless about the job market and what you need to do to succeed in finding a job. Let's face this new reality: It's your job to find a job. Good luck!

The Great Disconnect

Everything you've done thus far in college ostensibly should help you land a good job. But the truth is that there is a disconnect between what goes on in your academic world versus what goes on in the work world. Employers have a very simple need that seems quite different from the needs of colleges and universities – employers want to hire someone who can add **value** to their organization. In other words, they want to know what it is you can do for them and be able to predict your work behavior in reference to their particular needs. So what are you going to do to both find and convince employers that you are the one who can add the most value to their operations?

> *Employers have a very simple need – they want to hire someone who can add value to their organization.*

If you are good at conducting research, analyzing and synthesizing data, writing compelling copy, making brief presentations, and persuading others to both trust and like you, chances are you will be able to put together all the critical elements for organizing and implementing a successful job search. These are key skills involved in writing resumes and letters, researching employers, networking, and interviewing for a job. At the same time, if you are good at doing important things at the last minute, such as cramming for tests, you may be the perfect candidate for organizing and implementing an effective job search during your final 90 days in college.

90 Days and You're Out!

Let's not bemoan the fact that you probably should have done things differently when it comes time to look for a job. That's life, so you have to get over it and move on to more productive things. If you are like many other students, you've waited until the last 90 days of your senior year to start looking for a job. March of your senior year? Or right after Spring Break? Make sure it's not May!

While ideally you should have focused on your career the first day you started college and planned your college experience accordingly, including your major, course selections, and an internship experience, in reality you're doing what students have been doing for more than 200 years – putting off career planning issues and job search questions until the last few months of their senior year. That's okay. It's not a crime not to plan nor to procrastinate about your future. In fact, there's no evidence that students who plan their careers over a four-year period do any better landing a good job than those who wait until the final 90 days to focus on their career and job search. The truth is that it will probably take you 90 days to land a job whether or not you've planned this process over four years or in just 90 days! Once you intensely focus on finding a job, it will probably take you three months to get one you like.

As life goes on, you'll discover there's a season for everything. But your season is now and you can't procrastinate much longer. It's time to visit your career center, write your resume, and start getting job interviews lined up. Even though you may have started late in this process, you'll eventually get a job and hopefully launch a very productive career.

12 Months and You May Be History

But if you are like many students, you'll also probably quit your first post-college job within 12 months. That job you were so proud of landing may turn out to be a real bust. You'll usually know this within the first 90 days when you discover the job doesn't feel right. It's not what you really expected or want to continue doing for long. You'll either look for another job or decide to go back to college and become a student again in preparation for a wiser and more focused career. You may quickly discover you missed some important steps in your job search, such as self-assessment, that may have contributed to accepting the wrong job – one that looked good on the surface but which was not compatible with your interests, skills, abilities, and values.

There's no evidence that students who plan their careers over a four-year period do any better landing a good job than those who wait until the final 90 days.

Your Crash Course to Success

It's time to develop a 90-day crash plan for getting a job. In the pages that follow, we outline step-by-step what you need to do to organize and implement a smart job search over a 90-day period. Based on our many years of experience in working with college students and individuals in transition, we outline the key job search steps and skills that lead to success.

As you will quickly discover, becoming an effective job seeker is not rocket science. It requires **focus** and **skills** that you may not have developed well during your college days. Above all, these are key communication and interpersonal skills – from writing, speaking, and dressing appropriately to interacting in face-to-face situations and seeking help – that you have already acquired in college but which you now need to reorganize and focus on your job search. Once you finish this book, you should be well prepared to land your dream job within 90 days.

What's Your Hiring I.Q.?

Let's start by examining your current level of job search information, skills, and strategies as well as assess how prone you are to making job search mistakes. Respond to each of the following agree/disagree statements on a scale of 5 to 1 (strongly agree = 5; strongly disagree = 1):

1. I can identify my strongest abilities and skills.	5 4 3 2 1
2. I know what I like and dislike in work.	5 4 3 2 1
3. I know what motivates me at work.	5 4 3 2 1
4. I can list my seven top achievements and explain them to an employer.	5 4 3 2 1
5. I have a well-defined career objective that guides my job search from beginning to end.	5 4 3 2 1
6. I can clearly explain to employers what I do well and enjoy doing.	5 4 3 2 1
7. I can specify in 50 words or less why an employer should hire me.	5 4 3 2 1
8. I can write different types of effective resumes and job search letters.	5 4 3 2 1
9. I know whom to send resumes and letters.	5 4 3 2 1
10. I know how to properly close a cover letter and follow up.	5 4 3 2 1
11. I can identify and target employers I want to interview.	5 4 3 2 1
12. I can develop a job referral network.	5 4 3 2 1
13. I know how to use the Internet to conduct employment research and network.	5 4 3 2 1
14. I know which websites are best for posting my resume and browsing job listings.	5 4 3 2 1

15. I know how much time I should spend conducting an online job search.   5 4 3 2 1

16. I can persuade employers to interview me.   5 4 3 2 1

17. I have a list of at least 10 employer-centered questions I need to ask during interviews.   5 4 3 2 1

18. I know the best time to talk about salary.   5 4 3 2 1

19. I have a clear idea of what I want to accomplish at work this coming week.   5 4 3 2 1

20. I set priorities and follow through on the most important tasks first.   5 4 3 2 1

21. I make minor decisions quickly.   5 4 3 2 1

22. I know how to say "no" and do so.   5 4 3 2 1

23. I know what I want to do with my life over the next 10 years.   5 4 3 2 1

24. I have a clear pattern of accomplishments which I can explain with examples.   5 4 3 2 1

25. I plan to stay with an employer for three or more years.   5 4 3 2 1

26. I have little difficulty in making cold calls and striking up conversations with strangers.   5 4 3 2 1

27. I always arrive at a job interview on time or with a few minutes to spare.   5 4 3 2 1

28. I immediately return most phone calls and respond to important emails and letters.   5 4 3 2 1

29. I control my time well rather than let other people control it.   5 4 3 2 1

30. I usually take responsibility for my own actions rather than blame others.   5 4 3 2 1

TOTAL H.I.Q.

If your total H.I.Q. (Hiring I.Q.) score is 135 or above, you are least likely to make job search mistakes. If your H.I.Q. is below 110, you can benefit a great deal from reading this book and putting it into practice. Upon completion of this book, your H.I.Q. should increase substantially!

But which statements you disagreed with may indicate how difficult or easy it will be for you to take corrective actions. If, for example, most of your "disagrees" (3 through 1) were in response to the first 18 statements, taking corrective action may be relatively easy and most of the advice can be found within the pages of this book. The reason for this is that the first 18 statements relate to your **knowledge** in reference to conducting an effective job search. If you responded "disagree" to any of these statements, you can take corrective action by following "how to" advice or tips on learning new job search skills. However, if many of your "disagrees" were in response to the last 12 statements (19-30), you may be very mistake-prone; taking corrective action may be very difficult for you. The reason for this is that statements 19-30 relate to your **patterns of behavior**. Many of these behaviors deal with your attitudes, motivations, self-management practices, and social interactive skills. These patterns of behavior can be modified by changing your attitudes and orientations to people, things, and situations. They require breaking old habits that may lead to recurring mistakes rather than just acquiring more knowledge.

Resources for Organizing Your Future

The pages that follow reflect the very best career planning and job search advice offered by experienced career professionals who work with millions of job seekers each year. Our advice is very compatible with the serious work of your campus career center. It also incorporates the many experiences of CampusCareerCenter.com, one of the premier online employment resource centers that links college students to employers interested in recruiting them for entry-level positions. Through our many clients and users, we've learned a great deal about the needs of our two audiences – students and employers. The basic need is what we call a "good fit" between the applicant and the job. Whatever you do, your goal should be to find a job that is compatible with your interests, skills, and abilities. That's exactly what employers also want – highly motivated, enthusiastic, and talented employees who love what they do. They, too, are looking for a "good fit."

As you organize and implement your job search according to the advice outlined in this book, we recommend that you also use the following online resources for enhancing your job search:

www.campuscareercenter.com
www.impactpublications.com
www.winnningthejob.com

Used in conjunction with this book, these websites should assist you in every phase of your job search. They open up a whole new world of job insights and opportunities. Set aside time to focus on these websites over a 90-day period.

Whatever you do, make sure you use the next 90 days wisely. How well you organize and implement your job search at this stage in your life can have very important implications for your future career. Make sure your first career move is the right one. Don't discover during the first 90 days of your new job that you made a costly mistake – you accepted a job offer that wasn't a good fit for you. You can avoid doing so by doing first things first, as we outline in subsequent chapters.

Cramming for Success

We wish you the very best as you embark on the next phase of your life. You owe it to yourself and your loved ones to put your best effort into the next 90 days of your college life. Think of your job search as a cram course in finding the perfect job. If you're used to cramming for tests, you'll find cramming for a job to be even more rewarding than getting a high grade on a test. Only you can make this happen. We're here to assist you in putting your best foot forward in today's job market for college students. Keep in touch with us – now and in the future – through our career-related websites. After all, this is only one of many job and career transitions you will make during your work life. If you do this one right, you should put yourself on a path to career success. You'll use our job search knowledge and skills over and over again in the process of advancing your career. Serving you well both today and tomorrow, this book should become your guide to changing jobs in the future as well as getting off to a good start.

2

Do First Things First

WHY ARE SOME PEOPLE MORE SUCCESSFUL IN FINDING jobs than others? Are they smarter, more talented, better organized, or just luckier? Or do they know something about the job finding process that others don't?

Forget the Trendy Generation Talk

The truth is that most everyone can find a job, especially in an economy that boasts an unemployment rate of less than six percent. But finding a really good job – one you do well, enjoy doing, and truly reflects your value – is not something most people can do with ease.

Forget about the trendy Generation X, Y, or D talk. In many respects you are not much different from other generations that have passed your way – you have dreams, however vague at present, and you want a fulfilling job that will help you realize your current dreams as well as contribute to building new dreams. You need to connect with the right employer to whom you want to clearly communicate your qualifications in order to get the job. You need to organize yourself for job search success. At the same time, employers aren't much different from previous generations. They are looking for talented individuals who will bring value to their organizations. They want to know what it is you will do for them in exchange for the salary and benefits they offer you. The job search and recruitment processes are all about connecting with the right people.

But be careful what you wish for. You'll eventually get a job within a few months, but that "first job out" may not be a particularly good fit. Indeed, within a few weeks you may discover it was the wrong job for you. You may then reflect on how you went about finding that ill-fitting job – you should have done some things differently from the very start, from writing your resume to contacting employers and preparing for the job interview. In fact, you may conclude that you were too concerned with answering questions and therefore failed to ask important questions about the job and the employer – questions you may now, unfortunately, know the answers to!

Find the Right Job Proactively

How will you go about finding a job? Where will you start and what will you do first? Many job seekers start in all the obvious places – newspapers, Internet employment sites, and campus career centers. And they tend to engage in similar initial, and ritualistic, activities – write a resume and survey job listings. They then send their resume and cover letter in response to job vacancy announcements or schedule interviews with on-campus recruiters. Internet-savvy job seekers also post their resumes to online databases and respond to job postings in the hope of being discovered by employers. Viewed from this perspective, the job search is a relatively passive and reactive process which mainly involves writing, mailing, and interviewing activities as well as waiting, waiting, and waiting to hear from employers. For some job seekers, finding a job approximates the experience of being struck by lightning!

> *In many respects you're not much different from other generations . . . The job search is all about connecting with the right people.*

The traditional way of finding a job may not serve you well. In fact, we call this approach an **outdated job search**. If you largely approach your job search as a relatively passive process of writing resumes and letters, responding to job vacancies, and scheduling on-campus interviews, you'll eventually land a job. But chances are you will have missed out on some really great opportunities that you could have uncovered by taking a more proactive approach to your job search.

We call this latter approach an **updated job search**. The chart on page 12 summarizes the contrasting characteristics of these two different approaches to finding a job.

Characteristics of an Outdated Versus
Updated Job Search

Outdated Job Search	Updated Job Search
■ Passive job search.	■ Proactive job search.
■ Self-centered approach.	■ Employer-centered approach.
■ Primarily focuses on writing and distributing resumes and letters in response to job listings.	■ Focuses on entire job search process, with self-assessment and goal-setting playing important foundation roles.
■ Develops traditional chronological resume stressing employment dates and focusing on duties and responsibilities.	■ Develops performance-oriented resume stressing accomplishments and including an objective and summary of qualifications.
■ Brief cover letter politely repeats the contents of resume.	■ Cover letter expresses personality and includes a follow-up statement.
■ Major job search activities involve responding to classified ads with a resume and letter.	■ Research, networking, and follow-up play critical roles throughout the job search process.
■ Prepares answers to anticipated interview questions.	■ Prepares to both answer and ask questions at the interview.
■ Waits to hear from employers.	■ Uses effective follow-up techniques.
■ Primarily a paper writing and mailing exercise.	■ Focuses on e-mail, telephone, and face-to-face communications.
■ Job search tends to be spontaneous and serendipitous.	■ Planning and preparation play key roles throughout the job search.
■ Myth-based job search.	■ Reality-based job search.
■ Little use of the Internet beyond checking online job postings and and posting resumes online.	■ Fully integrates the Internet into the job search, with special emphasis on conducting research and networking.

15 Mistakes Job Seekers Make

We've heard numerous reasons why people don't get jobs or why finding a job seems to be so difficult and frustrating for the average job seeker:

- It's a bad economy.
- Unemployment is high.
- Employers aren't hiring right now.
- Everyone seems to be downsizing.
- There's too much competition for too few positions.
- You have to know someone to get an interview.
- I don't have enough experience.
- I'm probably over-qualified.
- There are no positions related to my level of experience.
- No one seems interested in my qualifications.
- I'm too old for most employers.
- I think it's because I'm a woman.
- I'm a student with little work experience.
- I'm being discriminated against because of my race.
- No one ever responds to my e-mail or returns my phone calls.
- There are few entry-level positions available.
- The jobs seem to be filled by the time I apply.
- I can't find a job that pays much.
- I'd probably fail the tests.
- I've been too busy to look for a job.
- I never get a chance to interview for a job.
- I cost too much – employers don't want to pay what I'm worth.
- I can't find anything I'm interested in.
- I didn't like any of the job offers.
- I guess I'm just unlucky.
- I don't know why it's such a problem. Is there something wrong with me?

Except for the last excuse, most of these reasons for job search failure tend to focus on external forces such as the economy, job market, and behavior of recruiters and employers. However, more often than not, we find the real reasons for job search ineffectiveness are much closer to home. Indeed, many job seekers tend to be their own worst enemies. They make numerous mistakes which result in sabotaging their own job search. In another job search book, *No One Will Hire Me!*, we identify 15 mistakes most job seekers make and how to overcome them. If you are like many other job seekers, chances are you will make several of these mistakes that can result in a frustrating and ineffective job search:

1. Abandon dreams and lack goals.
2. Possess self-defeating and negative attitudes.
3. Fail to organize an effective sequential job search.
4. Neglect to develop important networking skills.
5. Provide little evidence of key skills and accomplishments.
6. Write and distribute awful resumes and letters.
7. Mess up the critical job interview.
8. Fail to develop an appealing pattern of work behavior.
9. Appear honest but stupid or dishonest but smart.
10. Use a self-centered approach – appears needy or greedy.
11. Conduct an outdated job search or over-rely on technology.
12. Unwilling to take risks and handle rejections.
13. Fail to implement and follow through.
14. Avoid professional advice and assistance.
15. Resist changing behavior and acquiring new habits of success.

Taken together, these 15 mistakes constitute a volatile combination of behaviors employers wish to avoid when dealing with strangers who hope to become their new employees.

Seven Steps to Job Search Success

One of the major mistakes job seekers make is to primarily focus on the resume. In fact, most job seekers believe the first thing they need to do is to write a resume. Lacking information on their goals, skills, and accomplishments as well as jobs and employers, they proceed to craft a resume that often reflects the canned language of professional resume writers rather than reflecting what they have done, can do, want to do, and will do in the future.

Effective job seekers understand the sequential nature of the job search process and learn to do first things first within this process. In its simplest form, the job search consists of the seven steps outlined on page 15.

Doing first things involves understanding and implementing this well-defined seven-step job search process. An effective job search follows each step in sequence. For example, writing resumes and letters should take place only **after** you have identified your skills and abilities (#1), specified your goals (#2), and conducted research (#3). After completing your resume and letters, you should be well prepared to network (#5), interview (#6), and negotiate salary (#7). But if you start writing your resume and letters and responding to job listings without first identifying your skills and abilities, specifying your goals, and conducting research, chances are you will write weak resumes and letters, and your job search may lack focus. You'll eventually get a job, but it most likely won't be one that best reflects your objective, skills, abilities, values, and pattern of accomplishments.

Job Search Steps and Stages

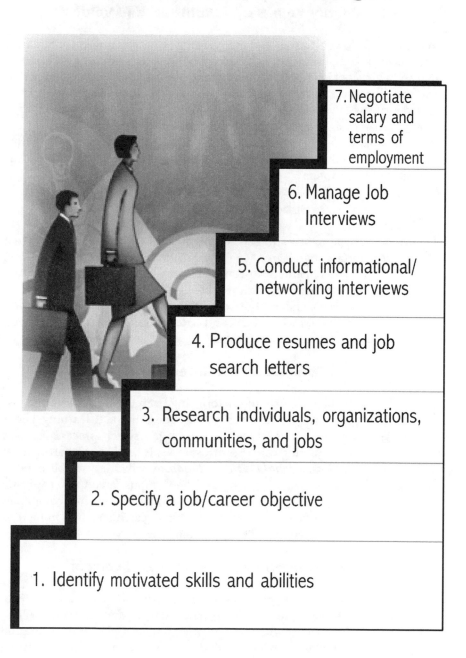

7. Negotiate salary and terms of employment

6. Manage Job Interviews

5. Conduct informational/ networking interviews

4. Produce resumes and job search letters

3. Research individuals, organizations, communities, and jobs

2. Specify a job/career objective

1. Identify motivated skills and abilities

Let's briefly examine each of these steps. As we will see in subsequent chapters, numerous do's and don'ts are associated with each step.

1. Identify Your Skills, Abilities, and Values

What exactly do you do well and enjoy doing? Can you quickly summarize your major accomplishments as evidence of your qualifications and performance? This set of job search activities generates a critical language of action verbs and keywords for communicating your qualifications to employers. Here you identify what you do well and enjoy doing – your key strengths centered around an analysis of your accomplishments. Once you complete this step, you'll be able to clearly communicate to employers your pattern of performance – skills, abilities, and expected benefits or outcomes. We address this critical step in Chapters 3 and 4.

2. Specify Your Career Goals

Knowing what you want to do and staying focused on your goals are two of the most important ingredients for job search success. Effective job seekers articulate their goals in employer-centered terms as they seek to focus their job search on the needs of employers. Having goals, they are able to communicate with vision and enthusiasm their particular passion for work. Employers know exactly what such candidates will most likely do for them. We examine this critical step in Chapter 5.

3. Conduct Job-Related Research

Research is something that should be ongoing from the first day to the last day of your job search. It involves asking questions and learning about companies, employers, jobs, careers, and the job search process. A good starting point for exploring careers, for example, is the U.S. Department of Labor's biannual *Occupational Outlook Handbook*, which is available in book form as well as online: www.bls.gov/oco. The CampusCareerCenter website (www.campuscareercenter.com) also includes profiles of numerous companies that recruit college students. We examine this research step and numerous resources in Chapter 6 and profile several major employers in Chapter 13.

4. Write Dynamite Resumes and Letters

Resumes and letters don't get jobs – they advertise you for job interviews. Writing and distributing resumes lie at the heart of any job search. When done right and in sequence with other job search steps, a powerful resume and letter clearly communicate what you have done, can do, and will do in the future for the employer. However, many job seekers make numerous mistakes related to writing, producing, distributing, and following up resumes and letters. We discuss these mistakes as well as offer advice on how to develop dynamite resumes and letters in Chapter 7.

5. Network for Information, Advice, and Referrals

While most job seekers spend a disproportionate amount of time responding to job listings in the advertised job market, they should be spending more of their time on developing and implementing an effective networking campaign centered around the use of the informational interview. The key to getting a job is knowing how to network for information, advice, and referrals in order to uncover opportunities in the hidden job market. As networking clearly demonstrates, success in finding a job is often more a function of whom you know than what you know. In Chapter 8 we address the whole issue of networking in reference to the larger job search process. We outline the importance of identifying, developing, building, and nurturing your network for job and career success.

6. Interview for Job Offers

The job interview is the single most important step in the job search process – no interview, no job offer, no job. However, many job seekers make numerous mistakes relating to the job interview from arriving late to failing to close and follow up. We examine the major mistakes in Chapter 9 as well as outline how to improve one's interview skills in order to go on to win the job.

7. Negotiate Salary and Terms of Employment

Most job seekers make numerous mistakes relating to salary, from prematurely discussing the subject to not knowing what they are really worth in today's job market. Many accept the very first offer without negotiating compensation and other terms of employment. Others expect salaries that have no basis except wishful thinking. Chapter 10 focuses on the many mistakes job seekers make relating to salaries. It offers useful tips for improving one's salary negotiation skills.

Organize a 90-Day Plan for Success

How long should it take to complete your job search? That's always a difficult question to answer because landing a job often seems like selling a house – it can take a day, a week, a month, three months, or six months. Success depends on your situation, potential buyers in the market, and the amount of time you are willing to devote to selling the product – yourself. Executive-level candidates, for example, often take longer because their job search is very focused on a few high-end jobs and they often work through executive re-cruiters. On average, however, expect to take 90 days to complete a well organized job search. You can shorten your job search time by accelerating various job search activities as outlined in the chart on page 19.

Our chart of job search activities emphasizes the importance of initiating each job search step in sequence. It also emphasizes that many job search activities, such as research and networking, should be ongoing activities. The key to making this process work for you over a 90-day period is persistence despite numerous rejections you may encounter.

Seek Assistance

While some people can pick up a book or follow the advice of others in organizing and implementing an effective job search, many others need assistance in completing critical steps in the process. Some need professional assistance throughout this process – from assessing skills to negotiating compensation. Most, however, fall somewhere along the assistance continuum – they can use professional assistance at various stages of their job search. Learning from a career expert can save them a great deal of time, provide them with a structure, and keep them focused on what's really important in their job search.

The good news for college students is that most campuses offer a wealth of free resources organized to assist them in conducting an effective job search. These come in the following forms:

- campus career resource centers
- testing centers
- career advisors, counselors, and psychologists
- resume writing clinics
- job search seminars and courses
- on-campus interviewing
- job fairs

Many student-oriented websites, such as www.campuscareercenter.com and www.jobweb.com, are specifically designed to respond to student employment needs by providing a combination of professional career advice along with actual employers, networking opportunities, job listings, and searchable resume databases.

The bad news is that many students do not take advantage of such assistance. Others wait to the very last minute to seek such assistance, or they focus on only one relatively passive job search activity – signing up for on-campus interviews. Except for some savvy business and engineering schools, most academic departments provide little career planning assistance to their majors – they don't see "nonacademic" job and career issues to be within their

Organization of Job Search Activities

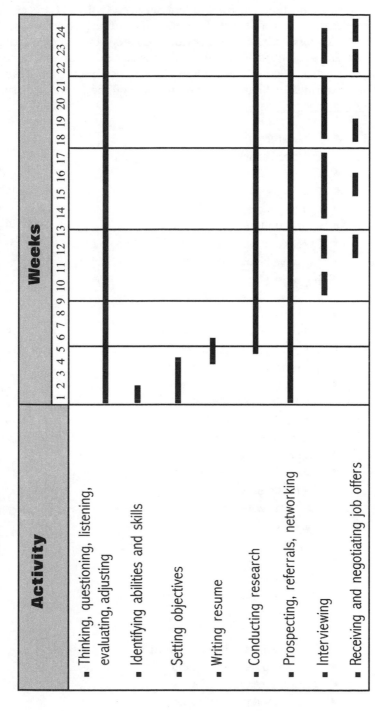

responsibilities. Most such assistance is offered to graduating students through administrative offices, such as Student Services, Office of Career Planning and Placement, or Career Services Center. Some alumni offices, women's centers, and professional schools may provide such assistance to special populations.

Several student-focused employment websites either complement or compete with on-campus career services with their own set of services and clients. These websites include some combination of the following assistance and services:

- Job search tips
- Featured articles
- Career experts or advisors
- Career tool kit
- Career assessment tests
- Community forums
- Discussion or chat groups
- Message boards
- Job alert ("push") e-mails
- Company research centers
- Networking forums
- Salary calculators or wizards
- Resume management center
- Resume and cover letter advice
- Multimedia resume software
- Job interview practice
- Relocation information
- Reference checkers
- Employment or career news
- Free e-mail for privacy
- Success stories
- Career newsletter
- Career events
- Online job fairs
- Affiliate sites
- Career resources
- Featured employers
- Polls and surveys
- Contests
- Online education and training
- International employment
- Talent auction centers
- Company ads (buttons and banners)

- Sponsored links
- Special channels for students, executives, freelancers, military, and other groups

Alternative Career Services

You'll find at least 12 alternative career planning and employment services available to job seekers. You may want to supplement or enhance your on-campus career resources with some of these off-campus employment services, especially those that are not well represented on campus. Once you leave campus and make future job and career changes, you may want to check out several of these services for career planning and job search assistance. In the meantime, explore several of our referenced websites to see if these services are worth pursuing at this stage in your career planning and job search.

While a few of the following career services are free, most charge fees which can be substantial for the level and intensity of professional assistance provided. Each service has certain advantages and disadvantages. Approach them with caution. Never sign a contract before you read the fine print, get a second opinion, and talk to former clients about the **results** they achieved through their services. With these words of caution, let's take a look at the variety of services available.

1. College/university placement offices

College and university placement offices provide in-house career planning services for graduating students. While some assist alumni, don't expect too much help if you have already graduated; contact the alumni office which may offer employment services. Many college placement offices are understaffed or provide only basic services, such as maintaining a career planning library, coordinating on-campus interviews for graduating seniors, and conducting workshops on how to write resumes and interview. Others provide a full range of well supported services including testing and one-on-one counseling. Many community colleges also offer such services to members of the community on a walk-in basis. You can use their libraries and computerized career assessment programs, take personality and interest inventories, or attend special workshops or full-semester career planning courses which will take you through each step of the career planning and job search processes. Check with your local campus to see what services you might use. Many of the college and university placement offices belong to the National Association of Colleges and Employers (NACE), which operates its own employment website: www.jobweb.com. This site includes a wealth of information on employment for college graduates. Its "Catapult" section provides direct links to hundreds of college and university placement

Meet the New Career Advisor

Tamara Kissane, Assistant Director,
Office of Career Services, Oberlin College

Individuals in the workforce now anticipate changing and/or losing several jobs during their lifetimes. They may even change careers completely. The result of this anticipated instability is an increasing focus on flexibility and transferable skills. To maintain employability, employees concentrate on developing skills that will enhance performance on the current job and will also help to secure a job in the future.

This presents a significant challenge for career counselors who are firmly entrenched in trait-and-factor methods. In today's world, occupational and skills inventories are unreliable due to the constantly changing definitions and responsibilities of jobs. Simply assessing present skills can no longer be the focus. In addition to assessment, career advisors must emphasize and educate individuals about the transferability of their skills. For the 'self-employed' workforce of today, self-knowledge and self-reliance are vital for successful career management.

Although students today rarely need an introduction to the events and viewpoints of the 'real world,' an appointment with a career advisor is often the first acknowledgment and confrontation with the approaching day when they will be full participants in the world of work.

For those students who consider young adulthood as an opportunity for positive personal growth and transformation, the 'real world' is simply a place to continue growing. These students consider life after college an exciting adventure, and the instability is positively interpreted as a means for 'keeping the options open.' For students who feel fragile and find the uncertainty of this time of life uncomfortable, the world may seem like a hazardous and un-friendly place. Students who yearn only for calm seas and safe harbors may find the notion of stabilizing in an unstable world overwhelming and impossible. In these cases, career advisors must balance the need for encour-agement and the careful introduction of materials with the need to prod students rather forcefully into action.

The changing definition of career has added additional tasks for career advisors. As in the past, we must discuss the present reality, including the current economy, demand (or lack of demand) for certain occupations, and the likelihood of securing a particular job based on one's skills and interests. We must also address the practicalities of how to locate job listings, write resumes, cover letters, personal statements, and standard interview techniques.

However, simply discussing occupational and practical information is not sufficient. Career advisors of the 21st century must also encourage the explo-ration of values and dreams. The instability and constant turnover of today's working world necessitates workers who know themselves well enough to speak confidently about transferable skills and abilities. They must also have enough self-knowledge to recognize opportunities in the workplace and assess 'fit' when considering new work environments. The goal is not only to leave college with a job and a resume, but also to leave college with a sense of self and a set of repeatable exercises and tools to reconnect self-interest with career-interest over the course of a lifetime. If we encourage young adults to seek jobs that reflect their values and enhance their skills, they will feel productive, active and connected. Work then is no longer just an economic support, but a vehicle for personal expression, and an opportunity to develop new skills and interests.

offices: www.jobweb.com/catapult. NACE's newly launched NACElink, in alliance with the E-Recruiting Association and several universities, includes job-posting, resume database, and interview-scheduling components integrated into a single online database. To find college alumni offices, visit the following websites: alumni.net, www.bcharrispub.com/isd/alumniconnections.html, and planetalumni.com.

2. Career fairs, job fairs, and career conferences

Career fairs, job fairs, and career conferences are organized by a variety of groups – from schools and government agencies to executive recruiters, employment agencies, and professional associations – to link applicants to employers. Held over one to two days in a hotel, conference center, or a college campus, employers give presentations on their companies, applicants circulate resumes, and employers interview candidates. Many such meetings are organized to attract hard-to-recruit groups. These are excellent sources for job leads and information on specific employers – if you are invited to attend or if the meeting is open to the public. Employers pay for this service, although some job fairs or career conferences may charge job seekers a nominal registration fee. Many colleges and universities regularly schedule career fairs. Numerous college students find their first post-graduation job through these events.

3. Women's centers and special career services

Women's centers and special career services for displaced workers, such as 40-Plus Clubs (40plus.org/chapters) and Five O'Clock Clubs (five oclockclub.com), have been established to respond to the employment needs of special groups. Women's centers are particularly active in sponsoring career planning workshops and job information networks. Special career services arise at times for different categories of employees. For example, unemployed aerospace engineers, teachers, veterans, air traffic controllers, and government employees have formed special groups for developing job search skills and sharing job leads.

4. Public employment services

Public employment services usually consist of a state agency which provides employment assistance as well as dispenses unemployment compensation benefits. Employment assistance largely consists of job listings and counseling services. Many employers still do not list with this service, especially for positions paying more than $40,000 a year. Many of these offices are literally "reinventing" themselves for today's new job market with One-Stop Career Centers, computerized job banks, and other innovative approaches. Many offer useful job services, including self-assessment and job search workshops as well as access to Internet job listings. Most are linked to America's Job Bank (www.ajb. dni.us), an electronic job bank which includes job listings throughout the U.S. and abroad, as well as the U.S. Department of Labor's two websites – America's CareerInfoNet (www.acinet.org) and America's Learning Exchange (www.servicelocator.org). If you are a veteran, you will find many of the jobs listed here give veterans preference in hiring.

5. Private employment agencies

Private employment agencies work for money, either from applicants or employers. Approximately 8,000 such agencies operate nationwide. Many are highly specialized in technical, scientific, and financial fields. The majority serve the interests of employers. While employers normally pay the placement fee, many agencies charge applicants 10 to 15 percent of their first year salary. These firms have one major advantage: job leads which you may have difficulty uncovering elsewhere. The major disadvantages are that they can be costly and the quality of the firms varies. Make sure you understand the fee structure and what they will do for you before you sign anything.

6. Temporary employment firms

Temporary employment firms offer a variety of employment services to both applicants and employers who are either looking for temporary work and workers, or who want to better screen applicants and employers. Many of these firms, such as Manpower (www.manpower.com), Olsten (olsten.com), and Kelly Services (kellyservices.com), recruit individuals for a wide range of positions and skill levels as well as full-time employment. Some firms specialize in certain types of workers, such as IT and computer personnel. If you are interested in "testing the job waters," you may want to contact these firms. Employers pay for these services. While most firms are listed in the community Yellow Pages, many also operate websites. The following websites are especially popular with individuals interested in part-time, temporary, or contract work: net-temps.com, www.rhii.com, eLance.com, brainbid.com, ework. com, a2zmoonlighter.com, contract-jobs.com, freeagent.com, talentmarket. monster.com, and www.talentgateway.com.

7. Private career and job search firms

Private career and job search firms help individuals acquire job search skills and coach them through the process of finding a job. They do not find you a job. Expect to pay anywhere from $1,500 to $10,000 for this service. If you need a structured environment for conducting your job search, contract these firms for assistance. One of the oldest such firms is Bernard Haldane Associates (jobhunting.com and bernardhaldane. com). Many of their pioneering career planning and job search methods are incorporated in this book as well as can be found in five other key job search books: *Haldane's Best Resumes for Professionals*, *Haldane's Best Cover Letters for Professionals*, *Haldane's Best Answers to Tough Interview Questions*, *Haldane's Best Salary Tips for Professionals*, and *Haldane's Best Employment Websites for Professionals*. This firm has over 90 branches located in the U.S., Canada, and the United Kingdom. Other firms offering related services include Right Management Associates (right.com) and R. L. Stevens & Associates (interviewing.com), and Lee Hecht Harrison (lhh.com/us).

8. Executive search firms and headhunters

Executive search firms work for employers in finding employees to fill critical positions in the $50,000 plus salary range. They also are called "headhunters," "management consultants," and "executive recruiters." Don't expect to contract for these services. Executive recruiters work for employers, not applicants. On the other hand, you may want to contact firms that specialize in recruiting individuals with your skill specialty. For a comprehensive listing of these firms, see the latest annual edition of *The Directory of Executive Recruiters* (Kennedy Information). Several companies we identify in Chapter 7, such as resumezapper.com, blastmy resume.com, and resumeblaster.com, offer e-mail resume blasting services that primarily target executive recruiters. For reasons which will become clearer in subsequent chapters, you should approach these services with a healthy sense of skepticism.

9. Marketing services

Marketing services represent an interesting combination of job search and executive search activities. They can cost $2,500 or more, and they work with individuals anticipating a starting salary of at least $75,000 but preferably over $100,000. A typical operation begins with a client paying a $150 fee for developing psychological, skills, and interests profiles. A marketing plan is outlined and a contract signed for specific services. The firm normally develops a slick "professional" resume and sends it by mail or e-mail, along with a cover letter, to hundreds – maybe thousands – of firms. Clients are then briefed and sent to interviews. Again, approach these services with caution and with the knowledge that you can probably do just as well – if not better – on your own by following the step-by-step advice of this and other job search books.

10. Testing and assessment centers

Testing and assessment centers provide assistance for identifying vocational skills, interests, and objectives. Usually staffed by trained professionals, these centers administer several types of tests and charge from $300 to $800 per person. You may wish to use some of these services if you feel our activities in Chapters 3 generate insufficient information on your skills and interests to formulate your job objective. If you use such services, make sure you are given one or both of the two most popular and reliable tests: *Myers-Briggs Type Indicator®* and the *Strong Interest Inventory®*. You should find both tests helpful in better understanding your interests and decision-making styles. The career office at your local community college or women's center may administer these tests at minimum cost. At the same time, many of these testing and assessment services are now available online. We identify several of these websites in Chapter 3.

11. Professional associations

Professional associations often provide placement assistance. This usually consists of listing job vacancies in publications, maintaining a resume database, and organizing a job information exchange at annual conferences. Many large associations operate their own online employment sites; members can include their resume in an electronic database and employers can access the database to search for qualified candidates. Annual conferences are good sources for making job contacts in different geographic locations within a particular professional field. But don't expect too much. Talking to people (networking) at professional conferences may yield better results than reading job listings, placing your resume in a database, or interviewing at conference placement centers. For online directories of professional associations, be sure to visit these sites: ipl.org/ref/AON, associationcentral.com, and www.asaenet.org.

12. Professional resume writers

Professional resume writers are increasingly playing an important role in career planning. Each year thousands of job seekers rely on these professionals for assistance in writing their resumes. Many of them also provide useful job search tips on resume distribution, cover letters, and networking. Charging from $100 to $500 for writing a resume, they work with the whole spectrum of job seekers – entry-level to senior executives making millions of dollars each year. While most are not certified career counselors, many of these professionals have their own associations and certification groups. If you are interested in using a professional resume writer, visit these websites for information on this network of career professionals: www.parw.com, www.prwra.com, and www.nrwa.com. Also, review several of our professional resume writing recommendations in Chapter 7.

Locate a Certified Career Professional

While most college campuses have certified career professionals associated with the career planning and counseling offices, you also can locate such professionals through various professional associations. If you are interested in contacting one for assistance, we advise you to first visit these websites of career professionals:

- **National Board of Certified Counselors, Inc.** nbcc.org
- **National Career Development Association** ncda.org
- **Certified Career Coaches** certifiedcareercoaches.com
- **Career Planning and Adult Development Network** careernetwork.org

Consider an Internship

Many students face the dilemma of approaching the job market with little or no work experience directly related to the types of jobs that interest them. One of the best ways to test the employment waters, acquire work experience, network, strengthen one's resume, and make contacts with employers is through an internship or co-op program experience.

You should check with your academic department, career center, or campus co-op program to see if they offer internship opportunities. Employers attending campus job fairs frequently offer internship opportunities. Many business and professional schools as well as political science and journalism departments and international programs offer internship programs. Some internship programs last for a few months whereas others may be for the summer, a semester, or a year.

For insightful student observations about their internship experiences, including both positives and negatives, and online internship opportunities, we recommend visiting the "Intern Zone," "Ask the Expert," and "Career Corner" sections of CampusCareerCenter's website:

www.campuscareercenter.com/students/intern.asp
www.campuscareercenter.com/students/expert.asp
www.campuscareercenter.com/students/career_corner.asp

For example, one international student recently shared these useful observations with fellow students:

> "Landing a summer internship is not difficult, even for international students if they tap into the right resources. The keywords are persistence and networking. The best places to look for internships are the career center and forums like CampusCareerCenter.com as well as online and actual career fairs and personal contacts. I secured an internship in three companies and I chose Honeywell Inc. (formerly AlliedSignal Inc.) because it offered me a very challenging project as well as excellent remuneration. What was strange was that they generally do not hire F-1 visa students. However, when they think you are suitable for the position, they often do take in a few F-1 students which is very heartening. I had a great time this summer . . . got to learn so many new things . . . and most importantly I not only developed software for the clients but also got to interact with them. It really broadened my horizons. I would really recommend a summer internship to anyone pursuing a Bachelor's or Master's degree."

Another student shared his internship experience with the *Texas Monthly*:

> "*Texas Monthly* was a great place to work. I was interning in the advertisement department and right away I was helping out on major presentations. I learned a lot while working there. Everyone is so nice and it feels like a family. It is also a very casual office. They even have beer and wine available in the kitchen if you are working after five. The internship helped me to understand what kind of office and job I would enjoy working in. I gained a lot of knowledge about the sales side of advertising and how important it is to a magazine. This is definitely a place I would like to work for."

And yet another student stressed the importance of the "real world experience" acquired through an internship:

> "Being an intern has really allowed me to grow and use the skills I learned in college. Even though I was an accounting major and went to work for the Air Force, many of the concepts that I learned in school had direct application to 'the real world.' Although I felt overwhelmed on many days, I also realized that this is a learning process for me, and being overwhelmed is just part of that process. If I could pass on one piece of advice, it would be to always ask questions if you don't know or aren't sure. All of my co-workers have been very supportive of me, and have always answered my questions, even if I asked them the same questions before. They realize that there is a lot to learn, and that Rome wasn't built in a day."

The most comprehensive listing of internships – over 50,000 paid and unpaid in the U.S. and abroad – can be found in the popular annual directory,

Internships (Peterson's). Students interested in international internships should acquire a copy of Charles Gliozzo's latest edition of the ***Directory of International Internships*** (Michigan State University). Several websites primarily focus on internship opportunities:

- Internships.com   www.internships.com
- Rising Star Internships   www.rsinternships.com
- Internship Programs   www.internshipprograms.com
- Internships-USA   www.internships-usa.com
- Intern Web   www.internweb.com
- Intern Jobs   www.internjobs.com
- Internship4America   www.internship4america.com

While you will discover numerous competitive sponsored internship programs through the above resources, many students easily find internships on their own by approaching employers directly with an internship proposal. They network through their contacts or make cold calls to employers inquiring about internship opportunities. Indeed, this is one of the best ways to get into the doors of employers and acquire experience. Consider contacting employers directly with a proposal. If you are willing to volunteer your time as an unpaid intern, you may find many employers will be receptive to your approach. Best of all, many students report receiving job offers from employers they worked for as interns. The internship experience gives both the intern and employer an excellent opportunity to examine each other carefully to determine whether or not they wish to work together in the future.

Your CampusCareerCenter Connection

Each day hundreds of student members log on to CampusCareerCenter.com for the latest career information and advice:

www.campuscareercenter.com

Unlike most other employment websites, CampusCareerCenter.com is the world's leading campus recruiting company. It specifically focuses on the job and career needs of college students and employers. Sponsored by employers who are interested in hiring students in a variety of fields, the site is free to student users who become registered members. It currently includes a rapidly growing database of over 100,000 top students around the world and clients who activity seek to hire new recruits from the pool. It includes the following useful information and services:

- Resume database
- Job listings
- Articles for improving one's job search
- Profiles of companies and employers
- Internship section ("internzone")
- Message board
- Diversity center
- International jobs
- Ask the expert
- Success stories and testimonials
- Online career resource center

We invite you to join this growing community of talented students who make CampusCareerCenter.com their one-stop shop for conducting an online job search. Be sure to sign up to access its numerous free services, acquire useful information and advice, and meet employers interested in your skills.

Important Prerequisites for Success

Over the years we have identified several factors that consistently contribute to job search success. While some of these factors relate to work skills and qualifications, most are personal factors related to attitudes and how one gets organized, uses time, relates to others, and handles disappointments. Make sure you incorporate many of these prerequisites in your job search.

1. **You should work hard at finding a job:** Make this a daily endeavor and involve others. Expect to spend 40 to 80 hours a week on organizing and implementing an effective job search. Focus on routinizing high-payoff job search activities, such as networking.

2. **You should not be discouraged by setbacks:** You are playing the odds, so expect disappointments and handle them in stride. You will have many *"no's"* before uncovering the one *"yes"* that's right for you.

3. **You should be patient and persevere:** Expect three months of hard work before you connect with the job that's right for you. Keep focused and active throughout this period.

4. **You should be honest with yourself and others – but not stupid:** Honesty is always the best policy. But don't confuse honesty with frankness and the confessional. Indeed, many people say the stupidest things about themselves in the name of honesty. Naive job seekers often volunteer their negatives and shortcomings to potential employers. They present an unfortunate image of someone who lacks

street smarts and who potentially will say the darnest things to clients and customers even about the inner workings of the business!

5. **You should develop a positive attitude toward yourself:** Nobody wants to employ guilt-ridden people with inferiority complexes and low self-esteem. Focus on your positives with enthusiasm. Sell your positive self – those things you do well and enjoy doing.

6. **You should associate with positive and successful people:** Finding a job largely depends on how well you relate to others. Avoid associating with negative and depressing people who complain and have a "you-can't-do-it" attitude. Run with winners who have a positive "can-do" outlook on life.

7. **You should set goals:** You should have a clear idea of what you want and where you're going. Without these, you will present a confusing and indecisive image to others. Clear goals help direct your job search into productive channels. Moreover, setting high goals will help you work hard in getting what you want.

8. **You should plan and implement for success:** Convert your goals into realistic action steps that are organized as short-, intermediate-, and long-range plans. Then put these plans into action by taking the necessary actions that should lead to success. Unfortunately, many people are good at planning their job search but they fail to implement properly. Planning without implementation is a waste of time.

9. **You should manage your time and get organized:** Translate your plans into activities, targets, names, addresses, telephone numbers, and materials. Develop an efficient and effective filing system and use a large calendar for setting time targets and recording appointments and useful information.

10. **You should be a good communicator:** Take stock of your oral, written, and nonverbal skills. How well do you communicate? Since most aspects of your job search involves communicating with others, and communication skills are one of the most sought-after skills, always present yourself well both verbally and nonverbally.

11. **You should be energetic and enthusiastic:** Employers are attracted to positive people who appear to be energetic and demonstrate that magical quality called **drive**. They don't like negative and depressing people who toil at their work. Generate enthusiasm both verbally and nonverbally. Check on your telephone voice – it may be more unen-

thusiastic than your voice in face-to-face situations. After all, your first interview is likely to take place over the telephone.

12. **You should ask questions:** Your best information comes from asking questions. Asking questions also communicates interest and intelligence. Learn to develop questions that are non-aggressive, probing, polite, and interesting to others. But don't ask too many questions and thereby dominate conversations and become an annoying inquisitor.

13. **You should be a good listener:** Being a good listener is often more important than being a good questioner and talker. Learn to improve your face-to-face listening behavior (nonverbal cues) as well as remember and use information gained from others. Make others feel they enjoyed talking with you, i.e., you are one of the few people who actually **listens** to what they say.

14. **You should be polite, courteous, and thoughtful:** Treat gatekeepers, especially receptionists, like human beings. Avoid being aggressive or too assertive. Try to be polite, courteous, and gracious. Your social graces are being observed. Remember to send thank-you letters – a very thoughtful thing to do in a job search. Even if rejected, thank employers for the "opportunity" given to you. After all, they may later have additional opportunities, and your letter will help them remember you.

15. **You should be inclusive, give credit to others, and help others look good:** Avoid the egocentrism of taking credit for everything by constantly referring to "I." Give credit to others by referring to "we" when discussing your accomplishments and "us" or the "company" when speculating about your future role. Employers love to work with competent employees who make them look good even though the credit belongs to others.

16. **You should be tactful:** Watch what you say to others about other people as well as yourself. Be very careful how you talk about previous employers and co-workers, especially anything negative about your relationships and their competence. Don't be a gossip, back-stabber, or confessor.

17. **You should demonstrate your intelligence and competence:** Present yourself as someone who gets things done and achieves results – a **producer**. Talk about your accomplishments by including examples of what you did and with what consequences. Employers

want to see proof of performance. They generally seek people who are bright, hard working, responsible, energetic, have drive, can communicate well, have positive personalities, maintain good interpersonal relations, are likable, observe dress and social codes, take initiative, are talented, possess expertise in particular areas, use good judgment, are cooperative, trustworthy, and loyal, generate confidence and credibility, and are conventional. In other words, they like people who can score in the "excellent" to "outstanding" categories of a performance evaluation.

18. **You should maintain a professional stance:** Be neat in what you do and wear, and speak with the confidence, authority, and maturity of a professional.

19. **You should not overdo your job search:** Don't engage in overkill and bore everyone with your "job search" stories. Achieve balance in everything you do. Occasionally take a few days off to do nothing related to your job search. Develop a system of incentives and rewards – such as two non-job search days a week if you accomplish targets A, B, C, and D.

20. **You should be open-minded and keep an eye open for "luck":** Too much planning can blind you to unexpected and fruitful opportunities. You should welcome serendipity. Learn to re-evaluate your goals and strategies. Seize new opportunities if appropriate.

21. **You should evaluate your progress and adjust:** Take two hours once every two weeks and evaluate your accomplishments. If necessary, tinker with your plans and reorganize your activities and priorities. Don't become too routinized and thereby kill creativity and innovation.

22. **You should focus on what's really important in conducting a successful job search:** If you spend most of your job search time sending your resume in response to job ads or submitting your resume in response to online job listings, you're not conducting a smart job search. Instead, focus most of your job search activities on research, networking, and making direct contacts with employers. Above all, use the Internet wisely for acquiring information and advice rather than only for responding to job listings.

3

Specify Your Motivated Abilities and Skills (MAS)

WHAT DO YOU DO WELL AND ENJOY DOING? WHAT are you particularly good at doing in the work world? What really turns you on – your primary passion? What motivates you to do your best professionally? Do you have a predictable and appealing pattern of behavior that you can communicate to employers? Does your resume provide evidence of several major accomplishments? Can you describe your five most important accomplishments which focus on benefits or outcomes for others? Can you communicate your accomplishments with a sense of purpose and enthusiasm?

All of these questions emphasize one of the most important errors made by job seekers – the failure to clearly communicate their skills, abilities, and accomplishments to employers. Always keep in mind what employers are looking for in candidates: They want to know how your skills, abilities, and accomplishments will translate into future value or benefits for their company. In other words, they want to know what you will do for them – your predictable pattern of accomplishments which should prove to be a good "fit" for the position.

What Can This Stranger Do for Me?

How well can you communicate your value to strangers? Can you convince a stranger within five minutes why they should give you $40,000 a year, a position, an office, laptop, cell phone, a 401k, stock options, and three weeks vacation each year? While the job search is by no means a form of panhandling, it does share one important characteristic – you're asking a stranger to give you money, perks, and benefits. But what are you prepared to give in return for a generous compensation package? You must offer a compelling and persuasive story to get strangers to take such actions.

You are a stranger to most employers who know little or nothing about your qualifications, accomplishments, and personality. They trust they are making the right decision largely based upon indirect evidence of your future potential to add value to their organization. So let's examine the nature of the evidence you are prepared to present to employers. We do this by first identifying your MAS – your pattern of Motivated Abilities and Skills. Not just abilities and skills but those that **motivate** you to do your very best.

> _Employers want proof of your past accomplishments so they can predict your future performance._

While employers may be interested in learning about your grade point average, courses taken, campus activities, and academic recognition, don't be surprised to discover that many of them show little interest in such evidence of your "qualifications." As you transition from college to career, their major concern is to predict your future performance in their work setting from college- and work-related experiences. If you have little direct work experience from which to make such predictions, they will look for other indicators of your skills, abilities, motivations, and personality. For example, what evidence can you give that you learn quickly, multi-task, take initiative, and are a team player, well organized, creative, and persistent? What motivates you to do your very best? Do you have a personality that fits well into the company's culture?

Employers want to know who you are in terms of your interests, skills, and abilities in reference to their hiring needs. They hire people whom they believe have the necessary knowledge, skills, and abilities to do the job in question. Above all, they want proof of past accomplishments so they can predict your future performance with them. In other words, they want to know what **benefits**, in the form of specific accomplishments, you will likely generate for them should they hire you.

Your immediate job search goal – from conducting research to writing resumes and networking – should be to get employers to interview you because you appear to be a good "fit" for their organization or team. You need to tell a very compelling **story** that persuades employers to invite you to interviews and offer you jobs. But first you need to know more about yourself – just who are you in terms of interests, skills, abilities, and accomplishments? What are your major strengths? Why should someone want to hire you?

Show Me the Evidence

Unfortunately, most job seekers are ill-equipped to discuss their accomplishments. Students, for example, are often preoccupied with talking about their college days – grade point, courses, activities – rather than who they are in terms of motivated abilities and skills that transcend the classroom and campus. Too often they approach employers without a good sense of what they have done, can do, and will do in the future. Instead, they tend to focus on activities and formal duties and responsibilities assigned to jobs rather than the knowledge, skills, and abilities they possessed in actually doing the job, which may be quite different from the position description. In fact, most job seekers define "experience" on their resumes and in job interviews as formal duties and responsibilities rather than what they accomplished in performing the duties and responsibilities. They give little evidence of actual outcomes of their work or behavior.

> *Most job seekers define "experience" as formal duties and responsibilities. They give little evidence of actual outcomes of their work or behavior.*

While employers understand job descriptions, they don't understand why candidates have so much difficulty articulating what they actually accomplished. Take, for example, the following "experience" statement on a resume:

Supervised a seven-person inventory management office.

Such a statement tells an employer nothing about your actual skills and accomplishments. It basically says you were a squatter – you held a position in which you were given the responsibility of supervising other people. So what? Many people sit in such positions. The question is how did you stand and perform in reference to the employer's needs? What distinguishes you from hundreds of other people in similar positions? Did you do well in that position? How well? With what effects? What exactly did you accomplish as a supervisor? Did you build an effective team that saved the company 20 percent in lost inventory? Were you given an award for your innovative inventory management system that reduced personnel costs by 30 percent? Or did you just occupy the position of "Supervisor" – you came to work, sat, gave orders, completed paperwork, and went home – with no distinguishing performance that separates you from the run-of-the-mill inventory managers?

If you define your "experience" as benefits, outcomes, or actual performance, you give an employer a very different and positive picture of your abilities and skills. Your accomplishments will be the basis for motivating employers to interview and hire you. Best of all, when you emphasize your accomplishments, you help set the focus for discussing your future performance with the employer who interviews you. Instead of leaving yourself open to performance questions about your duties and responsibilities – _"Tell me what you did as inventory supervisor"_ – you focus the discussion on your past performance as it might relate to future accomplishments with the employer interested in your qualifications. The employer might ask you the following:

> _"I find that very interesting. Tell me more about how you were able to achieve a 30 percent reduction in personnel costs in just 24 months. Let's take a look at our inventory system here. Based upon what we've talked about thus far, what do you think you could do here about reducing costs?"_

Contrast these two different experience statements about formal responsibilities versus actual accomplishments:

Experience Expressed as Responsibilities

Supervised a seven-person inventory management office.

Experience Expressed as Accomplishments

As inventory manager in charge of a seven-person office, reduced operating costs by 20 percent and personnel costs by 30 percent within 24 months. Received the "Best Employee of the Year Award" for designing and implementing a model inventory management system that eliminated the need for one of three warehouses. Annual savings: $735,000.

These are two very different ways of presenting your qualifications and experience to employers. Which one do you think presents the best impression and thus makes the job seeker look more attractive to a potential employer? If you were choosing between two candidates who might be equally qualified in terms of experience, which candidate would you be more interested in interviewing – the one who communicates responsibilities or the one who stresses accomplishments? There's no contest here: employers are impressed with candidates who use the language of the employer – focus on their accomplishments in reference to the needs of employers.

Identify Your Skills

The first step to communicating your qualifications to employers in the form of accomplishments is to identify your skills. Most people have hundreds of skills, but they have difficulty identifying and articulating the ones that are most important to employers. Many skills are related to specific jobs, such as operating a particular piece of equipment or working in various software programs. We call these **work-content skills** because they tend to be technical in nature, require some form of training and education, and are specific to particular jobs. Many of these skills become keywords and core competencies employers look for on resumes and which job seekers stress as part of their technical qualifications. For example, an employer may be looking for someone who has these specific work-content skills: QuarkXpress, PageMaker, Powerpoint, MS Word, Excel, Access, Lotus, C++, TMQ, spreadsheet, and Peachtree. Other skills tend to be more general and thus can be applied to many different jobs. We call these **functional or transferable skills**. For example, many job seekers possess these highly valued communication, organization, and decision-making skills:

- writing
- public speaking
- organization
- management
- leadership

- critical thinking
- dependability
- negotiating
- trouble-shooting
- supervision

Many people also possess several personal characteristics that are conducive to working in organizations and with groups:

- trustworthy
- punctual
- conscientious
- creative
- self-motivated
- reliable

- dependable
- patient
- resourceful
- responsible
- tenacious
- cooperative

These and many other transferable skills enable individuals to make job and career changes.

If you are a college student or recent college graduate and do not know what you do well or want to do, you probably should take a battery of vocational tests and psychological inventories to identify your interests and skills. Some of the most popular such tests, which may be available through your campus counseling center, include:

- *Myers-Briggs Type Indicator®*
- *Strong Interest Inventory®*
- *Self-Directed Search* (SDS)
- *Campbell Interest and Skill Survey*
- *Keirsey Character Sorter*
- *Birkman Method*
- *Enneagram*
- *FIRO-B*

- *California Psychological Inventory (CPI)*
- *16 Personality Factors Profile*
- *Edwards Personal Preference Schedule*
- *Kuder Occupational Interest Survey*
- *APTICOM*
- *Jackson Vocational Interest Survey*
- *Ramak Inventory*
- *Vocational Interest Inventory*
- *Career Assessment Inventory*
- *Temperament and Values Inventory*

If you have a great deal of work experience, chances are you don't need complex testing. You have experience, you have well defined values, and you know what you don't like in a job. You may be able to assess your interests, skills, and abilities, as well as specify your pattern of accomplishments, by completing a few self-directed exercises. Therefore, we outline several alternative skills identification exercises, ranging from simple to complex, for assisting you at this stage. We recommend using the most complete and extensive activity – Motivated Abilities and Skills (MAS) Exercise – to gain a thorough understanding of your strengths.

Use the following exercises to identify both your work-content and transferable skills. These self-assessment techniques stress your positives or strengths rather than identify your negatives or weaknesses. They should generate a rich vocabulary for communicating your "qualifications" to employers. Each exercise requires different investments of your time and effort as well as varying degrees of assistance from other people.

Simple Checklist Method

Most functional/transferable skills can be classified into two general skills and trait categories – organizational/interpersonal skills and personality/work-style traits. Review the following lists of transferable skills. Place a "1" in front of the skills that **strongly** characterize you; assign a "2" to those skills that describe you to a **large extent**; put a "3" before those that describe you to **some extent**. After completing this exercise, review the lists and rank order the 10 characteristics that best describe you on each list.

Organizational and Interpersonal Skills

__ communicating	__ trouble-shooting
__ problem solving	__ implementing
__ analyzing/assessing	__ self-understanding
__ planning	__ understanding
__ decision-making	__ setting goals

___ innovating
___ thinking logically
___ evaluating
___ identifying problems
___ synthesizing
___ forecasting
___ tolerating ambiguity
___ motivating
___ leading
___ selling
___ performing
___ reviewing
___ attaining
___ team building
___ updating
___ coaching
___ supervising
___ estimating
___ negotiating
___ administering

___ conceptualizing
___ generalizing
___ managing time
___ creating
___ judging
___ controlling
___ organizing
___ persuading
___ encouraging
___ improving
___ designing
___ consulting
___ teaching
___ cultivating
___ advising
___ training
___ interpreting
___ achieving
___ reporting
___ managing

Personality and Work-Style Traits

___ diligent
___ patient
___ innovative
___ persistent
___ tactful
___ loyal
___ successful
___ versatile
___ enthusiastic
___ outgoing
___ expressive
___ adaptable
___ democratic
___ resourceful
___ determining
___ creative
___ open
___ objective
___ warm
___ orderly
___ tolerant

___ honest
___ reliable
___ perceptive
___ assertive
___ sensitive
___ astute
___ risk taker
___ easygoing
___ calm
___ flexible
___ competent
___ punctual
___ receptive
___ diplomatic
___ self-confident
___ tenacious
___ discreet
___ talented
___ empathic
___ tidy
___ candid

___ frank   ___ adventuresome
___ cooperative   ___ firm
___ dynamic   ___ sincere
___ self-starter   ___ initiator
___ precise   ___ competent
___ sophisticated   ___ diplomatic
___ effective   ___ efficient

Autobiography of Accomplishments

Write a lengthy essay about your life accomplishments. This could range from 20 to 100 pages. After completing the essay, go through it page by page to identify what you most enjoyed doing (working with different kinds of information, people, and things) and what skills you used most frequently as well as enjoyed using. Finally, identify those skills you wish to continue using. After analyzing and synthesizing this data, you should have a relatively clear picture of your strongest skills.

Motivated Abilities and Skills (MAS) Exercise

Short of sitting down with a trained career professional and undergoing a thorough career assessment, this is the most thoroughgoing and useful self-assessment exercise we have found. While it is somewhat complex and time-consuming, it is time and effort well spent. It generates a great deal of data on your abilities and skills and then synthesizes them in terms of your major strengths – those things you do well and enjoy doing. This is precisely the type of information you need on yourself in order to best communicate your strengths and accomplishments to employers on resume and letters and in interviews.

The focus of this exercise is identifying your **pattern** of motivated abilities and skills rather than just coming up with a laundry list of abilities and skills. For example, while you may be a very good chef, you may not enjoy using all the wonderful abilities and skills that make you an excellent chef. Instead, you may discover what you really enjoy doing is organizing meetings and events and working with large groups of people – skills that served you well as a chef in the kitchen of a large hotel. Indeed, you may want to become a meetings planner rather than continue as a chef. Our MAS exercise is especially useful for those who feel they need a thorough analysis of their past achievements. This device is widely used by career counselors. Initially developed by Bernard Haldane Associates, this exercise is variously referred to as *Success Factor Analysis, System to Identify Motivated Skills,* or *Intensive Skills Identification.*

This technique helps you identify which skills you **enjoy** using. While you can use this technique on your own, it is best to work with someone else. Since you will need six to eight hours to properly complete this exercise, divide your time into two or three work sessions.

The exercise consists of six steps. The steps follow the basic pattern of generating raw data, identifying patterns, analyzing the data through reduction techniques, and synthesizing the patterns into a transferable skills vocabulary. You need strong analytical skills to complete this exercise on your own. The six steps include:

1. **Identify 15-20 achievements**: While ideally you should inventory over 100-150 achievements, let's start by focusing on a minimum of 15-20 achievements. These consist of things you enjoyed doing, believe you did well, and felt a sense of satisfaction, pride, or accomplishment in doing. You can see yourself performing at your best and enjoying your experiences when you analyze your achievements. This information reveals your motivations since it deals entirely with your voluntary behavior. In addition, it identifies what is right with you by focusing on your positives and strengths. Identify achievements throughout your life, beginning with your childhood. Your achievements should relate to specific experiences – not general ones – and may be drawn from work, leisure, education, military, or home life. Put each achievement at the top of a separate sheet of paper. For example, your achievements might appear as follows:

Sample Achievement Statements

"When I was 10 years old, I started a small paper route and built it up to the largest in my district."

_____

"I started playing chess in ninth grade and earned the right to play first board on my high school chess team in my junior year."

_____

"Learned to play the piano and often played for church services while in high school."

_____

"Designed, constructed, and displayed a dress for a 4-H demonstration project."

_____

"Although I was small compared to other guys, I made the first string on my high school football team."

_____

"I graduated from high school with honors even though I was very active in school clubs and had to work part-time."

_____

"I was the first in my family to go to college and one of the few from my high school. Worked part-time and summers. A real struggle, but I made it."

_____

"Earned an 'A' grade on my senior psychology project from a real tough professor."

_____

"Finished my master's degree while working full-time and attending to my family responsibilities."

_____

"Proposed a chef's course for junior high boys. Got it approved. Developed it into a very popular elective."

_____

"Designed the plans for our house and had it constructed within budget."

_____

2. Prioritize your seven most significant achievements.

Your Most Significant Achievements

1. _____
2. _____
3. _____
4. _____
5. _____
6. _____
7. _____

3. **Write a full page on each of your prioritized achievements.** For example, you should describe:

- How you initially became involved.
- The details of *what you did* and *how you did it*.
- What was especially enjoyable or satisfying to you.

Use copies of the "Detailing Your Achievements" form on page 45 to outline your achievements.

4. **Elaborate on your achievements:** Have one or two other people interview you. For each achievement have them note on a separate sheet of paper any terms used to reveal your skills, abilities, and personal qualities. To elaborate details, the interviewer(s) may ask:

   - What was involved in the achievement?
   - What was your part?
   - What did you actually do?
   - How did you go about that?

   Clarify any vague areas by providing an example or illustration of what you actually did. Probe with the following questions:

   - Would you elaborate on one example of what you mean?
   - Could you give me an illustration?
   - What were you good at doing?

   This interview should clarify the details of your activities by asking only "what" and "how" questions. It should take 45 to 90 minutes. Make copies of the "Strength Identification Interview" form on page 46 to guide you through this interview.

5. **Identify patterns by examining the interviewer's notes:** Together identify the recurring skills, abilities, and personal qualities **demonstrated** in your achievements. Search for patterns. Your skills pattern should be clear at this point; you should feel comfortable with it. If you have questions, review the data. If you disagree with a conclusion, disregard it. The results must accurately and honestly reflect how you operate.

6. **Synthesize the information by clustering similar skills into categories:** For example, your skills might be grouped or clustered in the manner as found at the top of page 47. This exercise yields a relatively comprehensive inventory of your skills. The information will better enable you to use a **skills vocabulary** when identifying your objective, writing your resume and letters, and interviewing. Your self-confidence and self-esteem should increase accordingly!

Detailing Your Achievements

ACHIEVEMENT # ___: _____

_____

_____

1. How did I initially become involved? _____

_____

_____

_____

2. What did I do? _____

_____

_____

_____

_____

3. How did I do it? _____

_____

_____

_____

_____

4. What was especially enjoyable about doing it?

_____

_____

_____

_____

Strength Identification Interview

Interviewee _____   Interviewer _____

INSTRUCTIONS: For each achievement experience, identify the **skills** and **abilities** the achiever actually demonstrated. Obtain details of the experience by asking *what* was involved with the achievement and *how* the individual made the achievement happen. Avoid "why" questions which tend to mislead. Ask for examples or illustrations of **what** and **how**.

Achievement #1:

Achievement #2:

Achievement #3:

Recurring abilities and skills:

Synthesized Skill Clusters

Investigate/Survey/Read Inquire/Probe/Question	Teach/Train/Drill Perform/Show/Demonstrate
Learn/Memorize/Practice Evaluate/Appraise/Assess Compare	Construct/Assemble/Put together
	Organize/Structure/Provide definition/ Plan/Chart course/Strategize/ Coordinate
Influence/Involve/Get participation/Publicize/ Promote	Create/Design/Adapt/Modify

More Self-Assessment Techniques

Several other self-assessment techniques and devices also can help you identify your motivated abilities and skills:

1. List all of your hobbies and analyze what you do in each, which ones you like the most, what skills you use, and your accomplishments.

2. Conduct a job analysis by writing about your past jobs and identifying which skills you used in each job. Cluster the skills into related categories and prioritize them according to your preferences.

3. Acquire a copy of Arthur F. Miller and Ralph T. Mattson's **The Truth About You** and work through the exercises found in the Appendix. This is an abbreviated version of the authors' SIMA (System for Identifying Motivated Abilities) technique used by People Management, Inc. (www. jobfit-pmi.com). If you need professional assistance, contact this firm directly. They can provide you with several alternative services consistent with the career planning approach outlined in this chapter.

4. Complete John Holland's *"The Self-Directed Search (SDS)."* You'll find it in his book, **Making Vocational Choices: A Theory of Vocational Personalities and Work Environments** or in a separate publication entitled **The Self-Directed Search – A Guide to Educational and Vocational Planning**. Also, check out the publisher's website for an online version of the SDS: self-directed-search. com.

5. Acquire **TalentSort: The Career Decision Cart Sort** as well as visit the producer's website for an online assessment: www.masteryworks.com.

Computerized Assessment Systems

While the previous self-directed exercises required you to either respond to checklists of skills or reconstruct and analyze your past job experiences, several computerized self-assessment programs also help individuals identify their skills. Some of the most widely used programs include:

- *Career Navigator*
- *Choices*
- *Discover II*
- *Guidance Information System* (GIS)
- *Self-Directed Search (SDS) Form R*
- *SIGI-Plus* (System of Interactive Guidance and Information)

Most of these computerized programs also integrate other key components in the career planning process – interests, goals, related jobs, college majors, education and training programs, and job search plans. These programs are widely available in schools, colleges, and libraries across the country. You might check with the career or counseling center at your college or local community college to see what computerized career assessment systems are available for your use. Relatively easy to use, they generate a great deal of useful career planning information. Many will print out a useful analysis of how your interests and skills are related to specific jobs and careers.

Online Assessment Options

Within the past few years, several companies have developed online assessment devices which you can quickly access via the Internet 24 hours a day in the comfort of your home. Some tests are self-scoring and free of charge while others require interacting with a fee-based certified career counselor or testing expert. CareerHub (careerhub.org), for example, is operated by the producers of the *Myers-Briggs Type Indicator®* and *Strong Interest Inventory®* – Consulting Psychologists Press. CareerLab (careerlab.com) offers one of the largest batteries of well regarded assessment tools: *Campbell Interest and Skills Survey, Strong Interest Inventory®, Myers-Briggs Type Indicator®, 16-Personality Factors Profile, FIRO-B, California Psychological Inventory (CPI), The Birkman Method*, and *Campbell Leadership Index*. The following seven websites are well worth exploring for both free and fee-based online assessments tools:

- **CareerHub**   careerhub.org
                                     cpp-db.com
- **CareerLab.com**   careerlab.com

- Self-Directed Search®   self-directed-search.com
- Personality Online   spods.net/personality
- Keirsey Character Sorter   keirsey.com
- MasteryWorks   www.masteryworks.com
- MAPP™   assessment.com
- PersonalityType   personalitytype.com

These 21 additional sites also include a wealth of related assessment devices that you can access online:

- Analyze My Career   analyzemycareer.com
- Birkman Method   review.com/career/article.cfm?id=
                                   career/car_quiz_intro
- Career Key   ncsu.edu/careerkey
- CareerLeader™   www.careerdiscovery.com/
                                   careerleader
- Career Services Group   careerperfect.com
- Careers By Design®   careers-by-design.com
- College Board   myroad.com
- Emode   www.emode.com
- Enneagram   ennea.com
- Fortune.com   fortune.com/careers
- Futurestep   futurestep.com
- Humanmetrics   humanmetrics.com
- Interest Finder Quiz   myfuture.com/career/interest.html
- Jackson Vocational
  Interest Inventory   jvis.com
- Keirsey Character Sorter   keirsey.com
- OnlineProfiles   onlineprofiles.com
- People Management
  International   www.jobfit-pmi.com
- Personality and IQ Tests   www.davideck.com
- Profiler   profiler.com
- QueenDom   queendom.com
- Tests on the Web   2h.com

Recommended Self-Assessment Books

For additional self-assessment resources, consult the following books for identifying your interests, skills, and abilities. Many of these resources also will assist you in setting career goals, the subject of the next chapter. Taken together, these books represent some of the best career assessment resources available. They will take you on a fascinating journey of self-discovery which could well change your life. Many of these resources can be found in libraries and bookstores or through Impact Publications' catalogs (see pages 266-273) and online career bookstore: www.impactpublications.com.

Do What You Are, Paul D. Tieger and Barbara Barron-Tieger (Little Brown & Company, 2001)

Do What You Love, the Money Will Follow: Discovering Your Right Livelihood, Marsha Sinetar (Dell Publishing Company, 1989)

Discover the Best Jobs for You, 4th Edition, Ron and Caryl Krannich (Impact Publications, 2001)

Discover What You're Best At, Linda Gale (Fireside, 1998)

Doing Work You Love: Discovering Your Purpose and Realizing Your Dreams, Cheryl Gilman (McGraw Hill, 1997)

Find a Job You Can Love, Ralph T. Mattson and Arthur F. Miller (Presbyterian & Reformed Publishing Company, 1999)

Finding a Career That Works for You, Wilma R. Fellman (Specialty Press, Inc., 2000)

Finding Your Perfect Work, Paul and Sarah Edwards (Putnam Publishing Group, 1995)

Follow Your True Colors to the Work You Love, Carolyn Kalil (True Colors, Inc., 1998)

A Fork in the Road: A Career Planning Guide for Young Adults, Susan Maltz and Barbara Grahn (Impact Publications, 2003)

Gifts Differing: Understanding Personality Type, Isabel Briggs Myers with Peter B. Myers (Davies-Black, 1995)

How to Find the Work You Love, Laurence G. Boldt (Arkana, 1996)

How to Find Your Mission in Life, Richard Nelson Bolles (Ten Speed Press, 2001)

I Could Do Anything If Only I Knew What It Was: How to Discover What You Really Want and How to Get It, Barbara Sher (Dell Publishing Company, 1995)

Live the Life You Love: In Ten Easy Step-By-Step Lessons, Barbara Sher (Dell Publishing Company, 1997)

Making Vocational Choices, John L. Holland (Psychological Assessment Resources, Inc., 1997)

Now, Discover Your Strengths, Marcus Buckingham (Free Press, 2001)

The Pathfinder: How to Choose or Change Your Career for a Lifetime of Satisfaction and Success, Nicholas Lore (Fireside, 1998)

Please Understand Me II, David Keirsey (Prometheus Nemesis Book Co., 1998)

The Practical Dreamer's Handbook, Paul and Sarah Edwards (Putnam Publishing, 2001)

The Truth About You, Arthur F. Miller and Ralph T. Mattson (Ten Speed Press, 1990)

What Type Am I? Discover Who You Really Are, Renee Baron (Penguin USA, 1998)

What's Your Type of Career? Donna Dunning (Consulting Psychologists Press, 2001)

Whistle While You Work: Heeding Your Life's Calling, Richard J. Leider and David A. Shapiro (Berrett-Koehler Publishing, 2001)

What Color Is Your Parachute? Richard Nelson Bolles (Ten Speed Press, 2003)

Make Discovering Your MAS a Top Priority

Identifying your motivated abilities and skills is one of the very first things you should do in your job search – before writing your resume, conducting research, networking, and responding to job opportunities. As noted in our seven-step job search process in Chapter 2, self-assessment is the **foundation** for everything else you do in the job search. But you want to do more than just identify your skills and abilities. You should focus on identifying your **motivated** abilities and skills – those things you do well and enjoy doing. For in the end, both you and the employer are looking for a good "fit" – a job that you approach with passion, enthusiasm, and productivity.

The sooner you discover what it is you do well and enjoy doing – your true passions – the more focused, energetic, fun, and fascinating will be your job search. You'll approach the job world and connect with the right people from a whole new and positive perspective. You'll be able to clearly communicate to employers what it is you will most likely do for them, because you have documented your accomplishments through self-assessment. Unlike other job seekers who make the mistake of not knowing their abilities and skills, and thereby have difficulty specifying an objective, you should stand out from the crowd because of your employer-centered approach. Employers will immediately know what you can do for them. Better still, they will want to invite you to an interview to learn more about your accomplishments in reference to their needs. At the interview, you will have an important and enthusiastic **story** to share with the interviewer(s) about who you are and what you will most likely do for them. When they say *"You're hired!"* it's probably because you convinced them that you had the right combination of motivated abilities and skills to do the job. You had the right MAS to solve their problems!

4

Discover Your Interests and Values

KNOWING WHAT YOU DO WELL IS ESSENTIAL FOR UNDER-standing your strengths, linking your capabilities to specific jobs, and communicating your strengths to employers. However, just knowing your abilities and skills will not give your job search its needed direction. You also need to know your work interests and values. These are the basic building blocks for setting goals and targeting your abilities toward certain jobs and careers.

Take, for example, individuals who type 120 words a minute or design Web pages. While these people possess highly marketable skills, if they don't regularly enjoy using these skills and are more interested in working outdoors or with people, these will not become **motivated skills**; these individuals will most likely not pursue jobs relating to word processing or the Internet. In the end, your interests and values will determine which skills should play a central role in your job search.

Vocational Interests

We all have interests. Most change over time. Many of your interests may center on your academic work and or a specific job whereas others relate to activities that define your hobbies and leisure activities. A good way to start identifying your interests is to examine the information and exercises found in both *The Guide to Occupational Exploration* and *The Enhanced Guide to*

Occupational Exploration. Widely used by students and others first entering the job market, it is also relevant to individuals who already have work experience. The guide classifies all jobs in the United States into 12 interest areas. Let's start by examining the following list of interest areas. In the first column check those work areas that appeal to you. In the second column rank order those areas you checked in the first column. Start with "1" to indicate the most interesting:

Your Work Interests

Yes/No (x)	Ranking (1-12)	Interest Area
___	___	**Artistic:** An interest in creative expression of feelings or ideas.
___	___	**Scientific:** An interest in discovering, collecting, and analyzing information about the natural world, and in applying scientific research findings to problems in medicine, the life sciences, and the nature sciences.
___	___	**Plants and animals:** An interest in working with plants and animals, usually outdoors.
___	___	**Protective:** An interest in using authority to protect people and property.
___	___	**Mechanical:** An interest in applying mechanical principles to practical situations by using machines or hand tools.
___	___	**Industrial:** An interest in repetitive, concrete, organized activities done in a factory setting.
___	___	**Business detail:** An interest in organized, clearly defined activities requiring accuracy and attention to details (office settings).
___	___	**Selling:** An interest in bringing others to a particular point of view by personal persuasion, using sales and promotion techniques.
___	___	**Accommodating:** An interest in catering to the wishes and needs of others, usually on a one-to-one basis.
___	___	**Humanitarian:** An interest in helping others with their mental, spiritual, social, physical, or vocational needs.

___ ___ **Leading and influencing:** An interest in leading and influencing others by using high-level verbal or numerical abilities.

___ ___ **Physical performing:** An interest in physical activities performed before an audience.

The Guide to Occupational Exploration also includes other checklists relating to home-based and leisure activities that may or may not relate to your work interests. If you are unclear about your work interests, you might want to consult these other interest exercises. You may discover that some of your home-based and leisure activity interests should become your work interests. Examples of such interests include:

Leisure and Home-Based Interests

___ Acting in a play or amateur variety show.

___ Advising family members on their personal problems.

___ Announcing or emceeing a program.

___ Applying first aid in emergencies as a volunteer.

___ Building model airplanes, automobiles, or boats.

___ Building or repairing radio or television sets.

___ Buying large quantities of food or other products for an organization.

___ Campaigning for political candidates or issues.

___ Canning and preserving food.

___ Carving small wooden objects.

___ Coaching children or youth in sports activities.

___ Collecting experiments involving plants.

___ Conducting house-to-house or telephone surveys for a PTA or other organization.

___ Creating or styling hairdos for friends.

___ Designing your own greeting cards and writing original verses.

___ Developing film.

___ Doing impersonations.

___ Doing public speaking or debating.

___ Entertaining at parties or other events.

___ Helping conduct physical exercises for disabled people.

___ Making ceramic objects.

___ Modeling clothes for a fashion show.

___ Mounting and framing pictures.

___ Nursing sick pets.

___ Painting the interior or exterior of a home.

___ Playing a musical instrument.

___ Refinishing or re-upholstering furniture.

___ Repairing electrical household appliances.

___ Repairing the family car.

___ Repairing or assembling bicycles.

___ Repairing plumbing in the house.

___ Speaking on radio or television.

___ Taking photographs.

___ Teaching in Sunday School.

___ Tutoring pupils in school subjects.

___ Weaving rugs or making quilts.

___ Writing articles, stories, or plays.

___ Writing songs for club socials or amateur plays.

Indeed, many people turn hobbies or home activities into full-time jobs after deciding that such "work" is what they really enjoy doing.

Other popular exercises designed to identify your work interests include John Holland's "The Self-Directed Search" which is found in his book, *Making Vocational Choices: A Theory of Careers*. It is also published as a separate testing instrument, *The Self-Directed Search – A Guide to Educational and Vocational Planning*. Developed from Holland's Vocational Preference Inventory, this popular self-administered, self-scored, and self-interpreted inventory helps individuals quickly identify what type of work environment they are motivated to seek – realistic, investigative, artistic, social, enterprising, or conventional – and aligns these work environments with lists of common occupational titles. An easy exercise to use, it gives you a quick overview of your orientation toward different types of work settings that interest you.

Holland's self-directed search is also the basic framework used in developing Bolles' "The Quick Job Hunting Map" as found in his *What Color Is Your Parachute?* and *The New Quick Job Hunting Map* books.

For more sophisticated treatments of work interests, which are also validated through testing procedures, contact a career counselor, women's center, or testing and assessment center for information on these tests:

- *Strong Interest Inventory®*
- *Myers-Briggs Type Indicator®*
- *Edwards Personal Preference Schedule*
- *Kuder Occupational Interest Survey*
- *Vocational Interest Inventory*
- *Career Assessment Inventory*
- *Temperament and Values Inventory*

Keep in mind that not all testing and assessment instruments used by career counselors are equally valid for career planning purposes. While the *Strong Interest Inventory*™ appears to be the most relevant for career decision-making, the *Myers-Briggs Type Indicator®* has become extremely popular during the past ten years. Based on Carl Gustav Jung's personality preference theory, the *Myers-Briggs Type Indicator®* is used extensively by psychologists and career counselors for identifying personality types. However, it is more useful for measuring individual personality and decision-making styles than for predicting career choices. It is most widely used in pastoral counseling, student personnel, and business and religious organizations for measuring personality and decision-making styles. For information on this test, contact: Consulting Psychologists Press, Inc. at 3803 East Bayshore Road, Palo Alto, CA 94303, Tel. 800-624-1765 (Website: cpp-db.com). In the meantime, many career counselors find Holland's *The Self-Directed Search* an excellent self-directed alternative to these professionally administered and interpreted tests.

Work Values

Work values are those things you like to do. They give you pleasure and enjoyment. Most jobs involve a combination of likes and dislikes. By identifying what you both like and dislike about jobs, you should be able to better identify jobs that involve tasks that you will most enjoy.

Several exercises can help you identify your work values. First, identify what most satisfies you about work by completing the following exercise:

My Work Values

I prefer employment which enables me to:

___ contribute to society	___ be creative
___ have contact with people	___ supervise others
___ work alone	___ work with details
___ work with a team	___ gain recognition
___ compete with others	___ acquire security
___ make decisions	___ make money
___ work under pressure	___ help others
___ use power and authority	___ solve problems
___ acquire new knowledge	___ take risks
___ be a recognized expert	___ work at own pace

Select four work values from the above list which are the most important to you and list them in the space below. List any other work values (desired satisfactions) which were not listed above but are nonetheless important to you:

1. _____

2. _____

3. _____

4. _____

_____

_____

Another approach to identifying work values is outlined in *The Guide to Occupational Exploration*. If you feel you need to go beyond the above exercises, try this one. In the first column check those values that are most important to you. In the second column rank order the five most important values:

Ranking Work Values

Yes/No (x)	Ranking (1-5)	Work Values
____	____	**Adventure:** Working in a job that requires taking risks.
____	____	**Authority:** Working in a job in which you use your position to supervise others.
____	____	**Competition:** Working in a job in which you compete with others.
____	____	**Creativity and self-expression:** Working in a job in which you use your imagination to find new ways to do or say something.
____	____	**Flexible work schedule:** Working in a job in which you choose your hours to work.
____	____	**Helping others:** Working in a job in which you provide direct services to persons with problems.
____	____	**High salary:** Working in a job where many workers earn a large amount of money.

___ ___   **Independence:** Working in a job in which you decide for yourself what work to do and how to do it.

___ ___   **Influencing others:** Working in a job in which you influence the opinions of others or decisions of others.

___ ___   **Intellectual stimulation:** Working in a job which requires a great amount of thought and reasoning.

___ ___   **Leadership:** Working in a job in which you direct, manage, or supervise the activities of other people.

___ ___   **Outdoor work:** Working out-of-doors.

___ ___   **Persuading:** Working in a job in which you personally convince others to take certain actions.

___ ___   **Physical work:** Working in a job which requires substantial physical activity.

___ ___   **Prestige:** Working in a job which gives you status and respect in the community.

___ ___   **Public attention:** Working in a job in which you attract immediate notice because of appearance or activity.

___ ___   **Public contact:** Working in a job in which you daily deal with the public.

___ ___   **Recognition:** Working in a job in which you gain public notice.

___ ___   **Research work:** Working in a job in which you search for and discover new facts and develop ways to apply them.

___ ___   **Routine work:** Working in a job in which you follow established procedures requiring little change.

___ ___   **Seasonal work:** Working in a job in which you are employed only at certain times of the year.

___ ___   **Travel:** Working in a job in which you take frequent trips.

___ ___   **Variety:** Working in a job in which your duties change frequently.

___ ___   **Work with children:** Working in a job in which you teach or care for children.

____   ____   **Work with hands:** Working in a job in which you use
your hands or hand tools.

____   ____   **Work with machines or equipment:** Working in a job in
which you use machines or equipment.

____   ____   **Work with numbers:** Working in a job in which you use
mathematics or statistics.

Second, develop a comprehensive list of your past and present **job frustrations and dissatisfactions**. This should help you identify negative factors you should avoid in future jobs.

My Job Frustrations and Dissatisfactions

List as well as rank order as many past and present things that frustrate or make you dissatisfied and unhappy in job situations:

Rank

1. _____   ____
2. _____   ____
3. _____   ____
4. _____   ____
5. _____   ____
6. _____   ____
7. _____   ____
8. _____   ____
9. _____   ____
10. _____   ____

Third, brainstorm a list of "Ten or More Things I Love to Do." Identify which ones could be incorporated into what kinds of work environments:

Ten or More Things I Love to Do

	Item	Related Work Environment
1.	_____	_____
2.	_____	_____
3.	_____	_____
4.	_____	_____
5.	_____	_____
6.	_____	_____
7.	_____	_____
8.	_____	_____
9.	_____	_____
10.	_____	_____

Fourth, list at least ten things you most enjoy about work and rank each item accordingly:

Ten Things I Enjoy the Most About Work

		Rank
1.	_____	____
2.	_____	____
3.	_____	____
4.	_____	____
5.	_____	____
6.	_____	____
7.	_____	____
8.	_____	____
9.	_____	____
10.	_____	____

Fifth, you should also identify the types of interpersonal environments you prefer working in. Do this by specifying the types of people you like and dislike associating with:

Interpersonal Environments

Characteristics of people I like working with:	Characteristics of people I dislike working with:
_____	_____
_____	_____
_____	_____
_____	_____
_____	_____
_____	_____
_____	_____
_____	_____
_____	_____
_____	_____

Computer Programs and Online Services

Several computerized self-assessment programs and online assessment services identified in Chapter 3 largely focus on career interests and values. Again, you may be able to get access to several major computerized assessment programs through your college career or counseling center. Several of the testing and assessment websites identified in Chapter 3 also include instruments for measuring interests and values.

Your Future as Objectives

All of these exercises are designed to explore your past and present work-related values. At the same time, you need to project your values into the **future**. What, for example, do you want to do over the next 10 to 20 years? We examine value questions when we address in Chapter 5 the critical objective-setting stage of the job search process.

5

Formulate an Employer-Oriented Objective

W E'VE ALL HAD IMPORTANT DREAMS ABOUT OUR future. Perhaps as a child you wanted to grow up and become a firefighter, policeman, teacher, soldier, or veterinarian. If you were on the high school basketball team, maybe you dreamed of someday becoming an NBA star. If you had a lead role in a school play, maybe you thought of becoming a star on Broadway. In college you may have been involved in an exciting summer marine biology project in the Galapagos Islands that convinced you to become an oceanographer. Or perhaps you're still dreaming of the perfect job or lifestyle – becoming the CEO of a major corporation or the U.S. Secretary of State or traveling to exotic places around the world.

While some dreams come true, others become fantasies we abandon as unrealistic. Others become **motivators** for setting and achieving goals.

The Next Step

Once you've identified your interests, values, and motivated abilities and skills – the subjects of Chapters 3 and 4 – you should be well prepared to develop a clear and purposeful objective for targeting your job search toward specific jobs, organizations, and employers. With a renewed sense of direction and versed in an appropriate language, you should be able to communicate to employers that you are a talented and purposeful individual who **achieves results**. Your objective must tell employers what you will **do for them** rather than what you want from them. It directly targets your accomplishments around employers' needs. In other words, your objective should become employer-centered rather than self-centered.

Goals and Objectives

Goals and objectives are statements of what you want to do in the future. When combined with an assessment of your interests, values, abilities, and skills and related to specific jobs, they give your job search needed direction and meaning for the purpose of targeting specific employers. Without them, your job search may founder as you present an image of uncertainty and confusion to potential employers.

When you identify your strengths, you also create the necessary database and vocabulary for developing your job objective. Using this vocabulary, you should be able to communicate to employers that you are a talented and purposeful individual who achieves results.

Try to find a job fit for you and your future rather than one you just think you can fit into.

If you fail to do the preliminary self-assessment work necessary for developing a clear objective, you will probably wander aimlessly in a highly decentralized, fragmented, and chaotic job market looking for interesting jobs you might fit into. Your goal, instead, should be to find a job or career that is compatible with your interests, motivations, skills, and talents as well as related to a vision of your future. In other words, try to find a job fit for you and your future rather than try to just fit into a job that happens to be advertised and for which you think you can qualify.

Analyze Your Past, View Your Future

Depending on how you approach your job search, your goals can be largely a restatement of your past MAS patterns (Chapter 3) or a vision of your future. If you base your job search on an analysis of your motivated abilities and skills, you may prefer restating your past patterns as your present and future goals. On the other hand, you may want to establish a vision of your future and set goals that motivate you to achieve that vision through a process of self-transformation.

The type of goals you choose to establish will involve different processes. However, the strongest goals will be those that combine your motivated abilities and skills with a realistic vision of your future.

So What Should a New Grad Do?

Robert L. Rostoni, Director of Career Services, Nyack College

From March madness to graduation gladness the race for the job market is officially on! I have noticed many tactics of the graduating seniors in regards to their job search and embracing life after college. Some seniors have been diligently working on their job search early on to secure their place in the work force (or graduate school). Some have embraced the task upon returning from the carefree bliss of Spring Break. Others see me (their career counselor) coming down the hall and dart the other way. It's time for *all* seniors to break through the starting gate of their career and life after college.

So, what does the market have for our graduating seniors? Will jobs adorn your feet on graduation day? Not necessarily. You have to market yourself. The old adage of 'it's who you know' is not enough in this competitive market. There's more to securing your place in this world than that. It's what you know, who you know, and who knows you. So market yourself and get networking. Let everyone know what you are looking for!

Size up your competition and know your market. Do you have something unique to offer the job market? Remember supply and demand? Know the market and where the jobs are at. As NACE (National Association of Colleges and Employers) states, "Don't look for petroleum industry jobs in the corn belt."

Market your worth! You need to present yourself as the 'best candidate,' one who is a good fit for the position. You need to go beyond just being a 'qualified' candidate. Meeting bare minimum requirements will not cut it.

Be cautious of the "I want it all" attitude and consider entry-level jobs which will give you the opportunity to prove yourself and move up. If you have stellar experience and can 'get it all,' then by all means do so. Also, remember to remain teachable. If being in college has prepared you for one thing, it's prepared you to be a lifelong learner.

So what's hot? Of course, technology fields are affording many opportunities, but many other fields are flourishing as well (communication services, insurance, computer services, hospitality/tourism, social services, and merchandising, to name a few). But should you pine after the hot jobs? Only if they truly interest you. You'll be better served to devote your time, expertise, and career to something that fits you. Do what you are!

For the many of you who will instinctively gravitate towards your career fields and dive in (much like the newly hatched sea turtles on the beach beelining to their new habitat, water), start your first year successfully. Learn how to work. There are so many nuances, inter-office politics, and rites of passage one needs to be aware of when entering the work force. Keep in mind you are not students anymore and you are not a professional yet. Learn the culture, manage a good impression, build allies and positive work relationships, please your boss, and earn the respect of those around you. Sounds basic, but even I have failed, at times, in those areas.

So with that, I leave my charges to the graduating senior class: Be world changers, do what you are, and suck the marrow out of life! Congratulations and welcome to the world of work!

Focus on Employers' Needs

Your objective should be a concise statement of what you want to do and what you have to offer to an employer. The position you seek is "what you want to do"; your qualifications are "what you have to offer." Your objective should state your strongest qualifications for meeting employers' needs. It should communicate what you have to offer an employer – not what you expect to get from the employer. In other words, your objective should be **work-centered**, not self-centered; it should not contain trite terms which emphasize what you want, such as give me a(n) "opportunity for advancement," "position working with people," "progressive company," or "creative position." Such terms are viewed as "canned" job search language which say little of value about you. Above all, your objective should reflect your honesty and integrity; it should not be "hyped."

Identifying what it is you want to do can be one of the most difficult job search tasks. Indeed, most job hunters lack clear objectives. Many engage in a random, often mindless, search for jobs by identifying available job opportunities and then adjusting their skills and objectives to fit specific job openings. While you can get a job using this approach, you may be misplaced and unhappy with what you find. You will try to fit into a job rather than find a job that is fit for you.

> *Your objective should be employer-centered rather than self-centered. It should reflect your honesty and integrity.*

Knowing what you want to do can have numerous benefits. First, you define the job market rather than let it define you. The inherent fragmentation and chaos of the job market should be advantageous for you, because it enables you to systematically organize job opportunities around your specific objectives and skills.

Second, you will communicate professionalism to prospective employers. They will receive a precise indication of your interests, qualifications, and purposes, which places you ahead of most other applicants.

Third, being purposeful means being able to communicate to employers what you really want to do. Employers are not interested in hiring indecisive and confused individuals who will probably have difficulty taking initiative because they really don't know what they should be doing in the first place. Employers want to know what it is you can and will do *for them*. With a clear objective – based upon a thorough understanding of your motivated skills and interests – you can take control of the situation as you demonstrate your value to employers.

Fourth, candidates with clear goals are better able to communicate their qualifications with energy and enthusiasm – key characteristics employers seek in candidates. Individuals without goals often appear uncertain and indecisive about what they want to do for employers.

Finally, few employers really know what they want in a candidate. Like most job seekers, employers lack clear employment objectives and knowledge about how the job market operates. If you know what you want and can help the employer define his or her "needs" as your objective, you will have achieved a tremendously advantageous position in the job market.

Be Purposeful and Realistic

Your objective should communicate that you are a **purposeful individual who achieves results**. It can be stated over different time periods as well as at various levels of abstraction and specificity. You can identify short-, intermediate-, and long-range objectives and very general to very specificobjectives. Whatever the case, it is best to know your prospective audience before deciding on the type of objective. Your objective should reflect your career interests as well as employers' needs.

Objectives also should be **realistic**. You may want to become President of the United States or solve all the world's problems. However, these objectives are probably unrealistic. While they may represent your ideals and fantasies, you need to be more realistic in terms of what you can personally accomplish in the immediate future given your particular skills, pattern of accomplishments, level of experience, and familiarity with the job market. What, for example, are you prepared to deliver to prospective employers over the next few months? While it is good to set challenging objectives, you can overdo it. Refine your objective by thinking about

> *The strongest goals combine your motivated abilities and skills with a realistic vision of your future.*

the next major step or two you would like to make in your career advancement. Develop a realistic action plan that focuses on the details of progressing your career one step at a time. By all means avoid making a grandiose leap outside reality!

State Manageable Goals

Dreams come in all sizes – big dreams, small dreams, and in-between dreams. They also can be stated within specific, measurable time frames: one week, three months, one year, five years, 10 years, or 25 years. Once your dreams become translated into career goals, some may be too big and complicated to operationalize; instead, they may frustrate you and thus lead you to abandon your dreams. Others may be too small to challenge you to achieve anything significant. Ideally, you want your dreams and goals to be big enough to motivate you to achieve greater things. For example, this may be your ultimate career dream:

Become President of the United States

Maybe it's attainable but don't let it frustrate you for the next 30 years. Try restating it as this more manageable goal:

Within the next 10 years, become the head of a terrific organization that enables me to fully use my skills and abilities to change other people's lives.

The two goals are basically the same but the second one is restated in more manageable terms. You can visualize what career steps you need to make in order to move to the top of such an organization. For example, you may decide as a prerequisite to achieving this goal that you need to get an accounting degree or an MBA. With the right amount of education, skills, connections, and drive, you may attain your 10-year goal. Eventually your organization just might become the country! The difference may be in the time frame – 30 years for the first goal and 10 years for the second goal. Whatever you do, don't abandon either goal, but at least get moving toward achieving the second goal within 10 years.

Let's take another example of setting realistic and manageable goals but in this case incorporate monetary considerations – a good indicator of how well you may do in comparison to others, the old "keeping score" approach to measuring progress. For example, if you are an ambitious 22-year old job seeker, perhaps this is your real dream:

Make $20 million by the age of 35.

Write yourself a check for $20 million and postdate it for your 35th, 50th, or 65th birthday. Then restate your objective as a more manageable step-by-step intermediate goal:

Increase my income by 20% a year over the next 10 years.

In this case, you can at least measure your progress in achieving your goal. Understanding the importance of moving from objectives to planning to implementation, you should next work out a weekly plan of action for achieving your yearly targeted goal. Without a plan of action for implementing your goals, your dreams are likely to remain unfulfilled fantasies and you may become frustrated with having so many dashed dreams and hopes of a better career and lifestyle.

Incorporate Your Dreams

Even after identifying your abilities and skills, specifying an objective can be the most difficult and tedious step in the job search process; it can stall the resume writing process indefinitely. This simple one-sentence, 25-word statement can take days or weeks to formulate and clearly define. Yet, it needs to be specified **prior to** writing the resume and engaging in other job search activities. It gives meaning and direction to everything you do in your job search.

Your objective should be viewed as a function of several influences. Since you want to build upon your strengths and you want to be realistic, your abilities and skills will play a central role in formulating your work objective. At the same time, you do not want your objective to become a function solely of your past accomplishments and skills. You may be very skilled in certain areas, but you may not want to use these skills in the future. As a result, your values and interests filter which skills you will or will not incorporate into your work objective.

Without a plan of action for implementing your goals, your dreams are likely to remain unfulfilled fantasies and frustrations.

Overcoming the problem of historical determinism – your future merely reflecting your past – requires incorporating additional elements into defining your objective. One of the most important is your ideals, fantasies, or dreams. Everyone engages in these, and sometimes they come true. Your ideals, fantasies, or dreams may include making $1,000,000 by age 27, owning a Porsche, taking frequent trips to Paris and Rome, owning your own business, developing financial independence, writing a best-selling novel, solving major social problems, or winning the Nobel Peace Prize. If your fantasies require more money than you are now making, you will need to incorporate monetary considerations into your work objective.

Our approach to developing a realistic objective is designed to provide you with sufficient corroborating data from several sources and perspectives so that you can make preliminary decisions. If you follow our steps in setting a realistic objective, you should be able to give your job search clear direction.

Talk the Language of Employers

Employers tend to favor candidates who are both purposeful and enthusiastic about their career and work. Enthusiasm is difficult to express unless you have a passion or purpose related to what you want to do.

Unfortunately, many job seekers make the mistake of communicating self-centered purposes or goals to employers. Rather, they should be developing work- or employer-centered goals that tell employers what they plan to do for the employer. Take, for example, these goals:

A marketing position in Biochemistry.

A challenging position in Public Relations that leads to career advancement.

These types of goals frequently appear at the beginning of resumes. Reading between the lines, these are essentially self-centered goals. They tell employers what it is you want from them. You essentially are saying the following:

I want this position because I want you to advance my career.

That's understandable from the perspective of the job seeker. But the prospective employer see you as another self-centered job seeker in search of a place to cut you generous paychecks and attractive benefits.

> ### The world of employers is all about exchanging benefits.

When you state an objective in such "me" terms, you basically tell an employer that he or she may have a nice platform from which you can realize your career goals. Okay. You want benefits from this job. But in exchange for what? So why should I hire you? So you can realize your career goals? So you can make more money on my payroll? So you can move on to another employer in six months with new skills and experience acquired through my company? Understandable, but that's not quite the way the world of employers works. That world is all about **exchanging** benefits.

The mind of the employer is very simple – the employer wants to hire people who will add value to the organization. He or she needs to know what it is you will bring to the organization. Talk to me about your **benefits for me** before I tell you about my **benefits for you**. What are you likely to accomplish for me? If I hire you, how much money will I save or how much additional income will you generate for this company? What is your predictable pattern of productivity? How will you solve my problems and with what outcomes for our organization? Give me some proof that you will do what you say you will do – not just make promises with the latest keywords and jargon about performance. Such employer-centered questions beg answers from job seekers who are often preoccupied with self-centered "me" issues.

Three Steps to Setting Realistic Goals

There's nothing really difficult about setting career goals or objectives. The major problem is making goal-setting a priority, allocating enough time to do it properly, and then just do it. At least in reference to your job search, one of the best ways to set goals and identify your career objective is to use the information you generated as you worked through the series of self-directed exercises in Chapters 3 and 4 as well as the remainder of this chapter which focuses on developing your own unique career objective.

It's important that you start with your career or job objective because it helps give direction to your job search. It will eventually be incorporated in your resume and discussed during job interviews. It should emphasize that you are a **purposeful individual who achieves results**. It should combine your interests and skills with the employer's needs. In so doing, it becomes a powerful work- or employer-centered rather than self-centered objective.

You will eventually want to develop a very succinct, one-sentence, 25-word objective. Doing so may take you many hours or days trying to refine what you really want to do. This is not something to take lightly. The more time you spend on specifying a career objective, the better organized and targeted will be your job search. One of the most thorough ways of developing a career objective is to follow this progressive three-step process:

1. Gather important data about your interests, skills, and abilities.

2. Project your values and preferences into the future.

3. Test and refine your objective against reality.

Each step includes a series of self-directed pencil and paper exercises as well as some external testing and the use of the Internet. When completed, you should be able to produce a very thoughtful work- or employer-centered objective that will serve you well when writing your resume, networking, and interviewing for jobs. Providing a renewed sense of purpose, this objective should give meaning to your whole job search and perhaps to your future work life.

Step 1

The first step is to gather information about yourself from others, tests, and you, yourself. Use the following resources for gathering such data:

A. **From others:** Ask three to five individuals whom you know well to evaluate you according to the questions in the "Strength Evaluation" form on page 72. Explain to these people that you plan to conduct a job search. You would greatly appreciate their candid appraisal so you can gain a better understanding of your strengths and weaknesses from the perspectives of others. Make copies of this form and ask your evaluators to complete and return it to a designated third party who will share the information – but not the respondent's name – with you.

Strength Evaluation

TO: _____

FROM: _____

I am going through a career assessment process and thought you would be an appropriate person to ask for assistance. Would you please candidly respond to the questions below? Your comments will be given to me by the individual designed below; s/he will not reveal your name. Your comments will be used for advising purposes only. Thank you.

What are my strengths?

What weak areas might I need to improve?

In your opinion, what do I need in a job or career to make me satisfied?

Please return to: _____

B. **From vocational tests**: While we prefer self-generated data, vocationally-oriented tests can help clarify, confirm, and translate your understanding of yourself into occupational directions. If you decide to use vocational tests, contact a professional career counselor who can administer and interpret the tests. They can be found through community colleges, local workforce development offices, and private testing and assessment companies. Check out the U.S. Department of Labor's America's CareerInfoNet website for assistance in locating a career professional near your community: www.acinet.org/acinet. This website also has lots of other useful career resources to help you in your job search. We recommend exploring several of the tests outlined on pages 38-39 and available through major websites identified on pages 48-49.

C. **From yourself**: Numerous alternatives are available for you to practice redundancy. Refer to the exercises in Chapter 4 which assist you in identifying your work values, job frustrations and dissatisfactions, things you love to do, things you enjoy most about work, and your preferred interpersonal environments.

Step 2

Project your values and preferences into the future by completing these simulation and creative thinking exercises:

A. **$30 Million Lottery Exercise**: First, assume that you have just won a $30 million lottery; now you don't have to work. After taxes, you have $20 million to work with. You decide the first $10 million will be for your use only – no giveaways or charities. What will you do with your time? At first? Later on? Second, you decide to give away the remaining $10 million. What kinds of causes, organizations, charities, etc. would you support? Complete the following exercise in which you answer these compelling questions:

What Will I Do With $20 Million?

First $10 million is restricted to my use only:

_____

_____

_____

_____

Second $10 million will be given away:

_____

_____

_____

_____

B. **Obituary Exercise:** Make a list of the most important things you would like to do or accomplish before you die. You can identify your "to do" list two different ways. First, make a list in response to this lead-in statement: *"Before I die, I want to..."*

Before I Die, I Want to . . .

1. _____

_____

2. _____

_____

3. _____

_____

4. _____

_____

5. _____

_____

6. _____

_____

7. _____

_____

8. _____

_____

9. _____

_____

10. _____

_____

Second, write a newspaper article which is actually your obituary for 10 years from now. Stress your accomplishments over the coming 10-year period.

My Obituary

Obituary for Mr./Ms. _____ to appear in the __
_____ Newspaper in the year 20____.

_____ _____

_____

_____

_____

_____

_____

_____

_____

_____

_____

_____

_____

_____

C. **My Ideal Work Week:** Starting with Monday, place each day of the week as the headings of seven sheets of paper. Develop a daily calendar with 30-minute intervals, beginning at 7am and ending at midnight. Your calendar should consist of a 118-hour week. Next, beginning at 7am on Monday (sheet one), identify the **ideal activities** you would enjoy doing, or need to do, for each 30-minute segment during the day. Assume you are capable of doing anything; you have no constraints except those you impose on yourself. Furthermore, assume that your work schedule consists of 40 hours per week. How will you fill your time? Be specific in completing this exercise.

D. **My Ideal Job Description:** Develop your ideal job. Be sure you include:

- Specific interests you want to build into your job
- Work responsibilities
- Working conditions
- Earnings and benefits
- Interpersonal environment
- Working circumstances, opportunities, and goals

Description of My Ideal Job

_____

_____

_____

_____

_____

_____

Use "My Ideal Job Specifications" on page 77 to outline your ideal job. After completing this exercise, synthesize the job and write a detailed paragraph which describes the job you would most enjoy.

Step 3

Test your objective against reality. Refine it by conducting market research, force field analysis, library research, and informational interviews.

A. **Market Research:** Based upon all other assessment activities, make a list of what you **do** or **make**:

Products/Services I Do or Make

1. _____

2. _____

3. _____

4. _____

5. _____

My Ideal Job Specifications

Job Interests	Work Responsibilities	Working Conditions	Earnings/Benefits	Circumstances/Opportunities/Goals

B. Conduct Online and Library Research: Research should strengthen and clarify your objective. Consult various reference materials on alternative jobs and careers. Most of these resources are available in print form at your local library or bookstore. Some are available in electronic versions online. If you explore the numerous company profiles and career sites available on the Internet, you should be able to tap into a wealth of information on alternative jobs and careers. Two of the best resources for initiating online research is Margaret Dikel and Frances Roehm's, *The Guide to Internet Job Search* and Pam Dixon's *Job Searching Online for Dummies*. For directories to key employment websites, see Ron and Caryl Krannich, *America's Top Internet Job Sites* and *The Directory of Websites for International Jobs*; Bernard Haldane Associates, *Haldane's Best Employment Websites for Professionals*; and Gerry Crispin and Mark Mehler, *CareerXroads*. Many of the resources traditionally found in libraries are available online. The following websites function as excellent gateway sites, online databases, and research tools:

- CEO Express   ceoexpress.com
- Hoover's Online   hoovers.com
- Dun and Bradstreet's
  Million Dollar Database   dnbmdd.com/mddi
- Corporate Information   corporateinformation.com
- BizTech Network   brint.com
- AllBusiness   www.allbusiness.com
- BizWeb   bizweb.com
- Business.com   business.com
- America's CareerInfoNet   www.acinet.org
- Newspapers USA   www.newspapers.com
- Salary.com   salary.com
- Forbes Lists   forbes.com/lists
- Annual Reports   annualreportservice.com
- Chambers of Commerce   www.chambers.com
- Daily Stocks   dailystocks.com
- The Corporate Library   thecorporatelibrary.com
- Forbes 500   forbes.com/lists
- Fortune 500   fortune.com
- Harris InfoSource   www.harrisinfo.com
- Inc. 500   inc.com/inc500
- Moodys   www.moodys.com
- NASDAQ   nasdaq.com
- One Source Corp Tech   onesource.com/products/
  Profiles   corptech.htm
- NASDAQ   nasdaq.com
- Standard & Poors   standardandpoors.com

- Thomas Regional   thomasregional.com
- Thomas Register   thomasregister.com
- Wall Street Research Net   wsrn.com

Career and Job Alternatives

- *Enhanced Guide for Occupational Exploration*
- *Guide to Occupational Exploration*
- *Occupational Outlook Handbook*
- *Occupational Outlook Quarterly*
- *O*NET Dictionary of Occupational Titles*

Industrial Directories

- *Bernard Klein's Guide to American Directories*
- *Dun and Bradstreet's Middle Market Directory*
- *Dun and Bradstreet's Million Dollar Directory*
- *Encyclopedia of Business Information Sources*
- *Geography Index*
- *Poor's Register of Corporations, Directors, and Executives*
- *Standard Directory of Advertisers*
- *The Standard Periodical Directory*
- *Standard and Poor's Industrial Index*
- *Standard Rate & Data Business Publications Directory*
- *Thomas' Register of American Manufacturers*

Associations

- *Encyclopedia of Associations*
- *National Trade and Professional Associations*
- Access thousands of associations online through: Ipl.org/ref/ AON, associationcentral.com, and www.asaenet.org.

Government Sources

- *The Book of the States*
- *Congressional Directory*
- *Congressional Staff Directory*
- *Congressional Yellow Book*
- *Federal Directory*
- *Federal Yellow Book*
- *Municipal Yearbook*
- *Taylor's Encyclopedia of Government Officials*
- *United Nations Yearbook*

- *United States Government Manual*
- *Washington Information Directory*

Newspapers

- Major city newspapers and trade newspapers. Many are available online through these gateway sites: Ipl.org/reading/news, newsdirectory.com, newspaperlinks.com, and www.newspapers. com.

- Your targeted city newspaper – the Sunday edition.

Business Publications

- *Business 2.0, Business Week, Economist, Fast Company, Forbes, Inc., Fortune, Harvard Business Review, Newsweek, Red Herring, Smart Money, Time,* and *U.S. News and World Report.* Many of these and other business-oriented publications can be viewed online through this terrific website: CEOExpress.com.

- Annual issues of publications surveying the best jobs and employers for the year: *Money, Fortune, Forbes,* and *U.S. News and World Report.* Several of these reports and publications are available online: money.com, fortune.com, and forbes.com/ lists.

Other Library Resources

- Trade journals
- Publications of Chambers of Commerce; state manufacturing associations; and government agencies
- Telephone books – The Yellow Pages
- Trade books on "how to get a job" (see order form at the end of this book and www.impactpublications.com)

C. **Conduct Informational Interviews:** This may be the most useful way to clarify and refine your objective. We'll discuss this procedure in Chapter 8.

After completing these steps, you will have enlarged your thinking to include what it is you would **like** to do (aspirations), and probed the realities of implementing your objective. Thus, setting a realistic work objective is a function of the diverse considerations outlined on page 81.

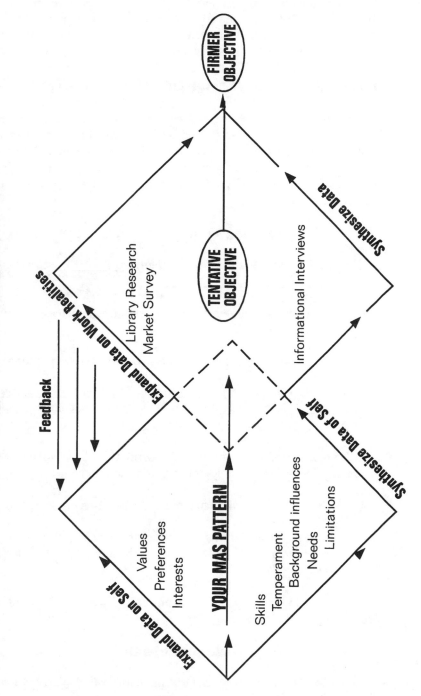

Objective Setting Process

Your strongest emphasis should be on your **competencies**. Your work objective is realistic in that it is tempered by your past experiences, accomplishments, skills, and current research. An objective formulated in this manner permits you to think beyond your past experiences.

State an Employer-Oriented Objective

Your job objective should be oriented toward skills and results or outcomes. You can begin by stating a job objective at two different levels: a general objective and a specific one for communicating your qualifications to employers both on resumes and in interviews. Thus, this objective-setting process sets the stage for other key job search activities. For the general objective, begin with the statement:

Stating Your General Objective

I would like a job where I can use my ability to _____which will result in _____.

The objective in this statement is both a **skill** and an **outcome**. For example, you might state:

Skills-Based and Results-Oriented Objective

I would like a job where my <u>experience in product management, supported by excellent organization and customer relations skills</u>, will result in <u>a significant increase in sales and a more profitable company</u>.

At a second level you may wish to re-write this objective to target various hospitality firms. For example, on your resume it becomes:

Job-Targeted Objective

A position as Operations Manager, where proven management abilities and customer relations skills will be used for expanding the profitability and performance of the company.

The following statements are examples of weak and strong objectives presented in various styles:

Weak Objectives

A challenging electrical engineering position with a leading energy firm that will provide opportunities for career advancement.

A position in computer security which will allow me to work with people and maintain high security standards.

A position in Sales with a progressive firm.

A Management Trainee position with opportunity for advancement.

Stronger Objectives

*To use innovative **landscape design** training for developing award-winning approaches to designing commercial properties.*

A public relations position focused on developing and implementing programs, organizing people and events, and communicating positive ideas and images. Effective in public speaking and in managing publicity/promotional campaigns.

A position as a General Sales Representative with a pharmaceutical house which will use chemistry background and ability to work on a self-directed basis in managing a marketing territory.

A position in banking where skills in sales, accounts management, and customer relations will result in a high retention rate of current clients and a rapid increase in new customers.

Retail Management position which will use sales/customer service experience and abilities to produce innovative displays and creative merchandising approaches. Long term goal: Merchandise Manager with corporate-wide responsibilities for promoting product lines.

Responsible position in investment research and analysis. Interests and skills include securities analysis, financial planning, and portfolio management. Long range goal: Chartered Financial Analyst.

It is important to relate your objective to your key audience – employers. While you want a good paying job, employers want to know what you can do for them in exchange for a good paying job.

Your objective says something very important about how you want to conduct your life with the employer. It gives them an important indicator of the value you will bring to this job. Most important of all, it tells them who you really are in terms of your key values and accomplishments – a short answer to the big question of *"Why should I hire you?"*

Gurus and Goal Setting Resources

Numerous resources are available to assist you in setting goals and achieving success. Many of the most popular resources are designed for individuals in sales occupations who must constantly stay motivated in the face of numerous rejections that might ordinarily discourage them from continuing to pursue their sales goals. These resources, in the form of audio tapes and books, are relevant to job seekers who face similar situations – approaching strangers (potential employers) who often reject them. As you will quickly discover, staying motivated throughout your job search can be a major challenge! Most of these resources can help you throughout your job search by focusing on goals, motivation, and personal achievement.

Staying motivated throughout your job search can be a major challenge.

Many of these resources focus on positive thinking, personal achievement, and thinking big. This is the literature of self-transformation in which **setting goals and staying focused** on achieving goals constitute a powerful approach to personal achievement and success. While most of these resources are filled with lots of hype, they do work for millions of individuals who have discovered the power of self-transformation.

We highly recommend reviewing many of the following books which are part of the huge positive thinking and self-transformation business. Authors with such names as Robbins, Tracy, Hill, Carnegie, Ziglar, and Sher have become gurus to millions of individuals who have changed their lives by following the positive thinking approaches of these "thinking big" personal achievement coaches. Each year they sponsor millions of dollars in revival-style seminars and promote back-of-the-room audio and book sales.

What these motivational gurus preach is a very simple yet effective message – you can achieve anything you want to *("Be whatever you want to be")* as long as you set goals and stay focused on achieving those goals. While intelligence, talent, and habits play important roles in achieving success, the single-minded pursuit of a clearly defined goal – a passion of purpose – may be your most important asset in achieving success.

Whatever you do, don't dismiss these resources as hocus-pocus. Instead, treat them as a form of hopeful-focus! We highly recommend reading several of the following books as you prepare for developing your job and career objective. Any one of these books could literally change your life!

Awaken the Giant Within, Anthony Robbins (Fireside, 1993)

Create Your Own Future: How to Master the 12 Critical Factors of Unlimited Success, Brian Tracy (John Wiley & Sons, 2002)

Dreams Into Action: Getting What You Want, Milton Katselas (Dove Books, 1997)

Eat That Frog!, Brian Tracy (Berrett-Koehler Publishing, 2001)

Focal Point, Brian Tracy (AMACOM, 2001)

Goal Setting 101: How to Set and Achieve a Goal, Gary Ryan Blair (The GoalsGuy, 2000)

Goals and Goal Setting, Larrie A. Rouillard (Crisp Publications, 1998)

High Performance Goal Setting, Beverly Potter (Ronin Publishing, 2000)

How to Get What You Want and Want What You Have, John Gray (HarperTrade, 2000)

I Could Do Anything If Only I Knew What It Was: How to Discover What You Really Want and How to Get It, Barbara Sher (Dell Publishing Company, 1995)

Life Strategies: Doing What Works, Doing What Matters, Philip C. McGraw (Hyperion, 2000)

The Magic Lamp: Goal Setting for People Who Hate Setting Goals, Keith Ellis (Crown Publishing Group, 1998)

The Magic of Believing, Claude M. Bristol (Simon & Schuster, 1991)

The Magic of Thinking Big, David Schwartz (Fireside, 1987)

Maximum Achievement, Brian Tracy (Fireside, 1995)

Motivation and Goal Setting, Jim Cairo (Career Press, 1998)

The Power of Focus, Jack L. Canfield, Leslie Hewitt, and Mark Victor Hansen (Health Communications, Inc., 2000)

The Power of Positive Thinking, Norman Vincent Peale (Ballantine Books, 1996)

The Power of Purpose, Richard J. Leider (Berrett-Koehler Publishing, 1997)

The Practical Dreamer's Handbook, Paul and Sarah Edwards (Putnam Publishing, 2001)

Secrets for Success and Happiness, Og Mandino (Fawcett Book Group, 1996)

Seven Habits of Highly Effective People, Steven P. Covey (Simon & Schuster, 1990)

Success Through a Positive Mental Attitude, Napoleon Hill and W. Clement Stone (Simon & Schuster, 1992)

Think and Grow Rich, Napoleon Hill (Fawcett Books, 1990)

Unlimited Power: A Black Choice, Anthony Robbins (Fawcett Books, 1996)

Wishcraft: How to Get What You Really Want, Barbara Sher (Ballantine Books, 1986)

You Can Become the Person You Want to Be, Dr. Robert H. Schuller (Jove Publications, 1995)

6

Conduct Research

THE OLD ADAGE THAT "KNOWLEDGE IS POWER" IS ESPE-cially true when conducting a job search. Your job search is only as good as the knowledge you acquire and use for finding the job you want.

Gathering, processing, and using information is the lifeblood of any job search. Given the numerous individuals and organizations involved in your job search, you must develop an information gathering strategy that will help you gain knowledge about, as well as access to, those individuals and organizations that will play the most important role in your job search.

Investigate Job and Career Alternatives

Your initial research should help familiarize you with **job and career alternatives**. For example, the U.S. Department of Labor now identifies over 1,100 job titles (condensed from over 13,000 job titles a few years ago). Most individuals are occupationally illiterate; they are unaware of the vast array of available jobs and careers. Therefore, it is essential to investigate occupational alternatives in order to broaden your perspective on the job market.

You should start your research by examining several key directories that provide information on alternative jobs and careers:

- *Occupational Outlook Handbook*
- *Enhanced Guide to Occupational Exploration*
- *Guide to Occupational Exploration*
- *O*NET Dictionary of Occupational Titles*

The latest version of the *Occupational Outlook Handbook,* most data related to the *O*NET,* and other useful career exploration information can be accessed online through these three U.S. Department of Labor websites:

- *OOH*   www.bls.gov/oco
- *O*NET*   www.onetcenter.org
- **America's CareerInfoNet**   www.acinet.org

You will also find several books that focus on alternative jobs and careers. McGraw-Hill, for example, produces one of the most comprehensive series of books on alternative jobs and careers. Their books address nearly 100 different job and career fields. Representative titles in their *Opportunities in . . .* series include:

- *Opportunities in Acting*
- *Opportunities in Aerospace*
- *Opportunities in Business Management*
- *Opportunities in Computer Systems*
- *Opportunities in Health and Medical Careers*
- *Opportunities in Laser Technology*
- *Opportunities in Pharmacy Careers*
- *Opportunities in Public Relations*
- *Opportunities in Teaching*
- *Opportunities in Visual Arts*

This company also publishes two other useful sets of career exploration books in a *Careers in...* and a *Careers for You* series. Titles in the *Careers in...* series include:

- *Careers in Business*   - *Careers in Journalism*
- *Careers in Communications*   - *Careers in Law*
- *Careers in Computers*   - *Careers in Marketing*
- *Careers in Education*   - *Careers in Medicine*
- *Careers in Engineering*   - *Careers in Science*
- *Careers in Environment*   - *Careers in Finance*

The nearly 50 books in the *Careers for You* series include such titles as:

- *Careers for Animal Lovers*
- *Careers for Caring People*

- *Careers for Computer Buffs & Other Technological Types*
- *Careers for Culture Lovers and Other Artsy Types*
- *Careers for Environmental Types*
- *Careers for Financial Mavens & Other Money Movers*
- *Careers for Foreign Language Aficionados*
- *Careers for History Buffs*
- *Careers for Music Lovers*
- *Careers for Sports Nuts*

Facts on File publishes 15 volumes on alternative jobs and careers in various industries, including such titles as:

- *Career Opportunities in Advertising and Public Relations*
- *Career Opportunities in Art*
- *Career Opportunities in Computers and Cyberspace*
- *Career Opportunities in Health Care*
- *Career Opportunities in the Music Industry*
- *Career Opportunities in Theater and Performing Arts*

Many other books examine a wide range of jobs and careers. Some are annual or biannual reviews of today's most popular jobs. You should find several of these books particularly helpful:

- *200 Best Jobs for College Graduates* (JIST Works)
- *America's Top Jobs for College Graduates* (JIST Works)
- *Best Jobs for the 21st Century*, Ron and Caryl Krannich (Impact)
- *Best Jobs for the 21st Century for College Graduates*, Michael Farr and LaVerne L. Ludden (JIST Works)
- *College Grad Job Hunter*, Brian D. Krueger (Adams Media)
- *Cool Careers for Dummies*, Nemko and Edwards (Wiley & Sons)

If you are unable to find these books in your local library or bookstore, they can be ordered directly from Impact Publications. Order information is found at the end of this book or online: www.impactpublications.com.

Target Organizations

After completing research on occupational alternatives, you should identify specific organizations which you are interested in learning more about. Next, compile lists of names, addresses, and telephone numbers of important individuals in each organization. You are well advised to browse the company profiles on campuscareercenter.com and in Chapter 13 of this book. Also, explore the home pages of companies on the Internet and write or telephone them for information, such as an annual report and recruiting literature.

Be an Opportunist – Find a Company That's Right for You

Robert L. Rostoni, Director of Career Services, Nyack College

The 'new graduate' is pining for opportunity in the 'new economy.' These graduates are confident that they will achieve their goals. Roadblocks are 'opportunities,' time is something to be conquered, not just passed. There's a sense of optimism in the air among the 'new graduate.' But what of the cutbacks? What of the flying pink slips? Should the new graduate embrace reality and settle for less? That depends on you and what you do with your bootstraps. The opportunist will see a buyer's potential in a bear market. the opportunist will look past acute national losses and see that overall we still have a growing economy. The opportunist will find a way around the word 'no.'

My first suggestion for the new graduate is to use your liberal arts critical thinking skills. Think about where the opportunity is and seize it! When it rains – sell umbrellas. When overall hiring is down – find out who they are still hiring (i.e., entry-level opportunities may rise, domestic, rather than international employment may increase, and markets may emerge from depths of doom and gloom). Take heart.

Graduates – align yourselves with companies that realize the value of an aspiring professional. Smart companies will recruit young talent during these times. For you painstakingly investigative students – look into companies' spending habits and go after the ones who aren't overspending (you just might have your job longer).

Whatever the wax and wane in our economy and hiring trends, the most employable mindset is to simply do what you are from an opportunist point of view.

The most important information you should be gathering concerns the organizations' goals, structures, functions, problems, and projected future opportunities and development. Since you invest part of your life in such organizations, treat them as you would a stock market investment. Compare and evaluate different organizations.

Several directories will assist you in researching organizations. Most are available in the reference sections of libraries and some can be found online. We identified several of these directories and websites on pages 78 and 79. If you have only time to visit a few of the business websites, make sure they include our top five:

- **CEO Express** — ceoexpress.com
- **Hoover's Online** — hoovers.com
- **Dun and Bradstreet's Million Dollar Database** — dnbmdd.com/mddi
- **Corporate Information** — corporateinformation.com
- **BizTech Network** — brint.com

If you are interested in jobs with a particular organization, you should visit their website for employment information and/or contact the human resources office for information on the types of jobs offered within the organization. Many companies include an extensive and relatively sophisticated employment section on their homepage that allows individuals to enter their resumes or brief profiles into a company database or apply online for specific positions. Indeed, companies are increasingly recruiting online for all types of positions, from entry-level to top management. Good examples include Cisco Systems (cisco.com), Motorola (motorola.com), Microsoft (microsoft.com), and the Boston Consulting Group (bcg.com). You may be able to examine vacancy announcements which describe the duties and responsibilities of specific jobs as well as survey the profiles of key company personnel. Some companies even include information about the company culture and tips on conducting an effective job search with the company! If you are interested in working for government, nonprofit organizations, and/or international employers, see our extensive list of relevant websites in Chapter 12.

Contact Individuals

While examining websites and directories and reading books on alternative jobs and careers will provide you with useful job search information, much of this material may be too general for specifying the right job for you. In the end, the best information will come directly from people in specific jobs in specific organizations. To get this information you must interview people. You especially want to learn more about the people who make the hiring decisions.

You might begin your investigations by contacting various professional and trade associations for detailed information on jobs and careers relevant to their members. Since most of these organizations have homepages on the Internet, you should be able to locate their websites by using one of the standard search engines, such as google.com and yahoo.com, or by visiting these two gateway websites to trade and professional associations:

- **Associations on the Net**   ipl.org/ref/AON
- **AssociationCentral**   associationcentral.com

For names, addresses, telephone numbers, websites, e-mails, and publications of such associations, consult the following key directories, which are available in most libraries:

- *The Encyclopedia of Associations* (Thomson Learning)
- *National Trade and Professional Associations* (Columbia Books)

Your most productive research activity will be talking to people or networking for information, advice, and referrals. Informal, word-of-mouth communication is still the most effective channel of job search information. In contrast to reading books or surfing the Internet, people have more current, detailed, and accurate information. Ask them about:

- Occupational fields
- Job requirements and training
- Interpersonal environments
- Performance expectations
- Their problems
- Salaries
- Advancement opportunities
- Future growth potential of the organization
- How to acquire more information and contacts in a particular field

You may be surprised how willingly friends, acquaintances, and strangers will give you useful information. But before you talk to people, do your research so that you are better able to ask thoughtful questions.

Ask the Right Questions

The quality of your research will only be as good as the questions you ask. Therefore, you should focus on a few key questions that will yield useful information for guiding your job search. Answers to these questions will help make important job search decisions relevant to informational and job interviews.

Who Has the Power to Hire?

Finding out who has the power to hire may take some research effort on your part. Keep in mind that human resources offices normally do not have the power to hire. They handle much of the paperwork involved in announcing vacancies, taking applications, testing candidates, screening credentials, and placing new employees on the payroll. In other words, personnel offices tend to perform auxiliary support functions for those who do the actual hiring – usually individuals in operating units.

If you want to learn who really has the power to hire, you need to conduct research on the particular organization that interests you. You should ask specific questions concerning who normally is responsible for various parts of the hiring process:

- Who describes the positions?
- Who announces vacancies?
- Who receives applications?

- Who administers tests?
- Who selects eligible candidates?
- Who chooses whom to interview?
- Who conducts the interview?
- Who offers the jobs?

If you ask these questions about a specific position you will quickly identify who has what powers to hire. Chances are the power to hire is **shared** between the human resources office and the operating unit. You should not neglect the personnel office, and in some cases it will play a powerful role in all aspects of the hiring. Your research will reveal to what degree the hiring function is centralized, decentralized, or fragmented in an organization.

How Does Organization X Operate?

It's best to know as much as possible about the internal operations of an organization before joining it. Your research may uncover information that would convince you that a particular organization is not one in which you wish to invest your time and effort. You may learn, for example, that Company X has a history of terminating employees before they become vested in the company retirement system. Or Company X may be experiencing serious financial problems and morale may be extremely low. They may lie to their employees or engage in unethical behavior. Or advancement within Company X may be very political, and company politics are vicious and debilitating.

You can get financial information about most companies by examining their annual reports as well as by talking to individuals who know the organization well. Information on the internal operations, especially company politics and power, must come from individuals who work within the organization. Ask them *"Is this a good organization to work for?"* and let them expand on specific areas you wish to probe – advancement opportunities, working conditions, relationships among co-workers and supervisors, growth patterns, internal politics, management style, work values, opportunities for taking initiative.

What Do I Need to Do to Get a
Job With Organization X?

The best way to find how to get a job in a particular organization is to follow the advice in the next chapter on prospecting, networking, and informational interviewing. This question can only be answered by talking to people who know both the formal and informal hiring practices.

You can get information on the formal hiring system by visiting the company's website or contacting the human resources office. A telephone call should be sufficient for this information.

But you must go beyond the formal system and human resources office in order to learn how best to conduct your job search. This means contacting people who know how one really gets hired in the organization, which may or may not follow the formal procedures. The best sources of information will be individuals who play a major role in the hiring process.

Identify the Right Community

Your final research target is central to all other research targets and it may occur at any stage in your research. Identifying the geographical area where you would like to work will be one of your most important decisions. Once you make this decision, other job search decisions and activities become easier. For example, if you live in a small college town, you probably need to move to a larger community that offers a wider range of job opportunities. If you decide to move to another community, you will need to develop a long-distance job search campaign which has different characteristics from a local campaign. It involves visiting community websites, writing letters, making long-distance phone calls, and visiting a community.

Deciding where you want to live involves researching various communities and comparing advantages and disadvantages of each. In addition to identifying specific job alternatives, organizations, and individuals in the community, you need to do research on other aspects of the community. After all, you will live in the community, buy or rent a residence, perhaps send children to school, and participate in community organizations and events. Often these environmental factors are just as important to your happiness and well-being as the particular job you accept. For example, you may be expecting to find a job paying $45,000 a year in your favorite community – San Francisco. But you may quickly find that $45,000 doesn't go very far if you have to pay 50 percent more for housing than in your present community – your current $800 a month apartment will be $1,600 in San Francisco. Consequently, it would be foolish for you to take a new job without first researching several facets of the community other than job opportunities.

Research on different communities can be initiated in a library or on the Internet. While most of this research will be historical in nature, several resources will provide you with a current profile of various communities. Statistical overviews and comparisons of states and cities are found in the *U.S. Census Data, The Book of the States,* and the *Municipal Yearbook.* Many libraries have a reference section of telephone books on various cities. If this section is weak or absent in your library, contact your local telephone company. They often have a relatively comprehensive library of telephone books. In addition to giving you names, addresses, and telephone numbers, the Yellow Pages are invaluable sources of information on the specialized structures of the public and private sectors of individual communities. Online telephone books, such as www.superpages.com, www.switchboard.com, www. bigbook.com, and www.yellowpages.com, also can be useful, if you know exactly what company you are looking for. The library may also have state and community directories as well as subscriptions to some state and community magazines and city newspapers.

The Internet has a wealth of information on the best places to live and work. For data and perspectives on the best places to live, visit these websites:

- **America's Best Online**   americasbestonline.com/
                                cities.htm
- **ChooseToCruise**   choosetocruise.com/america
                                two.html
- **Digital City**   digitalcity.com/bestplacestolive
- **Find Your Spot**   findyourspot.com
- **Kid Friendly Cities**   kidfriendlycities.org/2001
- **Money Magazine**   money.com/money/depts/
                                real_estate/bplive
- **Real Estate Journal**   homes.wsj.com/toolkit_res/
                                bestplaces.html
- **Sperling's BestPlaces**   www.bestplaces.net
- **School Report**   theschoolreport.com

For the best places to work, check out these websites:

- **BestJobsUSA**   bestjobsusa.com/sections/
                                CAN-bestplaces2001
- **EmploymentSpot**   employmentspot.com/lists
- **Forbes Magazine**   forbes.com/lists
- **Fortune Magazine**   fortune.com
                                (see "Fortune Lists")
- **Great Place to Work**   greatplacetowork.com/
                                100best/100best.html
- **Hoovers.com**   hoovers.com/company/
                                lists_best
- **iVillage**   ivillage.com/work
- **JobStar Central**   jobstar.org/hidden/bestcos.htm
- **Quintessential Careers**   quintcareers.com/best_places_
                                to_work.html

If you want to explore various communities, you should examine several of these gateway community sites:

- **Boulevards**   boulevards.com
- **CitySearch**   citysearch.com

- City Travel Guide   citytravelguide.com
- DigitalCity   digitalcity.com
- Insiders' Guides   insiders.com
- TOWD   www.towd.com
- USA City Link   usacitylink.com

Several relocation websites also provide a wealth of information on communities. Check these sites out for linkages to major communities:

- Homestore.com   homestore.com
- Monster.com   monstermoving.com
- Relocation Central   relocationcentral.com

Most major communities and newspapers have websites. You'll find a wealth of community-based information and linkages on such homepages, from newspapers and housing information to local employers, schools, recreation, and community services. Several employment sites include relocation information and salary calculators which provide information on the cost of living in, as well as the cost of moving to, different communities. These four websites provide linkages to thousands of newspapers:

- Internet Public Library   lpl.org/reading/news
- NewsDirectory.com   newsdirectory.com
- NewspaperLinks   newspaperlinks.com
- Newspapers.com   www.newspapers.com

If you are trying to determine the best place to live, you should start with the latest edition of David Savageau's and Richard Boyer's *Places Rated Almanac* (Simon & Schuster). This book ranks cities by various indicators. Both *Money* magazine and *U.S. News & World Report* publish annual surveys of the best places to live in the U.S.

Andrea Kay's *Greener Pastures: How to Find a Job in Another Place* (St. Martin's) outlines useful strategies for conducting a long-distance job search campaign, including the emotional and financial challenges.

You should also consult several city job banks that will give you contact information on specific employers in major metropolitan communities. Adams Media regularly publishes *The National JobBank* as well as several annual job bank guides, which may or may not continue being updated. Some of the most popular titles include:

- *The Atlanta JobBank*
- *The Austin/San Antonio JobBank*
- *The Boston JobBank*
- *The Chicago JobBank*
- *The Dallas/Fort Worth JobBank*

- *The Denver JobBank*
- *The Florida JobBank*
- *The Houston JobBank*
- *The Las Vegas JobBank*
- *The Los Angeles JobBank*
- *The Minneapolis/St. Paul JobBank*
- *The New York JobBank*
- *The Philadelphia JobBank*
- *The San Francisco JobBank*
- *The Seattle JobBank*
- *The Washington D.C. JobBank*

After narrowing the number of communities that interest you, further research them in depth. Start by exploring community homepages on the Internet (search by community name). Then kick off community-based research. Ask your relatives, friends, and acquaintances for contacts in the particular community; they may know people whom you can write, telephone, or e-mail for information and referrals. Once you have decided to focus on one community, visit it in order to establish personal contacts with key reference points, such as the local Chamber of Commerce, real estate firms, schools, libraries, churches, government agencies, and business firms and associations. Begin developing personal networks based upon the research and referral strategies in the next chapter. Subscribe to the local newspaper and to any community magazines which help profile the community. Follow the help-wanted, society, financial, and real estate sections of the newspaper – especially the Sunday edition. Keep a list of names of individuals who appear to hold influential community positions; you may want to contact them for referrals. Write letters to set up informational interviews with key people; give yourself two months of lead time to complete your letter writing campaign. Your overall research should focus on developing personal contacts which may assist you in both your job search and your move to the community.

Know What's Really Important

Reviewing online and print resources can be extremely time consuming, if taken to the extreme. While you should examine several such resources, do not spend an inordinate amount of time reading, clicking, taking notes, and responding with e-mail. Embrace the Internet, but don't fall in love with it! Like working the classified ads in newspapers, the Internet tends to be a passive medium that can give you a false sense of making progress with your job search – because you're keeping yourself busy entering your resume into several online resume databases and periodically reviewing job listings, message boards, and chat groups. There are too many other important proactive job search actions, such as interpersonal networking, that you need to focus your effort on. Your time will be best spent in gathering information through meetings and conversations with key people. Your primary goals in conducting research should be identifying people to contact, making appointments, and asking the right questions which lead to more information and contacts. If you engage in these activities you will know what is important when conducting research.

As you get further into your job search, networking for information, advice, and referrals will become an important element in your overall job search strategy. At that time you will come into closer contact with potential employers who can provide you with detailed information on their organizations and specific jobs. If you have a well defined MAS, specific job objectives, and a clearly focused resume, you should be in a good position to make networking pay off with useful information, advice, and referrals. You will quickly discover that the process of linking your MAS and objectives to specific jobs is an ongoing one involving several steps in your job search.

7

Create Winning Resumes and Letters

N OW THAT YOU KNOW WHAT YOU DO WELL, WHAT YOU enjoy doing, and what you want to do in the future – based on your assessment and objective-setting work in Chapters 3 and 4 – you should be in great shape for communicating your most important qualifications to employers. So what messages do you want to send to employers about your interests, skills, and accomplishments? How will you convey your messages – by telephone, letter, email, fax, or in person? If you have little direct work experience, how can you best present yourself to prospective employers?

Communicate Positive Images

At every stage of the job search you must communicate positive images. Remember, you are a stranger to most employers who make quick screening decisions based on first impressions. The **initial impression** you make on an employer through your application, resume, letter, email, telephone call, or informational interview will determine whether or not the employer is interested in interviewing you and offering you a position.

Developing and managing effective job search communication should play a central role in everything you do related to finding employment. While this communication will take several verbal and nonverbal forms, your first communication with employers will most likely be by letter, email, fax, or telephone. Your resume will most likely serve as your most important calling card for opening employers' doors. Essentially a nonverbal form of communication, this document should be written and distributed according to certain rules of effective communication.

A Love-Hate Relationship

Everyone, including employers, seems to have a love-hate relationship with resumes and letters. While we know these documents are important to the job search and recruitment processes, few people are really satisfied with the form and content of resumes and letters. Some people even go so far as to advise against writing resumes and letters. As a result, you'll receive all kinds of advice, some controversial, on how to make resumes and letters more effective, from writing each section to distributing them by mail, fax, or email. With so much written about resumes and letters, one might think there was something very magical about them. Let's examine the mystique as we hone in on what's really important with resumes and letters.

Many job seekers write awful resumes and letters that work against their best interests. Their resumes and letters are frequently "dead upon arrival" because of many common writing, production, and distribution errors. If they're not dead upon arrival, they often go nowhere because the writer fails to follow up. Worst of all, most job seekers are unaware how bad their resumes and letters may be in the eyes of employers. Intensely ego-involved with the writing process, like admiring a photo of themselves, most job seekers like their resumes and letters. They just don't understand why employers don't like them as much as they do!

Missing the Point

The most important error job seekers make in reference to resumes and letters is misunderstanding the role these documents play in the overall job search. They mistakenly believe that resumes and letters result in jobs. Accordingly, they try to put as much information as possible about their work history on their resume. Many job seekers can't understand how they could possibly get everything about themselves onto one or two pages – the preferred length of resumes for employers.

If there is only one thing you learn about resumes and letters that will serve you well throughout your job search, it's this: **resumes and letters are advertisements for interviews**. Like a good ad in a magazine, they should give just enough information to motivate the reader to acquire the product. That product is you; being invited to an interview is the sale. Always remember that **it's the job interview – not a resume or letter – that results in a job offer**. If you define resumes and letters as advertising mediums rather than summaries of one's history, you'll be surprised how many resume and letter mistakes you'll avoid. Indeed, you'll easily be able to produce a one- to two-page advertisement about what benefits you are likely to give the reader. You'll also be very careful in selecting language and you'll pay particular attention to making sure you produce picture-perfect and error-free copy.

Many myths surround resumes and letters. Some people still believe a resume should summarize their history. Others believe it will get them a job. And still others believe a resume should be mailed or emailed in response to classified ads and job listings or submitted to resume databases. The reality is closer to this: A resume advertises your qualifications to prospective employers. It is your calling card for getting interviews that lead to job offers. It should be used at any time to enhance your employability.

> *A resume advertises your qualifications to prospective employers. It is your calling card for getting interviews.*

Myths and Promising Realities

Numerous myths surround resumes and letters. Misunderstanding what these written documents are all about prevents many job seekers from taking effective action. Over the years we have catalogued nearly 30 myths and corresponding realities for clarifying the use of resumes and letters in an effective job search. Each myth and reality relates to various aspects of writing, producing, distributing, and following-up processes:

Winning the Job

MYTH 1: **The best way to find a job is to respond to classified ads, use employment agencies, submit applications, contact personnel offices, and put your resume online.**

REALITY: While many people get jobs by following such formal application procedures, these are not necessarily the most effective ways to get the best jobs – those offering good pay, advancement opportunities, and an appropriate "fit" with one's abilities and goals. Many of the best jobs are neither listed nor advertised; they are primarily uncovered through word-of-mouth and executive recruiters or by knocking on doors. As we note in Chapter 8 on networking, your most fruitful job search strategy will be to network for information, advice, and referrals in the "hidden job market." Make sure your job search includes a very active networking campaign to uncover such jobs.

MYTH 2:   A good resume and cover letter will get me a job.

REALITY: Resumes and letters don't get jobs – they advertise you for job interviews. Your resumes and letters are **marketing tools** designed to communicate your qualifications to employers. From the perspective of employers, resumes and letters are used to screen candidates for interviews.

MYTH 3:   The candidate with the best education, skills, and experience will get the job.

REALITY: Employers hire individuals for many different reasons. Education, skills, and experience are only a few of the various hiring criteria. Surprising to some candidates, these criteria may **not** be the most important in the eyes of many employers. Employers interview candidates because they want to see warm bodies – how you look and interact with them and how you will fit into their organization. The most important reason for hiring you is that the employer "likes" you. How "likes" is defined will vary from one employer and organization to another.

MYTH 4:   You can plan all you want, but getting a job is really a function of good luck.

REALITY: Luck is a function of being in the right place at the right time to take advantage of opportunities that come your way. But how do you plan your luck? The best way to have luck come your way is to plan to be in many different places at many different times through networking.

Deciding on Resume Content

MYTH 5:   The best type of resume is one that outlines employment history by job titles, responsibilities, and inclusive employment dates.

REALITY: This is the traditional chronological or "obituary" resume. It's filled with historical "what" information – what work you did, in what organizations, over what period of time. This type of resume may tell employers little about what it is you can do for them. You should choose a resume format that clearly communicates your major strengths. Your choices include variations of the chronological, functional, and combination resumes – each offering different advantages and disadvantages.

MYTH 6:   It's not necessary to put an objective on the resume.

REALITY: Recent survey research (The McLean Group and Career Masters Institute, February 2002) with employers validates the importance of objectives on resumes: employers are especially attracted to resumes that include objectives that either state an applicant's career goal (what he or she wants to do career-wise) or what an applicant can do for the organization. Employers are especially attracted to coherent resumes that are easy to read and interpret. An objective – stated at the very top of your resume – becomes the central focus from which all other elements in your resume should flow. The objective gives the resume organization, coherence, and direction. It tells employers exactly who you are in terms of your goals and skills. If properly stated, your objective will become one of the most powerful and effective statements on your resume. Without an objective, you force the employer to "interpret" your resume. Thus, it is to your advantage to set the agenda – control the flow and interpretation of your qualifications and capabilities by stating the objective. If nothing else, stating an objective on your resume is a thoughtful thing to do for the employer. And always remember, employers "like" thoughtful people!

MYTH 7:   **Employers prefer long resumes because they present more complete information for screening candidates than short resumes.**

REALITY: Employers prefer one- or two-page resumes. Longer resumes lose the interest and attention of readers. They usually lack a focus, are filled with extraneous information, need serious editing, and are oriented toward the applicant's past rather than the employer's future. But this one- to two-page rule does not apply to all employment situations. Individuals applying for academic and international jobs, for example, may be expected to write a five- to 10-page curriculum vitae (CV) rather than a one- to two-page resume. In these special situations the CV is actually a traditional chronological resume prominently displaying dates, job titles, responsibilities, and publications.

MYTH 8:   It's okay to put salary expectations on a resume.

REALITY: One of the worst things you can do is to mention salary on your resume. Remember, the purpose of your resume is to get an interview – not negotiate terms of employment. Only during the interview – and preferably toward the very end – should you discuss salary. Before you discuss salary, you want to demonstrate your **value** to employers as well as learn about the **worth** of the position. If you prematurely discuss salary, you will most likely put yourself at a disadvantage when it comes time to talk about money.

MYTH 9:   **Contact information (your name, address, phone, email) should appear in the left-hand corner of your resume.**

REALITY: You can choose from a variety of resume formats which place the contact information in several different positions at the top of the resume. Choose the one that best complements the remaining layout and style of the resume.

MYTH 10:   **You should not include your hobbies or any personal statements on a resume.**

REALITY: In general this is true. However, there are exceptions which would challenge this rule as a myth. If you have a hobby or a personal statement that can strengthen your objective in relation to the employer's needs, do include it on your resume. For example, if a job calls for someone who is outgoing and energetic, you would not want to include a hobby or personal statement that indicates that you are a very private and sedentary person, such as *"enjoy reading and writing"* or *"collect stamps."* But *"enjoy organizing community fund drives"* and *"compete in the Boston Marathon"* might be very appropriate statements for your resume. Such statements further emphasize the "unique you" in relation to your capabilities, the requirements for the position, and the employer's needs.

MYTH 11:   **You should list your references on the resume so the employer can check them before the interview.**

REALITY: Never include references on your resume. The closest you should ever get to doing so is to include this statement at the very end: "References available upon request." **You** want to control your references for the interview.

Producing the Resume

MYTH 12:   **You should try to get as much as possible on each page of your resume.**

REALITY: Each page of your resume should be appealing to the eye. It should make an immediate favorable impression, be inviting and easy to read, and look professional. You achieve these qualities by using a variety of layout, type style, highlighting, and emphasizing techniques. When formatting each section of your resume, be sure to make generous use of white space. Bullet and underline items for emphasis. If you try to cram a great deal on each page, your resume will look cluttered and uninviting to the reader.

MYTH 13:   **You should have your resume produced by a graphic designer and professionally printed.**

REALITY: You may want to go to the expense of hiring a graphic designer and printing, depending on your audience. However, it is not necessary for most positions to go to such an extreme in order to impress your reader. Just make sure your resume looks first-class and professional. Employers are more interested in the content of your resume – documented work history, accomplishments, skills, education, and objective related to their specific hiring needs – than in the "dress for success" visual elements. They are looking for behavior patterns that help them predict your potential future performance in their organization.

MYTH 14:   **The weight and color of the resume's paper and ink are unimportant to employers.**

REALTY: Weight, paper color, and ink do count, but how much they count in comparison to resume content is difficult to say. These are the very first things the employer sees and feels when receiving your resume. They make an important initial impression. If your resume doesn't look and feel right during the first five seconds, the reader may not feel good about reading the contents of your resume. Make a good initial impression by selecting a good weight and color of paper. Your resume should have a substantive feel to the touch – use nothing less than 20-pound paper which also has some texture. But don't go to extremes with a very heavy and roughly textured paper. Stay with conservative paper colors: white, off-white, ivory, light tan, or light grey.

MYTH 15:   **You should make at least 100 copies of your resume.**

REALITY: Make only as many as you need – which may be only one. If you word-process your resume, you can customize it for each position for which you apply. Your production needs should be largely determined by your strategy for distributing your resume.

Writing Job Search Letters

MYTH 16:   **It's okay to send your resume to an employer without an accompanying cover letter.**

REALITY: Only if you want the employer to think his or her position and employment opportunity are not important. Sending a resume without a cover letter is like going to a job interview barefoot – your application is incomplete and your resume is not being properly communicated for action. Cover letters should always accompany resumes that are sent through the mail. A cover letter ties together and thus completes your application or inquiry package.

MYTH 17:   **The purpose of a cover letter is to introduce your resume to an employer.**

REALITY: A cover letter should be much more than mere cover for a resume. If written properly, a cover letter enables you to express important qualities sought by employers in the job interview – your personality, style, energy, and enthusiasm. Like good advertising copy, your cover letter should be the "sizzle" or headline accompanying your resume. After all, the purpose of a cover letter should be to get the employer to **take action** on your resume. Consequently, the whole structure of your cover letter should focus on persuading the employer to invite you for a job interview.

MYTH 18:   **End your letter indicating that you expect to hear from the employer:** *"I look forward to hearing from you."*

REALITY: What do you expect will happen when you close your letter in this manner? Probably nothing. You want specific **action** to result from your written communication. Any type of action – positive or negative – should help you move on to the next stage of your job search with this or other potential employers. It's best to close your letter with an action statement like this one:

> *I'll give you a call Thursday afternoon to answer any questions you may have regarding my interests and qualifications.*

Such a follow-up statement, in effect, invites you to a telephone interview – the first step to getting a face-to-face job interview. While some employers may avoid your telephone call, at least you will get some action in reference to your letter and resume.

MYTH 19: **The cover letter should attempt to sell the employer on your qualifications.**

REALITY: The cover letter should command attention and nicely provide a cover for an enclosure – your resume. This letter should be professional, polite, personable, and to the point. Avoid repeating in this letter what's on your resume.

MYTH 20: **Handwritten cover letters have a greater impact on employers than typed cover letters.**

REALITY: Handwritten cover letters are inappropriate as are scribbled notes on or attached to a resume. They are **too** personal and look unprofessional when applying for a job. You want to demonstrate that you can present yourself to others in the most professional manner possible. Confine your handwriting activities to your signature only.

MYTH 21: **Letters are not very important in a job search. The only letter you need to write is a formal cover letter.**

REALITY: Your letters actually may be more important than your resume. In fact, cover letters are only one of several types of letters you should write during your job search:

- Resume letters
- Approach letters
- Thank-you letters

Different types of thank-you letters should be written on various job search occasions:

- Post-job interview
- After an informational interview
- Responding to a rejection
- Withdrawing from consideration
- Accepting a job offer
- Terminating employment

These are some of the most neglected yet most important forms of written job search communications. If you write these letters, your job search may take you much further than you expected!

Distributing Resumes and Letters

MYTH 22:   **It is best to send out numerous resumes and letters to prospective employers in the hope that a few will invite you to an interview.**

REALITY: Yes, if you play the odds, someone might call you. In fact, if you broadcast resumes and letters to 1,000 employers, you may have two or three invite you to an interview. However, this approach is more appropriate for people who are in desperate need of a job or who don't know what they want to do. Some inexpensive executive resume email blasting services ($50+ to email a resume to 10,000 ostensibly interested parties – see blastmyresume.com, resumeblaster.com, executiveagent.com), which primarily email resumes to headhunters, claim remarkable results. This non-focused approach will initially give you a false sense of making progress with your job search. You should concentrate on targeting your resume on particular organizations, employers, and positions that most interest you. This approach will require you to network for information and job leads. As such, you will seldom send a resume and cover letter through the mail or by email.

MYTH 23:   **You should present your resume at the beginning of an informational interview.**

REALITY: Never ever introduce yourself with your resume. Instead, your resume should be presented at the very **end** of the informational interview. Keep in mind that the purpose of an informational interview is to get information, advice, and referrals. You are not asking for a job. If you present your resume at the beginning of such an interview, you give the impression that you are looking for a job. Near the end of the interview you want to ask the interviewer to review your resume and give you advice on how to strengthen it and to whom to send it.

Following Up

MYTH 24:   **Once you distribute your resume and letters, there is little you can do other than wait to be called for an interview.**

REALITY: If you do nothing, you are likely to get nothing. There are many things you can do. First, you can write more letters to inquire about your application status. Second, you can telephone the employer for more information on when the interview and hiring decisions will take place. Third, you can telephone to request an interview at a convenient time. The first approach will likely result in no response. The second approach will probably give you an inconclusive answer. The third approach will give you a *"yes"* or *"no."* We prefer the third approach. See Dana Quist's insightful follow-through article on page 124.

MYTH 25:   **The best way to follow up on your application and resume is to write a letter of inquiry.**

REALITY: Employers are busy people who do not have time to read all their email and snail mail, much less sit down to write letters. Use the telephone instead. It's much more efficient and effective. Be sure to keep good records of all correspondence, telephone conversations, and meetings. Keep a paper or electronic file on each prospective employer.

Using New Types of Resumes

MYTH 26:   **Electronic resumes are the wave of the future. You must write and distribute them to get a good job.**

REALITY: During the past eight years electronic resumes (scannable, emailable, HTML, video, and multimedia) have played an increasingly important role in the job search and recruitment processes. However, numerous changes have taken place during the past two years due to rapid advances in resume screening and processing technology. For example, scannable resumes have become obsolete. Ugly duckling ASCII resumes are disappearing as employers increasingly receive formatted resumes via the Internet. Many employers now require applicants to complete an online form that produces a "profile" in lieu of a regular resume. At present no one electronic resume fits all employers. Electronic resumes are structured around "keywords" or nouns which stress capabilities. While such resumes may be excellent candidates for searchable resume databases and online applicant systems, they may be weak documents for human readers. Since human beings interview and hire, you should first create a resume that follows the principles of human communication. For now, we also recommend developing a separate resume designed for email transmission. We're less enthusiastic about HTML, video, and multimedia resumes. For the most recent update on the changing technology of employers for receiving, screening, and processing resumes, see Joyce Lain Kennedy's fourth edition of *Resumes for Dummies* (John Wiley & Sons) where she focuses on the return of the "beautiful resume" with the new technology. At the same time, keep in mind that the resume requirements differ given the size of the company. A company with 50,000 employees will more likely be on the technological cutting edge for receiving, screening, and processing electronic resumes than a company with only 25 employees which still accepts mailed and faxed resumes.

MYTH 27:   **Individuals who include their resumes in resume banks or post them online in resume databases are more likely to get high-paying jobs than those that don't.**

REALITY: During the past 10 years most electronic resume banks have become victims of the "free" Internet. They have either gone out of business or have transformed their operations by becoming resume databases on the Internet. While some resume banks and databases still charge users monthly or yearly membership fees, most are now supported by employers who advertise on the sites and/or pay fees to access resumes online. Essentially a high-tech approach for broadcasting resumes, inclusion of your resume in these resume banks and databases means your resume literally works 24 hours a day. Employers increasingly use these resume banks and databases for locating qualified candidates, especially for screening individuals with technical skills. While many individuals do get jobs through such online efforts, there is no evidence that they get higher paying jobs. The real advantage of such groups is this: they open new channels for contacting employers whom you might not otherwise come into contact with. Indeed, some employers only use these resume banks and databases for locating certain types of candidates rather than use more traditional channels, such as newspapers and employment offices, for advertising positions and recruiting candidates. Employers find the Internet to be a much cheaper way of recruiting personnel than through the more traditional approach of purchasing classified ads or hiring employment firms or headhunters.

MYTH 28:   **The video resume is the wave of the future. You are well advised to develop a video resume and send it to prospective employers.**

REALITY: The video resume is a novel approach to the employment process. However, since it is video-based, it's really a misnomer to call these videos a form of "resume." The so-called video resume functions more as a screening interview than a resume. Remember, the purpose of a resume is to get an interview. A video includes key elements that are best presented in a face-to-face interview – verbal and nonverbal communication. Unless requested by an employer in lieu of a traditional resume, we recommend avoiding the use of the video resume. However, if you are applying for a position that requires good presentation skills best demonstrated in the video format, such as in sales, broadcasting, and entertainment, the video resume may be the perfect approach to employers. But make sure you do a first-class job in developing the video. Avoid amateur products which will probably reflect badly on your skills.

MYTH 29: **You should develop your own homepage on the Internet and direct employers to your site.**

REALITY: Do this only if you are a real professional and can customize your site to particular employers. Like the video resume, homepages can be double-edged swords. Some employers may like them, but others may dislike them. Your particular site may reflect poorly on your qualifications, especially if it is not designed like a resume, i.e., stresses your accomplishments and goals. Furthermore, since most employers are too busy trying to get through traditional paper and electronic resumes and letters, few have the time or desire to spend time accessing your Internet site – unless your paper resume and letter sufficiently motivate them to do so. Like viewing videos, accessing sites on the Internet takes time. Remember, employers can still screen a paper resume and letter within 30 seconds! Why would they want to spend 15 minutes trying to access and review your site when they could be dispensing with another 30 resumes and letters during that time? If you decide to go this route, you'll need to give employers a good reason why they should invest such time looking for you on the Internet!

Resume Writing Mistakes

Many resumes are literally "dead upon arrival" because the job seeker made serious writing errors. Employers frequently report the following common mistakes resume writers make which often eliminate them from competition. Most of these mistakes center on issues of focus, organization, trustworthiness, intelligence, and competence. Reading between the lines, employers often draw conclusions about the individual's personality, competence, and honesty based upon the number of errors found on the resume. If you make any of these errors, chances are your **credibility** will be called into question. Make sure your resume does not commit any of these writing errors:

1. Unrelated to the position in question.
2. Too long or too short.
3. Unattractive with a poorly designed format, small type style, and crowded copy.
4. Misspellings, poor grammar, wordiness, and redundancy.
5. Punctuation errors.
6. Lengthy phrases, long sentences, and awkward paragraphs.
7. Slick, amateurish, or "gimmicky" – appears over-produced.
8. Boastful, egocentric, and aggressive.
9. Dishonest, untrustworthy, or suspicious information.
10. Missing critical categories, such as experience, skills, and education.
11. Difficult to interpret because of poor organization and lack of focus. Uncertain what the person has done or can do.
12. Unexplained time gaps between jobs.
13. Too many jobs in a short period of time – a job hopper with little evidence of career advancement.
14. No evidence of past accomplishments or a pattern of performance from which to predict future performance. Primarily focuses on formal duties and responsibilities that came with previous jobs.
15. Lacks credibility and content – includes much fluff and "canned" resume language.
16. States a strange, unclear, or vague objective.
17. Appears over-qualified or under-qualified for the position.
18. Includes distracting personal information that does not enhance the resume nor candidacy.
19. Fails to include critical contact information (phone number and email address) and uses an anonymous address (P.O. Box).
20. Uses jargon and abbreviations unfamiliar to the reader.
21. Embellishes name with formal titles, middle names, and nicknames which make him or her appear odd or strange.
22. Repeatedly refers to "I" and appears self-centered.
23. Includes obvious self-serving references that raise credibility questions.
24. Sloppy, with handwritten corrections – crosses out "married" and writes "single"!
25. Includes "red flag" information such as being fired, lawsuits or claims, health or performance problems, or starting salary figures, including salary requirements that may be too high or too low.

Your resume, instead, should incorporate the characteristics of strong and effective resumes. It should:

1. Clearly communicate your purpose and competencies in relation to employers' needs.
2. Be concise and easy to read.
3. Outline a pattern of success highlighted with examples of key accomplishments.
4. Motivate the reader to read it in-depth.
5. Tell employers that you are a responsible and purposeful individual – a doer who can quickly solve their problems.

Keep in mind that most employers are busy people who normally glance at a resume for only 20 to 30 seconds. Your resume, therefore, must sufficiently catch their attention to pass the 20- to 30-second evaluation test. Above all, it must **motivate the reader to take action**. When writing your resume, ask yourself the same question asked by employers: *"Why should I read this or contact this person for an interview?"* Your answer should result in an attractive, interesting, unique, and skills-based resume.

Production, Distribution, and Follow-Up Errors

Assuming you have written a great resume and a very persuasive cover letter, your next challenge is to make sure you don't make several errors relating to the production, distribution, and follow-up stages of your resumes and letters. Here are the most common such errors you must avoid:

1. Poorly typed and reproduced – hard to read.
2. Produced on odd-sized paper.
3. Printed on poor quality paper or on extremely thin or thick paper.
4. Soiled with coffee stains, fingerprints, or ink marks.
5. Sent to the wrong person or department.
6. Mailed, faxed, or emailed to "To Whom It May Concern" or "Dear Sir."
7. Emailed as an unsolicited attachment which could have a virus if opened.
8. Enclosed in a tiny envelope that requires the resume to be unfolded and flattened several times.
9. Arrived without proper postage – the employer gets to pay the extra!
10. Sent the resume and letter by the slowest postage rate possible.
11. Envelope double-sealed with tape and is indestructible – nearly impossible to open by conventional means!

12. Back of envelope includes a handwritten note stating that something is missing on the resume, such as a telephone number, email address, or new mailing address.
13. Resume taped to the inside of the envelope, an old European habit practiced by paranoid letter writers. Need to destroy the envelope and perhaps the resume as well to get it out.
14. Accompanied by extraneous or inappropriate enclosures which were not requested, such as copies of self-serving letters or recommendations, transcripts, or samples of work.
15. Arrives too late for consideration.
16. Comes without a cover letter.
17. Cover letter repeats what's on the resumes – does not command attention nor move the reader to action.
18. Sent the same or different versions of the resume to the same person as a seemingly clever follow-up method.
19. Follow-up call made too soon – before the resume arrives!
20. Follow-up call is too aggressive or the candidate appears too "hungry" for the position – seems very needy or greedy.

Whatever you do, make sure you write, produce, and distribute error-free resumes and letters. If you commit any of the errors outlined in this chapter, chances are you will be eliminated from consideration or your candidacy will be greatly diminished.

Types of Resumes

You have four basic types of resumes to choose from: chronological, functional, combination, or resume letter. Each form has various advantages and disadvantages, depending on your background and purpose. For example, someone first entering the job market or making a major career change should use a functional resume. On the other hand, a person who wants to target a particular job may choose to use a powerful resume letter that may also function as a "T" letter or Focus Piece. Examples of these different types of resumes and letters are included at the end of this chapter. Further assistance for developing each section of your resume can be found in our resume development books, *High Impact Resumes and Letters*, *Dynamite Resumes*, and *The Savvy Resume Writer*.

> *Employers are busy people who normally only glance at a resume for 20 or 30 seconds.*

The **chronological resume** is the standard resume used by most applicants who are not very job search savvy. It often comes in two forms: traditional and improved. The **traditional chronological resume** is also known as the "obituary resume," because it both "kills" your chances of getting a job and is a good source for writing your obituary. Summarizing your work history, this resume lists dates and names first and duties and responsibilities second; it includes extraneous information such as height, weight, age, marital status, gender, and hobbies. While relatively easy to write, this is the most ineffective resume you can produce. Its purpose at best is to inform people of what you have done in the past as well as where, when, and with whom. It tells employers little or nothing about what you want to do, can do, and will do for them.

The **improved chronological resume** better communicates to employers your purpose, past achievements, and probable future performance. This resume works best for individuals who have extensive experience directly related to a position. This resume should include a clear work objective. The experience section should include the names and locations of former employers followed by a brief description of relevant accomplishments, skills, and responsibilities; inclusive employment dates should appear at the end, stressing your **accomplishments** and **skills** rather than formal duties and responsibilities – that you are a productive and responsible person who gets things done, a doer. While this resume performs better than the traditional chronological resume, it still has major limitations because of its chronological format. It simply doesn't highlight very well major accomplishments and a pattern of success.

> *Functional resumes are appropriate for individuals first entering the job market, with little or no experience, or for those making a significant career change.*

Functional resumes should be used by individuals first entering the workforce, making a significant career change, or re-entering the job market after a lengthy absence. This resume should stress your accomplishments and transferable skills regardless of previous work settings and job titles. This could include accomplishments as a student, volunteer worker, Sunday school teacher, or housewife. Names of employers and dates of employment should not appear on this resume.

Functional resumes have certain weaknesses. While they are important bridges for the inexperienced and for those making a career change, some employers dislike these resumes. Since many employers still look for names, dates, and direct job experience, this resume does not meet their expectations. You should use a functional resume only if you have limited work experience or your past experience doesn't strengthen your objective when making a career change.

Combination resumes, also known as hybrid resumes, combine the best features of both chronological and functional resumes. Having more advantages than disadvantages, this resume best communicates accomplishments to employers. It's an ideal resume for experienced professionals who are advancing in their careers and for those making a career change.

Combination resumes have the potential to both **meet** and **raise** employers' expectations. You should stress your accomplishments and skills as well as include your work history. Your work history should appear as a separate section immediately following your presentation of accomplishments and skills in the "Areas of Effectiveness," "Experience," or "Achievements" section. It is not necessary to include dates unless they enhance your resume. This is the perfect resume for someone with work experience who wishes to change to a job in a related career field.

Resume letters are substitutes for resumes. Appearing as a job inquiry or application letter, resume letters highlight various sections of your resume, such as work history, experience, areas of effectiveness, objective, or education, in relation to employers' needs. These letters are used when you prefer not sending your more general resume. Resume letters have one major weakness: they give employers insufficient information and thus may prematurely eliminate you from consideration.

Structuring Resume Content

After choosing an appropriate resume format, you should generate the necessary information for structuring each category of your resume. You developed much of this information when you identified your motivated abilities and skills and specified your objective in Chapters 3 and 4. Include the following information on separate sheets of paper:

Contact Information:	Name, street address, and telephone/fax numbers, email address.
Work Objective:	Refer to your data in Chapter 5 on writing an objective.
Education:	Degrees, schools, dates, highlights, special training.
Work Experience:	Paid, unpaid, civilian, military, and part-time employment. Include job titles, employers, locations, dates, skills, accomplishments, duties, and responsibilities.
Achievements:	Things you did that provided **benefits** to others, especially initiatives that resulted in outcomes for previous employers.

Other Experience:	Volunteer, civic, and professional memberships. Include your contributions, demonstrated skills, offices held, names, and dates.
Special Skills or Licences/ Certificates:	Computer, Internet, foreign languages, teaching, paramedical, etc. relevant to your objective.
Other Information:	References, expected salary, willingness to relocate/travel, availability dates, and other information supporting your objective.

Producing Drafts

Once you generate the basic data for constructing your resume, your next task is to reduce this data into draft resumes. If, for example, you write a combination resume, the internal organization of the resume should be as follows:

- Contact information
- Work objective
- Summary statement
- Qualifications/experience/achievements
- Work history or employment
- Education

If you have limited work experience and education is your most important qualification, put the education section immediately after the summary statement. Be careful about including any other type of information on your resume. Other information most often is extraneous or negative information. You should only include information designed to strengthen your objective.

While your first draft may run more than two pages, try to get everything into one or two pages for the final draft. Most employers lose interest after reading the first page. If you produce a two-page resume, one of the best formats is to attach a supplemental page to a self-contained one-page resume.

Your final draft should conform to the following rules for creating an excellent resume:

Rules for Effective Resumes

Resume "Don'ts"

- **Don't** use abbreviations except for your middle name.
- **Don't** create a cramped and crowded look.
- **Don't** make statements you can't document.

- **Don't** use the passive voice.
- **Don't** change tense of verbs.
- **Don't** use lengthy sentences and descriptions.
- **Don't** refer to yourself as "I."
- **Don't** include negative information.
- **Don't** include extraneous information.

Resume "Do's"

- **Do** include an employer-centered objective.
- **Do** focus on your major accomplishments as they relate to the needs of the employer.
- **Do** use action verbs and the active voice.
- **Do** include nouns so your resume can be scanned for keywords.
- **Do** be direct, succinct, and expressive with your language.
- **Do** appear neat, well organized, and professional.
- **Do** use ample spacing and highlights (all caps, underlining, bulleting) for different emphases (except if it's an electronic resume).
- **Do** create an eye-pleasing balance of elements.
- **Do** check carefully your spelling, grammar, and punctuation.
- **Do** clearly communicate your purpose and value to employers.
- **Do** communicate your strongest points first.

Evaluating the Final Product

You should subject your resume drafts to two types of evaluations. An **internal evaluation** consists of reviewing our lists of "do's" and "don'ts" to make sure your resume conforms to these rules. An **external evaluation** should be conducted by circulating your resume among three or more individuals whom you believe will give you frank, objective, and useful feedback. Avoid people who tend to flatter you. The best evaluator would be someone in a hiring position similar to one you will encounter in the actual interview. Ask these people to critique your draft resume and suggest improvements in both form and content. This will be your most important evaluation. After all, the only evaluation that counts is the one that helps get you an interview. Asking someone to critique your resume is one way to spread the word that you are job hunting. As we will see in Chapter 8, this is one method for getting invited to an interview!

Final Production

It's best to word-process your resume and print it on a laser printer (600 dpi or higher preferred). Dot matrix and near-letter-quality printers make your resume look both unprofessional and mass produced. Word-processed resumes give you the greatest flexibility to custom design your resume for individual employers. If you lack good word-processing skills, take your resume to a printer or quick copy center, such as Kinkos, which should be able to give you first-class production for under $50.00.

Be sure to proofread the final copy. Don't spend good money on production only to later find typing errors. Better still, have someone else proofread your resume. You may be too close to your subject to catch all errors.

When reproducing the resume, you must consider the quality and color of paper as well as the number of copies you need. By all means use good quality paper. You should use 20-pound or heavier bond paper. Costing 3¢ to 7¢ per sheet, this paper can be purchased through stationery stores and printers. It is important not to cut corners at this point by purchasing cheap paper or using copy machine paper. You may save $5 on 100 copies, but you also will communicate an unprofessional image to employers.

> *Remember, your resume is your calling card – it should represent your best professional image.*

Use one of the following paper colors: white, cream, light tan, light gray, or light blue. Avoid blue, yellow, green, pink, orange, red, or any other bright or pastel colors. Conservative, light, neutral colors are the best. Any of these colors can be complemented with black. However, be very careful in using any color other than white since some employers still electronically scan resumes. Resumes printed on colored papers do not scan well.

Your choices of paper quality and color say something about your personality and professional style. They communicate nonverbally your potential strengths and weaknesses. Employers will use these as indicators for screening you in or out of an interview. At the same time, these choices may make your resume stand out from the crowd of standard black-on-white resumes.

Whatever your choices, do not try to cut costs when it comes to producing your resume. It simply is not worth it. Remember, your resume is your calling card – it should represent your best professional image. Put your best foot forward at this stage. Go in style; spend a few dollars on producing a first-class resume.

Job Search Letters

Regardless of how you send your resume, it should be accompanied by a cover letter. Indeed, certain types of cover letters – especially powerful "T" letters and Focus Pieces developed by Bernard Haldane Associates – are often more important than resumes. After interviewing for information or a position, you should send a thank you letter. Other occasions will arise when it is both proper and necessary for you to write different types of job search letters. Numerous examples of job search letters are presented in our *High Impact Resumes and Letters, Dynamite Cover Letters*, and *201 Dynamite Job Search Letters*. For a unique set of powerful "T" letters and Focus Pieces, see *Haldane's Best Cover Letters for Professionals*.

Your letter writing should follow the principles of good resume and business writing. Job hunting letters are like resumes – they advertise you for interviews. Like good advertisements, these letters should follow four basic principles for effectiveness:

1. Catch the reader's attention.
2. Persuade the reader of your benefits or value.
3. Convince the reader with evidence.
4. Move the reader to acquire the product – you!

In addition, the content of your letters should be the basis for conducting screening interviews as well as a face-to-face interviews.

Basic Preparation Rules

Before you begin writing a job search letter, ask yourself several questions to clarify the content of your letter:

- What is the **purpose** of the letter?
- What are the **needs** of my audience?
- What **benefits** will my audience gain from me?
- What is a good opening sentence or paragraph for grabbing the **attention** of my audience?
- How can I maintain the **interest** of my audience?
- How can I best end the letter so that the audience will be **persuaded** to contact me?
- If accompanied by a resume, how can my letter best **advertise the resume**?
- Have I spent enough **time** revising and proofreading the letter?
- Does the letter represent my **best professional effort**?

Since your letters are a form of business communication, they should conform to the rules of good business correspondence:

- Organize what you will say by outlining the content of your letter.
- Know your purpose and structure your letter accordingly.
- Clearly communicate your message in a logical and sequential manner.

- State your purpose immediately in the first sentence and paragraph; main ideas always go first.
- End by stating what your reader can expect next from you.
- Use short paragraphs and sentences; avoid complex sentences.
- Punctuate properly and use correct grammar and spelling.
- Use simple and straightforward language; avoid jargon.
- Communicate your message as directly and briefly as possible.

The rules stress how to both **organize and communicate** your message with impact. At the same time, you should always have a specific purpose in mind as well as know the needs of your audience.

Types of Letters

Cover letters provide cover for your resume. You should avoid overwhelming a one-page resume with a two-page letter or repeating the contents of the resume in the letter. A short and succinct one-page letter which emphasizes one or two points in your resume is sufficient. Three paragraphs will suffice. The first paragraph should state your interest and purposes for writing. The second paragraph should highlight your possible value to the employer. The third paragraph should state that you will call the individual at a particular time to schedule an interview.

However, do not expect great results from cover letters. Many professional job search firms use computers and mailing lists to flood the job market with thousands of unsolicited resumes and cover letters each day. Other job seekers use "canned" job search letters produced by computer software programs, such as *WinWay Resumes*, designed to generate model job search letters. As a result, employers are increasingly suspicious of the authenticity of such letters. To cope with the sheer volume of communications, many employers use resume management software to scan, store, and retrieve such communications – or they throw away most of the unsolicited resumes and letters they receive.

Approach letters are written for the purpose of developing job contacts, leads, or information as well as for organizing networks and getting interviews – the subjects of Chapter 9. Your primary purposes should be to get employers to engage in the 5R's of informational interviewing:

- **Reveal** useful information and advice.
- **Refer** you to others.
- **Read** your resume.
- **Revise** your resume.
- **Remember** you for future reference.

These letters help you gain access to the hidden job market by making important networking contacts that lead to those all-important informational interviews.

Approach letters can be sent out en masse to uncover job leads, or they can target particular individuals or organizations. It is best to target these letters since they have maximum impact when personalized for a specific position.

The structure of approach letters is similar to other letters. The first paragraph states your purpose. In so doing, you may want to use a personal statement for openers, such as *"Mary Tillis recommended that I write to you..."* or *"I am familiar with your..."* State your purpose, but do not suggest that you are asking for a job – only career advice or information. In your final paragraph, request a meeting and indicate you will call to schedule such a meeting at a mutually convenient time.

> *Approach letters should get employers to engage in the 5R's of informational interviewing.*

Thank you letters may well become your most effective job search letters. They especially communicate your thoughtfulness. These letters come in different forms and are written for various occasions. The most common thank you letter is written after receiving assistance, such as job search information and advice or a critique of your resume. Other occasions include:

- **Immediately following an interview**: Thank the interviewer for the opportunity to interview for the position. Repeat your interest in the position.

- **Receive a job offer**: Thank the employer for his or her faith in you and express your appreciation.

- **Rejected for a job**: Thank the employer for the "opportunity" to interview for the job. Ask to be remembered for future openings.

- **Terminate employment**: Thank the employer for the experience and ask to be remembered for future reference.

- **Begin a new job**: Thank the employer for giving you this new opportunity and express your confidence in producing the value he or she is expecting from you.

Examples of these letters are included at the end of this chapter.

Several of these thank you letters are unusual, but they all have the same goal – to be remembered by potential employers in a positive light. In a job search, being remembered by employers is the closest thing to being invited to an interview and offered a job.

Distribution and Management

The only good resumes are the ones that get read, remembered, referred, and result in a job interview. Therefore, after completing a first-rate resume, you must decide what to do with it. Are you planning to only respond to classified ads with a standard mailing piece consisting of your conventional or electronic resume and a formal cover letter? Do you prefer posting your resume online with resume databases or emailing it to potential employers? But wait a minute; classified ads and resume databases only represent one portion of the job market. What other creative distribution methods might you use, such as sending it to friends, relatives, and former employers; mailing it in a shoe box with a note (*"Now that I've got my foot in the door, how about an interview?"*); gift wrapping it; or having it delivered by a singing messenger? What's the best way to proceed?

Responding to Classified Ads

Most of your writing activities should focus on the hidden job market where jobs are neither announced nor listed. At the same time, you should respond to job listings in newspapers, magazines, human resources offices, and on websites as well as get your resume into online resume databases. While this is largely a numbers game, you can increase your odds by the way you respond to the listings.

You should be selective in your responses. Since you know what you want to do, you will be looking for only certain types of positions. Once you identify them, your response entails little expenditure of time and

> *Keep your letter brief and concise and highlight your qualifications that best meet the expectations as stated in the employer's ad.*

effort – a quick email, fax, or a paper envelope, letter, stamp, resume, and some of your time. You have little to lose. While you have the potential to gain by sending a letter and resume in response to an ad, remember the odds are usually against you.

It is difficult to interpret job listings, regardless of whether they are in print or electronic format. Some employers place blind ads with P.O. Box numbers and email addresses in order to collect resumes for future reference. Others wish to avoid aggressive applicants who telephone or "drop in" for interviews. Many employers work through professional recruiters who place these ads, or they post job listings on websites. While you may try to second guess the rationale behind such ads, it's always best to respond to them as you would to ads with an employer's name, address, or telephone number. Assume there is a real job behind each ad.

Effective Job Seekers Follow Through
Dana Quist, Assistant Director, Career Management Center,
Old Dominion University

Like a golfer who only concentrates on making contact with the ball, a job searcher who only concentrates on sending out resumes is likely to be disappointed in the results of his or her effort. In so many sports – baseball, hockey, golf, and tennis, striking the ball is only the halfway point. The same holds true for the job search – submitting the resume is only one part of the job search. The part that many job searchers (and athletes!) forget to concentrate on or consider at all is the follow through. The majority of the students I work with want to send out a resume and wait for someone to call. But for many employers, the extra effort of following up once a resume has been submitted is what separates the serious job searchers from the rest of the pack. The days of posting a resume and waiting for a recruiter to call are all but over.

Following through on every resume sent allows you to:

1. Restate your qualifications and interest in the position.
2. Ensure that your resume was actually received.
3. Make the personal contact with the hiring official allowing you to become more than just a paper resume.
4. Get a better sense of the time frame of the search, which means less worrying and guessing.
5. Ask for networking contacts if the position has been filled or no longer exists.

The benefit to following through on the resumes you submit are broad and far reaching with virtually no downside. If the employer already intends to call you for an interview and you call first, you are actually saving the employer time and you will certainly win points for that. If the employer hasn't selected you to interview, your call may encourage him or her to reconsider you – at worst it gets your resume a second look. Lastly, if only a few of the applicants call to follow through, you automatically distinguish yourself from the rest of the pool.

The most effective follow through is a phone call that states your major, your school, the position you're interested in, and the fact that you've already submitted a resume. Your goal is to confirm that your resume has been received, to state your interest in the position and the company/organization and to ask if there is a convenient time for you to come in to discuss the position in more detail. You should be prepared to leave a voice mail message as well as to speak in person on the phone. Often it is easier to catch someone at his or her desk first thing in the morning or after 4:30pm.

As a general rule, follow up with a phone call 3-5 days after you believe your resume should have been received. Two phone messages, 3-5 days apart is probably sufficient. You need to use good judgment in deciding what is appropriate and what is annoying!

Employers want to see that students have the interest level and motivation to go beyond just submitting a nice cover letter and resume. They are looking for interns and employees that go beyond what is required and thorough follow through is an excellent way to demonstrate that you have this quality.

Most ads request a copy of your resume. Employers increasingly request that it be sent by email and accompanied by a letter. You should respond with a cover letter and resume as soon as you see the ad. Depending on how much information about the position is revealed in the ad, your letter should be tailored to emphasize your qualifications vis-a-vis the ad. Examine the ad carefully. Underline any words or phrases which relate to your qualifications. In your cover letter, you should use similar terminology in emphasizing your qualifications. The most powerful letter you can send is the classic "T" letter, which literally matches your skills and accomplishments with each of the employer's requirements. Keep the letter brief and to the point. An example of such a letter is found on page 137.

If the ad asks you to state your salary history or salary requirements, state "negotiable" or "open." If you decide to include a figure, make sure the amount is based upon salary comparables which you acquired through your research in Chapters 6 and 10. For example, you might state:

"$35,000 to $40,000, which is the average salary range for similar positions in the Chicago metropolitan area."

Use your own judgment in addressing the salary question. There is no hard and fast rule on stating a figure or range. We recommend that you *"be honest but not stupid."* A figure helps the employer screen out individuals with too high a salary expectation. However, most people prefer to keep salary considerations to the end of the final interview – after they have demonstrated their value and have more information about the position. This may occur during the initial interview but most likely during the second, third, or even fourth interview.

Keep in mind that your cover letter and resume may be screened among 400 other resumes and letters. Thus, you want your cover letter to be eye-catching and easy to read. Keep it brief and concise and highlight your qualifications as stated in the employer's ad. Don't spend a great deal of time responding to an ad or waiting anxiously at your mailbox, telephone, or computer for a reply. Keep moving on to other job search activities.

Self-Initiated Methods

Your letters and resumes can be distributed and managed in various ways. Many people broadcast or "shotgun" hundreds of cover letters and resumes to prospective employers. This is a form of gambling where the odds are always against you. For every 100 people you contact in this manner, expect one or two who might be interested in you. After all, successful direct-mail experts at best expect only a 2 percent return on their mass mailings!

If you choose to use the broadcast method, you can increase your odds by using the **telephone**. Call the prospective employer within a week after he or she receives your letter. This technique will probably increase your effectiveness rate from 1 to 5 percent.

However, many people are broadcasting their resumes today and more and more employers are using automated resume management systems. As more resumes and letters descend on employers, the effectiveness rates may be even lower. This also can be an expensive marketing method. You would be much better off posting an electronic version of your resume on various online employment sites where your exposure rate will be much higher and more targeted to the needs of specific employers. In addition to using Campus CareerCenter.com (www.campuscareercenter.com), survey online job listings and post your resume on these top Internet sites:

- directemployers.com
- monster.com
- careerbuilder.com
- jobs.com
- www.ajb.dni.us

- hotjobs.com
- nationjob.com
- flipdog.com
- jobsonline.com
- jobsniper.com

Your best distribution strategy will be your own modification of the following procedure:

1. Selectively identify with whom you are interested in working.
2. Send an approach letter.
3. Follow up with a telephone call requesting a meeting.

In more than 50 percent of the cases, you will get an interview. It is best not to include a copy of your resume with the approach letter. If you include a resume, you communicate the wrong message – you want a job rather than information and advice. Keep your resume for the very end of the interview. Chapter 8 outlines procedures for conducting this informational interview.

Useful Books and Software

Numerous books focus on resumes and letters. Covering almost every occupation, many are appropriate for recent college graduates and individuals pursuing professional careers. Most books fall into one of three categories:

1. Emphasize the process of writing each resume and letter section as well address the production, distribution, and follow-up issues.

2. Present examples of excellent resumes and letters produced by professional resume writers and/or talented job seekers.

3. Focus on the special case of electronic and Internet resumes.

The majority of resume and letter books primarily present examples with very little information on how to write, produce, distribute, and follow up. The following books should prove useful:

Primary Focus on Process With Examples

Cover Letters for Dummies, 2nd Edition, Joyce Lain Kennedy (John Wiley & Sons, 2000)

Dynamite Cover Letters, 4th Edition, Ron and Caryl Krannich (Impact Publications, 1998)

Dynamite Resumes, 4th Edition, Ron and Caryl Krannich (Impact Publications, 1998)

Haldane's Best Cover Letters for Professionals, Bernard Haldane Associates (Impact Publications, 1999)

Haldane's Best Resumes for Professionals, Bernard Haldane Associates (Impact Publications, 1999)

High Impact Resumes and Letters, 8th Edition, Ronald L. Krannich and William J. Banis (Impact Publications, 2003)

Resumes for Dummies, 4th Edition, Joyce Lain Kennedy (John Wiley & Sons, 2003)

Primary Focus on Presenting Examples

101 Best Resumes for Grads, Jay A. Block and Michael Betrus (McGraw-Hill, 2002)

175 High-Impact Resumes, 3rd Edition, Richard Beatty (John Wiley & Sons, 2002)

201 Dynamite Job Search Letters, 4th Edition, Ron and Caryl Krannich (Impact Publications, 2001)

America's Top Resumes for America's Top Jobs, 2nd Edition, J. Michael Farr (JIST Works, 2002)

Best Resumes and CVs for International Jobs, Ronald L. Krannich and Wendy S. Enelow (Impact Publications, 2002)

Best Resumes for College Students and New Grads, Louise M. Kursmark (JIST Works, 2003)

The Complete Resume and Job Search Book for College Students, Bob Adams (Adams Media, 1999)

Cover Letters That Knock 'em Dead, Martin Yate (Adams Media, 2002)

The Damn Good Resume Guide, 2nd Edition, Yana Parker (Ten Speed Press, 2002)

Gallery of Best Cover Letters, David F. Noble (JIST Works, 1999)

Gallery of Best Resumes, David F. Noble (JIST Works, 2000)

Resume Catalog: 200 Damn Good Examples, Yana Parker (Ten Speed Press, 1996)

Resumes for College Students and Recent Graduates, 2nd Edition (NTC/Contemporary Publishing Company, 1998)

Resumes That Knock 'Em Dead, 4th Edition, Martin Yate (Adams Media, 2000)

Sure-Hire Resumes, Robbie Miller Kaplan (Impact Publications, 1998)

Special Case of Electronic and Internet Resumes

Cyberspace Resume Kit, 2nd Edition, Fred Jandt and Mary Nemnich (JIST Works, 2000)

Electronic Resumes and Online Networking, 2nd Edition, Rebecca Smith (Career Press, 2000)

e-Resumes, Susan Britton Whitcomb and Pat Kendall (McGraw-Hill, 2001)

Resumes in Cyberspace, 2nd Edition, Pat Criscito (Barrons Educational Series, 2001)

Several software programs assist individuals in quickly producing resumes that follow standard computer-generated formats. While quick and easy to use, most of these programs encourage using canned resume language and editing (i.e., plagiarizing) cover letter examples – not a recommended way to write quality resumes and letters that represent you. The three most popular resume software programs are:

> *ResumeMaker®*: Offers "Entry Level" and "Professional/Executive" versions of this popular software program (Individual Software)

> *Resumes Quick & Easy 4.0*: Includes thousands of pre-written phrases and 100 sample resumes (Individual Software)

> *WinWay Resume Deluxe*: Includes 100,000+ job-related phrases, 13,000+ customizable resumes, 400+ cover letters, resume and letter examples (Nova Sun Publishing)

Online Writing Assistance and Services

Several websites provide useful tips on how to write resumes and letters:

▪ Monster.com	resume.monster.com
▪ America's CareerInfoNet	www.acinet.org/acinet
▪ JobStar	jobstar.org/tools/resume
▪ CareerBuilder	careerbuilder.com
▪ Quintessential Careers	quintcareers.com
▪ Wetfeet	wetfeet.com
▪ Jobsonline	jobsonline.com
▪ WinningTheJob	www.winningthejob.com

A few sites, such as vault.com, even provide a free online resume review by a career professional. Other sites, such as careerbuilder.com (see the "Candidate Resource Center"), primarily include sponsored links to companies that offer fee-based resume and distribution services. Several resume writing professionals, such as Rebecca Smith, maintain their own websites (eresumes.com) with tips on writing an electronic resume.

If you feel you could benefit from the services of a professional resume writer, who charges from $100 to $500 to develop and produce a resume, check out these websites for assistance:

▪ Professional Association of Resume Writers and Career Coaches	www.parw.com
▪ Professional Resume Writing and Research Association	prwra.com
▪ National Resume Writers' Association	nrwa.com

For an online state-by-state directory of professional resume writers – which also includes a useful comparative chart for surveying service fees, years of experience, certification, samples, and free critiques – visit the NetWorker Career Services' (NCS) site: careercatalyst.com/resume.htm.

At the same time, check out some of these websites which are sponsored by professional resume writers. Most of them will give you a free resume critique prior to using their fee-based services:

▪ A&A Resume	aandaresume.com
▪ A-Advanced Resume Service	topsecretresumes.com
▪ Advanced Career Systems	resumesystems.com
▪ Advanced Resumes	advancedresumes.com
▪ Advantage Resume	advantageresume.com
▪ Best Fit Resumes	bestfitresumes.com
▪ Cambridge Resume Service	cambridgeresume.com
▪ Career Resumes	career-resumes.com
▪ CertifiedResumeWriters	certifiedresumewriters.com
▪ eResume (Rebecca Smith's)	eresumes.com
▪ e-resume.net	e-resume.net
▪ Free-Resume-Tips	free-resume-tips.com
▪ Impact Resumes	impactresumes.com
▪ Leading Edge Resumes	leadingedgeresumes.com
▪ Resume Agent	resumeagent.com
▪ Resume.com	resume.com
▪ Resume Creators	resumecreators.com
▪ ResumeMaker	resumemaker.com
▪ Resume Writer	resumewriter.com
▪ ResumeWriters.com	resumewriters.com

Resume Blasting Services

Resume distribution approaches have always been controversial, whether offline or online. Indeed, career counselors usually caution job seekers about literally "throwing money to the wind" by shotgunning, or blasting, their resumes to hundreds of employers. This approach usually gives job seekers a false sense of hope – they feel they are actually doing something to advance their job search by reaching out by mail or email to literally touch potential employers! However, this is usually the approach of unfocused, and often desperate and unrealistic, job seekers.

As the Internet increasingly plays an important role in the job search, several companies now specialize in blasting resumes via email to hundreds individuals possibly interested in receiving such resumes. For a fee ranging from $50 to $200, they will email your resume to a special list of executive recruiters and employers, but primarily to executive recruiters.

We're very dubious about this approach, despite many self-serving testimonials to the contrary. You'll probably get what you pay for using this borderline spam approach to resume distribution – little to nothing and lots of false hopes. If you're interested in this approach, check out these resume blasting sites which include information on their services:

- BlastMyResume — blastmyresume.com
- CareerPal — careerpal.com
- Careerxpress.com — careerxpress.com
- E-cv.com — e-cv.com
- Executiveagent.com — executiveagent.com
- HotResumes — hotresumes.com
  (posts to multiple job boards)
- Job Search Page — jobsearchpage.com
  (international focus)
- Job Village — jobvillage.com
- Nrecruiter.com — nrecruiter.com
- ResumeBlaster — resumeblaster.com
- Resume Booster — resumebooster.com
- ResumeBroadcaster — resumebroadcaster.com
- Resume Path — resumepath.com
- ResumeZapper — resumezapper.com
- ResumeXpress — resumexpress.com
- RocketResume — rocketresume.com
- See Me Resumes — seemeresumes.com
- Your Missing Link — yourmissinglink.com
- WSACORP.com — www.wsacorp.com

Tooting Your Horn With Focus

Regardless of all the myths, mistakes, and cautionary notes about writing, producing, distributing, and following up resumes and letters, many job seekers continue to abuse this important step in their job search. Perhaps it's because there is still something very mystical about these highly ego-involved documents that also seem to violate one of mother's early childhood rules – don't talk about yourself to others! Lacking practice in tooting their horn, many job seekers appear confused about how to best present themselves on resumes and in letters. However, presenting your best self on paper should be a relatively easy task if you stay focused on what employers really look for in candidates – evidence of past, present, and future performance relevant to their needs. If you can keep this focus and remember the central purpose of resumes, you should be able to avoid most of the resume and letter sins outlined in this chapter. Your resume should grab the attention of employers who will want to interview you for a job.

Chronological Resume

MARCY EVERS
2231 Wilson Drive
Syracuse, NY 19999
Tel. 219-123-4567
Email: mevers@aol.com

Objective

A MANAGEMENT CONSULTING POSITION, where strong research, problem solving, and communication skills will be used for expanding clientele in the area of small business development, with special emphasis on e-commerce.

Qualifications Summary

DETAILED AND RESULTS-ORIENTED INDIVIDUAL with strong entrepreneurial skills focused on small business development. Areas of competency include:

- E-commerce
- Strategic Planning
- Accounting
- Project Management
- Research
- Web Development

Education

SYRACUSE UNIVERSITY   B.A., Finance   May 2003
- Developed award-winning e-commerce model for student businesses
- Interned with P.C. Consulting Group as a research assistant
- Graduated with Honors, 3.8/4.0
- Worked part-time, earning 50% of educational and personal expenses

Work Experience

P.C. CONSULTING GROUP, Pittsburgh, PA   Summer Intern, 2002
    Research Assistant: focused on small business e-commerce and accounting.

SUMMIT ACCOUNTING, Pittsburgh, PA   Summer Intern, 2001
    Accounting Associate: assisted in reviewing new client accounts.

SYRACUSE UNIVERSITY, Syracuse, NY   Part-time, 2000-2002
    Various part-time positions as office assistant and researcher.

Activities

VICE-PRESIDENT: Student Entrepreneurs Club, Syracuse University, 2002.
CHAPTER PRESIDENT: Young Business Leaders, Syracuse University, 2001.
VOLUNTEER: Super Seniors on the Internet, Sunrise Acres, 2001-2002.

Functional Resume

MARCY EVERS
2231 Wilson Drive
Syracuse, NY 19999
Tel. 219-123-4567
Email: mevers@aol.com

Objective

A MANAGEMENT CONSULTING POSITION, where strong research, problem solving, and communication skills will be used for expanding clientele in the area of small business development, with special emphasis on e-commerce.

Qualifications Summary

DETAILED AND RESULTS-ORIENTED INDIVIDUAL with strong entrepreneurial skills focused on small business development. Areas of competency include:

- E-commerce
- Accounting
- Research
- Strategic Planning
- Project Management
- Web Development

Education

SYRACUSE UNIVERSITY   B.A., Finance   May 2003
- Developed award-winning e-commerce model for student businesses
- Interned with P.C. Consulting Group as a research assistant
- Graduated with Honors, 3.8/4.0
- Worked part-time, earning 50% of educational and personal expenses

Experience

- **Research:** Conducted several research projects as both a university student and a summer intern with P. C. Consulting in Pittsburgh.

- **Problem-solving:** Solved a major accounting problem that saved a client over $50,000 and resulted in extending an important consulting contract. Frequently called upon to assist others in resolving problems.

- **Communication:** Wrote several research papers, contributed articles to the student newspaper, gave several classroom presentations, and briefed supervisors on research findings. Enjoy both writing and public speaking.

Activities

VICE-PRESIDENT: Student Entrepreneurs Club, Syracuse University, 2002.
CHAPTER PRESIDENT: Young Business Leaders, Syracuse University, 2001.
VOLUNTEER: Super Seniors on the Internet, Sunrise Acres, 2001-2002.

Combination Resume

MARCY EVERS
2231 Wilson Drive
Syracuse, NY 19999
Tel. 219-123-4567
Email: mevers@aol.com

Objective

A MANAGEMENT CONSULTING POSITION, where strong research, problem solving, and communication skills will be used for expanding clientele in the area of small business development, with special emphasis on e-commerce.

Qualifications Summary

DETAILED AND RESULTS-ORIENTED INDIVIDUAL with strong entrepreneurial skills focused on small business development. Areas of competency include:

- E-commerce
- Strategic Planning
- Accounting
- Project Management
- Research
- Web Development

Education

SYRACUSE UNIVERSITY   B.A., Finance   May 2003

- Developed award-winning e-commerce model for student businesses
- Interned with two consulting firms in research and accounting
- Graduated with Honors, 3.8/4.0
- Worked part-time, earning 50% of educational and personal expenses

Work Experience

P.C. CONSULTING GROUP, Pittsburgh, PA   Summer Intern, 2002

Research Assistant: Focused on small business e-commerce and accounting. Worked with team in developing an e-commerce model for increasing client revenues by 20 percent over a 12-month period. Focused on converting bookkeeping system to an online accounting system. Cited by employer for *"dependability, strong analytic and problem solving capabilities, and an ability to meet deadlines in a timely manner."*

SUMMIT ACCOUNTING, Pittsburgh, PA   Summer Intern, 2001

Accounting Associate: Assisted in reviewing new client accounts. Solved a major accounting problem that saved a client over $50,000 and resulted in extending an important consulting contract. Cited by employer as one of their most *"energetic, enthusiastic, and results-oriented interns."*

SYRACUSE UNIVERSITY, Syracuse, NY　　　　　　　　　Part-time, 2000-2002

Various part-time positions as office assistant and research assistant in the Department of Finance. Worked closely with faculty members in completing projects. Contributed to major study involving the gathering and analyzing of longitudinal data on small business practices in New York State. Cited by the department chair as *"an exceptionally responsible, competent, and inquisitive researcher with the potential to excel in the field of finance."*

Activities

VICE-PRESIDENT: Student Entrepreneurs Club, Syracuse University, 2002

Increased membership from 53 to 147 within six months of becoming vice-president of this innovative student business club. Promoted the development of four new Internet-based student businesses each month.

CHAPTER PRESIDENT: Young Business Leaders, Syracuse University, 2001

Participated in national conference as a seminar leader on "The New Face of Student Business Leaders in the Work Force." Developed important linkages to the presidents of all fraternities and sororities at Syracuse University who encourage members to participate in monthly meetings on developing micro businesses in college.

VOLUNTEER: Super Seniors on the Internet, Sunrise Acres, 2001-2002

Assisted seniors in developing computer skills with special emphasis on using the Internet to communicate with family members. Trained more than 100 seniors over an 18-month period. Established a very popular Internet Club at Sunrise Acres.

References

Available upon request. Complete credentials file available through the Office of Career Services, Syracuse University.

"T" Letter

July 21, 20 ___

Darlene Compton
Timberlake-Thompson Company
892 Champion Drive
Austin, TX 77889

Dear Ms. Compton:

I'm responding to your job posting that appears on the CampusCareerCenter website for a Public Relations Specialist. My profile is available online (#1234321) with CCC and I emailed a copy of my resume to you today as you requested.

I believe I am an excellent candidate for this position given my interests, educational background, and recent internship experience in Public Relations:

Your Requirements	**My Qualifications**
1+ years of experience in PR	Served as a PR intern during the past three summers with special focus on sales and marketing strategies.
Strong interpersonal skills	Praised by professors and supervisors for working well in teams and with both co-workers and clients. Received the "Intern of the Year" Award in 2001.
Ability to develop compelling ad copy	Developed copy for three ad campaigns which were used in major television and radio spots. Client realized a 30% increase in sales due to these efforts.
Energetic and willing to travel	Work well with deadlines and stressful situations. "Energy and enthusiasm" cited as major characteristics in receiving the internship award. Love to travel.

In addition, I know the importance of building strong customer relations and developing innovative approaches to today's new PR mediums. I love taking on new challenges, working in multiple team and project settings, and seeing clients achieve results from my company's efforts.

I believe there is a strong match between your needs and my professional interests and qualifications. Could we meet soon to discuss how we might best work together? I'll call your office Tuesday at 11am to see if your schedule might permit such a meeting.

I appreciate your consideration and looking forward to speaking with you on Tuesday.

Sincerely,

Sterling Richards

Sterling Richards

Cover Letter

1 Sherman Avenue
Gainesville, FL 34444
May 21, 20 _____

Wendy Jackson
Director of Personnel
Bank of Atlanta
245 Central Plaza
Atlanta, GA 33333

Dear Ms. Jackson:

My accompanying resume is in response to your listing in the *Atlanta Constitution* for a junior loan officer.

I am especially interested in this position because of my dual interest in community banking and small business development. During this past year I had an opportunity to intern with the loan department at the Gainesville Community Bank. The experience was invaluable as I acquired a greater understanding of the financial needs and problems of the local business community. I wish to use this experience with a bank that has strong roots in the local community and works closely with small businesses and community leaders.

I would appreciate an opportunity to meet with you to discuss how my experience could best meet your needs. My ideas on how to improve small business financing may be of particular interest to you. Therefore, I will call your office on the morning of May 28 to inquire if a meeting can be scheduled at a convenient time.

I look forward to meeting you.

Sincerely yours,

Sharon North

Sharon North

Approach Letter
Referral

341 Mountain Drive
Colorado Springs, CO 75555
February 26, 20 ____

Bacey Perry
Director of Personnel
e-Recruit Solutions
722 Fulton Boulevard
Denver, CO 77777

Dear Ms. Perry:

Tom Peterson suggested that I contact you about my interest in human resource development. He said you are one of the best people to talk to in regards to careers in this field.

I will graduate from the University of Colorado in May with a degree in business management. During the past two years I've become fascinated with e-recruitment – an area your company has pioneered over the past decade. I am especially interested in working with a small- to medium-size firm. However, before I venture further into the job market, I want to benefit from the experience of others in the field who might advise me on opportunities for someone with my interests and qualifications.

Perhaps we could meet briefly sometime during the next two weeks to discuss my career interests. I have several questions about my career direction, which I believe you could help me plan better. I will call your office on Wednesday, April 5, to schedule a meeting time.

I look forward to meeting you and learning from your experience.

Sincerely yours,

Karen Utley

Karen Utley

Approach Letter
Cold Turkey

929 Great Falls Parkway
Portland, OR 93333
March 8, 20 ____

Greta Paulson, Director
Stevenson Learning Center
148 Washington Boulevard
Portland, OR 93321

Dear Ms. Paulson:

I have been very impressed with your work on learning disabilities. In fact, I had a chance to attend your excellent presentation at Portland State University last month. Your organization had done some pioneering work on ADHD, an area in which I'm especially interested in pursuing a career.

I am anxious to meet you and learn more about your work. In May I will graduate with a B.S. in Special Education. During the past two years I've served as a volunteer at New Beginnings Education where I worked closely with ADHD clients. From these experiences I decided I preferred working primarily with the learning disabled.

However, before I pursue my interests further, I need to talk to people with experience in this field. In particular, I would like to know more about careers relating to learning disabilities as well as how my background might best be used in this field. For example, would you recommend continuing studies at the graduate level or first getting work experience in this field?

I am hoping you can assist me in this matter. I would like to meet with you briefly to discuss several of my concerns. I will call next week to see if your schedule permits such a meeting.

I look forward to meeting you.

Sincerely,

Wanda Lessons

Wanda Lessons

Thank You Letter
Post-Informational Interview

6722 Terrace Drive
St. Louis, MO 65432
April 29, 20 ___

Sharon Everts, Director
Finance One Corporation
330 Wall Street West
St. Louis, MO 65423

Dear Ms. Everts:

Thanks so much for taking the time from your busy schedule to meet with me today. Your advice was most helpful in clarifying several questions on careers in finance. I am now reworking my resume and have included many of your thoughtful suggestions. I will send you a copy next week.

I will follow up on your suggestion to see Steven Gray about opportunities with St. Louis Finance Corporation. From what you said, their entry-level training program for account executives may be the perfect fit for my interests and skills. I'll let you know how my job search story ends, which hopefully will be soon, as I graduate from Washington University within the next three weeks.

Sincerely,

Edwardo Sanchez

Edwardo Sanchez

Thank You Letter
Post-Job Interview

632 Ocean Avenue
Seattle, WA 98321
May 3, 20 ____

Owen Watts
Director of Marketing
Pacific Net Group
23 Overlook Drive
San Francisco, CA 94111

Dear Mr. Watts:

Thank you again for the opportunity to interview for the trainee position in international marketing. I appreciated your hospitality and enjoyed meeting with you and members of your staff.

The interview convinced me of how compatible my background, interests, and skills are with the goals of the Pacific Net Group. My semester abroad marketing internship program in Shanghai last year reinforced what I really want to do – focus my career efforts on newly emerging markets within the Pacific Rim. Your work in agricultural exports to China especially intrigues me given my language background in Chinese and my familiarity with the Pearl River Delta regional expansion. I see a very exciting future for your company in this rapidly emerging market. And I would love to be a part of that future. I am confident my work for you would contribute substantially to increasing your market share in China.

For more information on the new business promotion associations operating in Shanghai which we spoke about, please contact Professor Jason Wilson in the Marketing Department at the University of Washington (Tel. 245-245-2455). I talked to him this morning about your interest in his work. He would be delighted to share his recent research findings with you.

I look forward to meeting you again.

Sincerely,

Devon Chandler

Devon Chandler

Thank You Letter
Job Rejection

251 College Campus Way
Phoenix, AZ 85333
April 21, 20 ___

Jason Wise, Director
Management Training
The Phoenix Group
131 West Desert Road
Phoenix, AZ 85322

Dear Mr. Wise:

I appreciated your considering me for the Manager in Training Program. While I am disappointed in not being selected, I learned a great deal about your company, and I enjoyed meeting with you and your talented staff. I felt particularly good about the professional manner in which you conducted the interview. I would have loved to join your company as an Operations Manager.

Please keep me in mind for future consideration. I have a strong interest in your company. I believe we would work well together. I will be closely following the progress of your company over the coming months. Perhaps we will be in touch with each other at some later date.

Best wishes.

Sincerely,

Morris Profitt

Morris Profitt

Thank You Letter
Job Offer Acceptance

541 Graduation Lane
Boston, MA 04153
June 7, 20 ____

Wanda Nelson
Vice President
Forecast Electronics
24 West 83rd Street
New York, NY 10111

Dear Ms. Nelson:

I am pleased to accept your offer, and I am looking forward to joining you and your staff next month.

The sales and marketing position is ideally suited to my background and interests. I assure you I will give you my best effort in making this an effective position within your company.

I understand I will begin work on July 8th. If, in the meantime, I need to complete any paperwork or take care of any other matters, please contact me.

I enjoyed meeting with you and your staff and appreciated the professional manner in which the hiring was conducted.

Sincerely,

Teresa Newton

Teresa Newton

8

Network Your Way
to a Great Job

CONDUCTING A SUCCESSFUL JOB SEARCH DEPENDS A
great deal on whom you know and how they help you connect with
the right people who have the power to hire. One of your most
important job search assets will be your network of relationships –
your relatives, friends, professors, classmates, and acquaintances you interact
with and who might be helpful in giving you useful information, advice, and
referrals. You'll also want to build your network by developing new relationships based upon referrals and cold calls. How well you identify, build, and
nurture your networks throughout your job search may determine how
successful you are in landing a really good job.

Advertised and Hidden Job Markets

Savvy job seekers know that advertised jobs – those found in classified ads of
newspapers or posted on Internet sites – represent perhaps less than 30
percent of all jobs available at any time. Most jobs are unadvertised. They are
found through word-of-mouth, employment firms, or by knocking on doors.
Found on the "hidden job market," these jobs often turn out to be the best
jobs. They are usually less competitive, pay better, and have a more promising
future than those found on the advertised job market.

Since most job seekers think the majority of jobs are found on the advertised job market, they primarily conduct a passive job search of sending their

resume and letters in response to classified job ads or job postings. Not surprising, this market is characterized by high competition and frustration for many job seekers. The symbol of this type of job seeker is often someone who waits, waits, and waits in anticipation of hearing good news in response to their mailed, faxed, or e-mailed resumes and letters. Moving paper and e-mails gives them a false sense of making progress in this deceptive job market.

From students to CEOs, savvy job seekers play the advertised job market game, but they also know that the best and least competitive jobs are found on the hidden job market. Navigating this job market requires interpersonal skills for acquiring information, advice, and referrals. Your goal should be to learn as much as possible about jobs appropriate for you that may or may not be advertised. In the process of networking, you communicate your interests, skills, and abilities to individuals in your network who refer you to other individuals who might be interested in giving you more advice and referrals. If you develop an active networking campaign that involves making five new contacts a day, you should quickly accelerate your job search. Best of all, you will soon be invited to job interviews which hopefully will turn into job offers.

Are You a Savvy Networker?

Savvy networkers know the importance of conducting a well organized job search that involves three critical networking activities: (1) connecting with others, (2) building networks, and (3) nurturing relationships within those networks. Once you learn how to connect, build, and nurture your network, you should be able to quickly and successfully navigate the hidden job market.

Just how savvy are you when it comes to finding a job and advancing your career? Do you have the necessary networking skills for success? Can you quickly network your way to job and career success, or do you need to focus on developing specific networking skills? Let's start by testing your "Savvy Networking I.Q." You do this by responding to the following set of agree/disagree statements:

Your Savvy Networking I.Q.

INSTRUCTIONS: Respond to each statement by circling the number to the right that best represents your situation. The higher your score, the higher your "Savvy Networking IQ."

SCALE: 5 = strongly agree   2 = disagree
           4 = agree   1 = strongly disagree
           3 = maybe, not certain

1. I enjoy going to business and social
    functions where I have an opportunity to
    meet new people. (CONNECT/BUILD)   5   4   3   2   1

Resume Letter

2231 Wilson Drive
Syracuse, NY 19999
April 3, 20 ___

Kevin Daly
Delta Five
7211 Independence Way
Philadelphia, PA 18888

Dear Mr. Daly:

Delta Five is one of today's most respected management consulting firms.
I know because I recently completed a major research project on America's top
management consulting firms for a Business Development class at Syracuse University.
In addition to being a leader in the field of small business development, Delta Five has
one of the best employee training and development programs in the business. Given
my interests, educational background, and experience, this is the type of organization
I would love to join.

I am seeking a training position with a management consulting firm which would
use my business background and strong research, analytical, problem solving, and
communication abilities. My experience includes:

- Research: Conducted several research projects as both a university student and
  a summer intern with P. C. Consulting in Pittsburgh.

- Problem-solving: Solved a major accounting problem that saved a client
  over $50,000 and resulted in extending an important consulting contract.
  Frequently called upon to assist others in resolving problems.

- Communication: Wrote several research papers, contributed articles to
  the student newspaper, gave several classroom presentations, and briefed
  supervisors on research findings. Enjoy both writing and public speaking.

Could we meet to discuss your training program as well as how I might best meet
your needs? I will call your office on Thursday morning, April 8, to arrange
a convenient time to meet with you.

I particularly want to show you the work I did on management consulting firms,
especially some of the challenges facing your competition. I discovered some
fascinating new Internet solutions which may be of interest to you.

Sincerely,

Marcy Evers

Marcy Evers

2. I usually take the initiative in introducing
   myself to people I don't know. (CONNECT)   5   4   3   2   1

3. I enjoy being in groups and participating
   in group activities. (CONNECT/BUILD)   5   4   3   2   1

4. On a scale of 1 to 10, my social skills
   are at least a "9." (BUILD/NURTURE)   5   4   3   2   1

5. I listen carefully and give positive
   feedback when someone is speaking
   to me. (CONNECT/BUILD)   5   4   3   2   1

6. I have a friendly and engaging
   personality that attracts others to me.
   (CONNECT/BUILD/NURTURE)   5   4   3   2   1

7. I make a special effort to remember
   people's names and frequently address
   them by their name. (CONNECT)   5   4   3   2   1

8. I carry business cards and often give
   them to acquaintances from whom I
   also collect business cards. (CONNECT)   5   4   3   2   1

9. I have a system for organizing business
   cards I receive, including notes on the
   back of each card. (BUILD)   5   4   3   2   1

10. I seldom have a problem starting a
    conversation and engaging in small
    talk with strangers. (CONNECT)   5   4   3   2   1

11. I enjoy making cold calls and persuading
    strangers to meet with me. (CONNECT)   5   4   3   2   1

12. I usually return phone calls in a timely
    manner. (CONNECT)   5   4   3   2   1

13. If I can't get through to someone on the
    phone, I'll keep trying until I do, even if it
    means making 10 more calls. (CONNECT)   5   4   3   2   1

14. I follow up on new contacts by phone,
    e-mail, or letter. (BUILD)   5   4   3   2   1

15. I have several friends who will give me
    job leads. (BUILD)   5   4   3   2   1

16. I often give and receive referrals. (BUILD)   5   4   3   2   1

17. I have many friends. (BUILD/NURTURE)   5   4   3   2   1

18. I know at least 25 people who can give
     me career advice and referrals. (BUILD)   5   4   3   2   1

19. I don't mind approaching people with my
     professional concerns. (CONNECT/BUILD)   5   4   3   2   1

20. I enjoy having others contribute to my
     success. (BUILD)   5   4   3   2   1

21. When I have a problem or face a
     challenge, I usually contact someone
     for information and advice. (BUILD)   5   4   3   2   1

22. I'm good at asking questions and getting
     useful advice from others. (BUILD)   5   4   3   2   1

23. I usually handle rejections in stride by learn-
     ing from them and moving on. (BUILD)   5   4   3   2   1

24. I can sketch a diagram, with appropriate
     linkages, of individuals who are most
     important in both my personal and
     professional networks. (BUILD)   5   4   3   2   1

25. I regularly do online networking by
     participating in Usenet newsgroups,
     mailing lists, chats, and bulletin boards.
     (CONNECT/BUILD)   5   4   3   2   1

26. I regularly communicate my accomplish-
     ments to key members of my network.
     (NURTURE)   5   4   3   2   1

27. I make it a habit to stay in touch with
     members of my network by telephone,
     e-mail, and letter. (NURTURE)   5   4   3   2   1

28. I regularly send personal notes, birthday
     and holiday greeting cards, and letters
     for special occasions to people in my
     network. (NURTURE)   5   4   3   2   1

29. I still stay in touch with childhood
     friends and old schoolmates. (NURTURE)   5   4   3   2   1

30. I have a great network of individuals
    whom I can call on at anytime for
    assistance, and they will be happy to
    help me. (BUILD/NURTURE)   5   4   3   2   1

31. I belong to several organizations,
    including a professional association.
    (CONNECT/BUILD)   5   4   3   2   1

32. I consider myself an effective networker
    who never abuses his relationships.
    (CONNECT/BUILD/NURTURE)   5   4   3   2   1

33. Others see me as a savvy networker.
    (CONNECT/BUILD/NURTURE)   5   4   3   2   1

TOTAL I.Q.

If your total composite I.Q. is above 155, you're most likely a savvy net-worker. If you're below 120, you're probably lacking key networking skills. Each of the above items indicates a particular connect, build, or nurture behavior or skill that contributes to one's overall networking effectiveness. Concentrate on improving those skills on which you appear to be weak. For example, you may discover you are particularly savvy at "connecting" with people but you're weak on "building" and "nurturing" relationships – or vice versa – that define your network.

Focus on Getting Interviews

Everything you do up to this point in your job search should be aimed at **getting a job interview.** The skills you identified, the goals you set, the resume you wrote, and the information you gathered are carefully related to one another so you can clearly communicate your best qualifications to employers who, in turn, will decide to invite you to a job interview.

But there are secrets to getting a job interview you should know before continuing further with your job search. The most important secret is the **informational interview** – a type of interview which yields useful job search information and **may** lead to job interviews and offers. Based on prospecting and networking techniques, these interviews minimize rejections and com-petition as well as quickly open the doors to organizations and employers. If you want a job interview, you first need to understand the informational interview and how to initiate and use it for maximum impact.

Prospecting and Networking

What do you do after you complete your resume? Most people send cover letters and resumes in response to job listings; they then wait to be called for a job interview. Viewing the job search as basically a direct-mail operation, many are disappointed in discovering the realities of direct mail – a 2 percent response rate is considered successful!

Successful job seekers break out of this relatively passive job search role by orienting themselves toward face-to-face action. Being proactive, they develop interpersonal strategies in which the resume plays a **supportive** rather than a central role in the job search. They first present themselves to employers; the resume appears only at the end of a face-to-face conversation.

Throughout the job search you will acquire useful names and addresses as well as meet people who will assist you in contacting potential employers. Such information and contacts become key building blocks for generating job interviews and offers.

> *The most effective means of communication are face-to-face and word-of-mouth.*

Since the best and most numerous jobs are found on the hidden job market, you must use methods appropriate for this job market. Indeed, research and experience clearly show the most effective means of communication are face-to-face and word-of-mouth. The informal, interpersonal system of communication is the central nervous system of the hidden job market. Your goal should be to penetrate this job market with proven methods for success. Appropriate methods for making important job contacts are **prospecting and networking**. The best methods for getting these contacts to provide you with useful job information are **informational and referral interviews**. Taken together, these methods will enable you to successfully penetrate and navigate the hidden job market for interviews and offers.

Communicate Your Qualifications

These interpersonal methods help you **communicate your qualifications to employers**. Although many job seekers may be reluctant to use this informal communication system, they greatly limit their potential for success if they do not become proactive in using these methods.

Put yourself in the position of the employer for a moment, especially one that is not fully staffed nor automated to handle hundreds of resumes and phone, fax, and e-mail inquiries. You have a job vacancy to fill. If you advertise the position, you may be bombarded with hundreds of resumes, applications, phone calls, faxes, e-mails, and walk-ins. While you do want to hire the best qualified individual for the job, you simply don't have time nor patience to review scores of applications. Even if you use a P.O. Box number, the paperwork may quickly overwhelm you. Furthermore, with limited information from application forms, cover letters, and resumes, you find it hard to identify the best qualified individuals to invite for an interview; many look the same on paper.

So what do you do? You might hire a professional job search firm or use the services of a temporary employment agency to take on all of this additional work. Or you may try recruiting on the Internet by doing keyword searches of various online resume databases or posting a job announcement on your homepage and on a few commercial recruitment sites. On the other hand, you may want to better control the hiring process, especially since it appears to be filled with uncertainty and headaches. You want to minimize your risks and time so you can get back to what you do best – accomplishing the external goals of the organization. Like many other employers, you begin by calling your friends, acquaintances, and other business associates and ask if they or someone else might know of any good candidates for the position. If they can't help, you ask them to give you a call should they learn of anyone qualified for your vacancy. You, in effect, create your own hidden job market – an informal information network for locating desirable candidates. Best of all, your trusted contacts initially screen the candidates in the process of referring them to you. This both saves you a lot of time and minimizes your risks in hiring a stranger.

Based on this understanding of the employer's perspective, what should you do to best improve your chances of getting an interview and job offer? Networking for information, advice, and referrals should play a central role in your overall job search. Remember, employers need to solve personnel problems. By conducting **informational interviews and networking** you help employers identify their needs, limit their alternatives, and thus make decisions and save money. Most important, such interviews and networking activities help relieve their anxiety about hiring an unknown applicant.

At the same time, you gain several advantages by conducting these interviews:

1. You are less likely to encounter rejections since you are not asking for a job – only information, advice, referrals, and to be remembered.

2. You go after better positions.

3. You encounter little competition.

4. You go directly to the people who have the power to hire.

5. You are likely to be invited to job interviews based upon the referrals you receive.

Most employers want more information on candidates to supplement the "paper qualifications" represented in application forms, resumes, and letters. Studies show that employers in general seek candidates who have these skills: communication, problem solving, analytical, assessment, and planning. Surprising to many job seekers, technical expertise ranks third or fourth on employers' lists of most-desired skills. These findings support a frequent observation made by employers: the major problems with employees relate to communication, problem solving, and analysis; most individuals get fired because of political and interpersonal conflicts rather than for technical incompetence.

Employers seek individuals they **like** both personally and professionally. Therefore, communicating your qualifications to employers entails more than just informing them of your technical competence. You must communicate that you have the requisite personal **and** professional skills for performing the job. Informal prospecting, networking, and informational interviewing are the best methods for communicating your "qualifications" to employers.

Develop Networks

Networking is the process of purposefully developing relations with others. Networking in the job search involves connecting and interacting with other individuals who can possibly help you.

Your network consists of you and people you know, who are important to you, and whom you interact with most frequently. Many of these people influence your behavior. Others may also influence your behavior but you interact with them less frequently. As illustrated on page 153, your network may consist of family friends, faculty members, other students, your boss, if you have a part-time job, and other who can assist you. Your network of relationships involves **people** – not data, things, or knowledge of a particular subject area. The more you develop, maintain, and expand your networks, the more successful should be your job search.

Your network is your interpersonal environment. While you know and interact with hundreds of people, on a day-to-day basis you may encounter no more than 20 people. You frequently contact these people in face-to-face situations. Some people are more **important** to you than others. You **like** some more than others. And some will be more **helpful** to you in your job search than others. Your basic network may encompass the following individuals and groups: friends, acquaintances, immediate family, distant relatives, fellow students, faculty members, spouse, supervisor, fellow workers, close friends and colleagues, and local businessmen and professionals, such as your banker, doctor, minister, and insurance agent. You should contact many of these individuals for advice relating to your job search.

You need to **identify everyone in your network** who might help you with your job search. You first need to expand your basic network to include

Your Network of Relationships

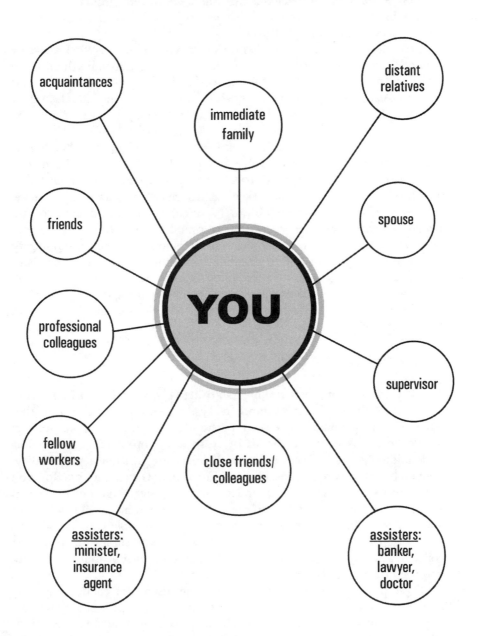

individuals you know and have interacted with over the past 10 or more years. Make a list of at least 200 people you know. Include friends, relatives, past and present neighbors, former classmates, politicians, business persons, previous employers, professional associates, ministers, insurance agents, lawyers, bankers, doctors, dentists, accountants, and social acquaintances – even your postman and UPS driver.

After identifying your extended network, you should try to **link your network to others' networks**. The figure on page 155 illustrates this linkage principle. Individuals in these other networks also have job information and contacts. Ask people in your basic network for referrals to individuals in their networks. This approach should greatly enlarge your basic job search network.

What do you do if individuals in your immediate and extended network cannot provide you with certain job information and contacts? While it is much easier and more effective to meet new people through personal contacts, on occasion you may need to **approach strangers without prior contacts**. In this situation, try the "cold turkey" approach. Write a letter to someone you feel may be useful to your job search. Research this individual so you are acquainted with their background and accomplishments. In the letter, refer to their accomplishments, mention your need for job information, and specify a date and time you will call to schedule a meeting. Another approach is to introduce yourself to someone by telephone and request a meeting and/or job information. While you may experience rejections in using these approaches, you also will experience successes. And those successes should lead to further expansion of your job search network.

Prospect for Leads

The key to successful networking is an active and routine **prospecting campaign**. Salespersons in insurance, real estate, Amway, Shaklee, and other direct-sales and pyramid businesses understand the importance of prospecting; indeed, many have turned the art of prospecting into a science as well as billion-dollar global businesses! The basic operating principle is **probability**: the number of sales you make is a direct function of the amount of effort you put into developing new contacts and following through. Expect no more than a 10 percent acceptance rate: for every 10 people you meet, nine will reject you and one will accept you. Therefore, the more people you contact, the more acceptances you will receive. If you want to be successful, you must collect many more "no's" than "yeses." In a 10 percent probability situation, you need to contact 100 people for 10 successes.

These prospecting principles are extremely useful for conducting a job search or making a career change. Like sales situations, the job search is a highly ego-involved activity often characterized by numerous rejections accompanied by a few acceptances. While no one wants to be rejected, few people are willing and able to handle more than a few rejections. They take

Linking Your Networks to Others

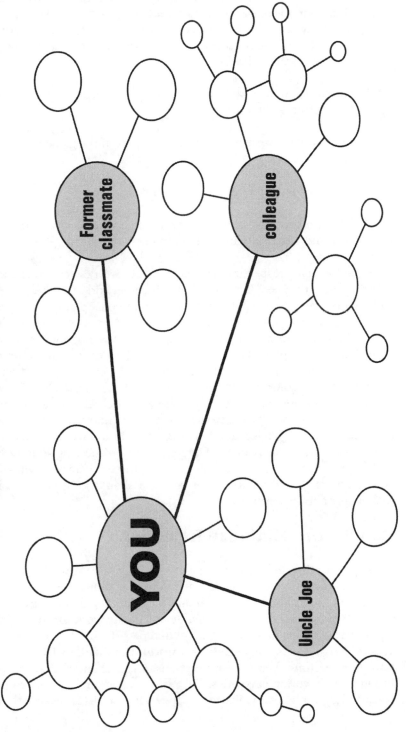

a "no" as a sign of personal failure – and quit prematurely. If they persisted longer, they would achieve success after a few more "no's." Furthermore, if their prospecting activities were focused on gathering information rather than making sales, they would considerably minimize rejections. Therefore, you are well advised to do the following:

- Develop a well organized and active prospecting campaign for uncovering quality job leads.

- Be positive by accepting rejections as part of the game that leads to acceptances.

- Link prospecting to informational interviewing.

- Keep prospecting for more information and "yeses" which will eventually translate into job interviews and offers.

A good initial prospecting pace is to make two new contacts each day. Start by contacting people in your immediate network. Let them know you are conducting a job search, but emphasize that you are only doing research. Ask for a few moments of their time to talk about what you are doing. You are only seeking **information and advice** at this time – not a job.

It should take you about 20 minutes to make a contact by letter or telephone. If you make two contacts each day, by the end of the first week you will have 10 new contacts for a total investment of less than seven hours. By the second week you may want to increase your prospecting pace to four new contacts each day or 20 each week. The more contacts you make, the more useful information, advice, and job leads you will receive. If your job search bogs down, you probably need to increase your prospecting activities.

Expect each contact to refer you to two or three others who will also refer you to others. Consequently, your contacts should multiply considerably within only a few weeks.

Handle and Minimize Rejections

These prospecting and networking methods are effective, and they can have a major impact on your job search, and your life. While they are responsible for building, maintaining, and expanding multi-million dollar businesses, they work extremely well for job hunters. But they only work for those who have a positive attitude and who are patient and persist. **The key to networking success is to focus on gathering information while also learning to handle rejections**. Learn from rejections, forget them, and go on to more productive networking activities. The major reason direct-sales people fail is because they don't persist. The reason they don't persist is because they either can't take, or they get tired of taking, rejections. This should not happen to you. Always welcome rejections: they lead to acceptances.

Rejections are no fun, especially in such an ego-involved activity as a job search. But you will encounter rejections as you travel on the road toward job search success. This road is strewn with individuals who quit prematurely because they were rejected four or five times. Don't be one of them!

Our prospecting and networking techniques differ from sales approaches in one major respect: we have special techniques for minimizing the number of rejections. If handled properly, at least 50 percent – maybe as many as 90 percent – of your prospects will turn into "yeses" rather than "no's." The reason for this unusually high acceptance rate is how you introduce and handle yourself before your prospects. Many insurance agents and direct distributors expect a 90 percent rejection rate, because they are trying to sell specific products potential clients may or may not need. Most people don't like to be put on the spot – especially when it is in their own home or office – to make a decision to buy a product.

> *The job search is a highly ego-involved activity often characterized by numerous rejections accompanied by a few acceptances.*

Be Honest and Sincere

The principles of selling yourself in the job market are similar. People don't want to be put on the spot. They feel uncomfortable if they think you expect them to give you a job. Thus, you should never introduce yourself to a prospect by asking them for a job or a job lead. You should do just the opposite: relieve their anxiety by mentioning that you are not looking for a job from them – only job information and advice. You must be honest and sincere in communicating these intentions to your contact. The biggest turn-off for individuals targeted for informational interviews is insincere job seekers who try to use this as a mechanism to get a job.

Your approach to prospects must be subtle, honest, and professional. You are seeking **information, advice, and referrals** relating to several subjects: job opportunities, your job search approach, your resume, and contacts who may have similar information, advice, and referrals. Most people gladly volunteer such information. They generally like to talk about themselves, their careers, and others. Like advice columnists, they like to give advice. This approach flatters individuals by placing them in the role of the expert-advisor. Who doesn't want to be recognized as an expert-advisor, especially on such a critical topic as one's employment?

This approach should yield a great deal of information, advice, and referrals from your prospects. One other important outcome should result from using this approach: people will **remember** you as the person who made them feel at ease and who received their valuable advice. If they hear of job opportunities for someone with your qualifications, chances are they will contact you with the information. After contacting 100 prospects, you will have created 100 sets of eyes and ears to help you in your job search!

Practice the 5R's of Informational Interviewing

The guiding principle behind prospecting, networking, and informational interviews is this: **The best way to get a job is to ask for job information, advice, and referrals; never ask for a job**. Remember, you want your prospects to engage in the 5R's of informational interviewing:

- **Reveal** useful information and advice.
- **Refer** you to others.
- **Read** your resume.
- **Revise** your resume.
- **Remember** you for future reference.

If you network according to this principle, you should join the ranks of thousands of successful job seekers who have experienced the 5R's of informational interviewing. Largely avoiding the advertised job market, you may find your perfect job through such powerful networking activities.

Approach Key People

Whom should you contact within an organization for an informational interview? Contact people who are busy, who have the power to hire, and who are knowledgeable about the organization. The least likely candidate will be someone in the human resources department. Most often the heads of operating units are the most busy, powerful, and knowledgeable individuals in the organization. However, getting access to such individuals may be difficult. Some people at the top may appear to be informed and powerful, but they may lack information on the day-to-day personnel changes or their influence is limited in the hiring process. It is difficult to give one best answer to this question.

Therefore, we recommend contacting several types of people. Aim for the busy, powerful, and informed, but be prepared to settle for less. Secretaries, receptionists, and the person you want to meet may refer you to others. From a practical standpoint, you may have to take whomever you can schedule an appointment with. Sometimes people who are less powerful can be helpful. Talk to a secretary or receptionist sometime about their boss or working in the organization. You may be surprised by what you learn!

Nonetheless, you will conduct informational interviews with different types of people. Some will be friends, relatives, or acquaintances. Others will be referrals or new contacts. You will gain the easiest access to people you already know. This can usually be done informally by telephone. You might meet at their home or office or at a restaurant.

You should use a more formal approach to gain access to referrals and new contacts. The best way to initiate a contact with a prospective employer is to **send an approach letter** and follow it up with a phone call. Examples of approach letters are found at the end of Chapter 7. This letter should include the following elements:

> _The best way to get a job is to ask for job information, advice, and referrals; never ask for a job._

OPENERS

If you have a referral, tell the individual you are considering a career in _____. His or her name was given to you by _____ who suggested he or she might be a good person to give you useful information about careers in _____.
Should you lack a referral to the individual and thus must use a "cold turkey" approach to making this contact, you might begin your letter by stating that you are aware he or she has been at the forefront of _____ business – or whatever is both truthful and appropriate for the situation. A subtle form of flattery will be helpful at this stage.

REQUEST

Demonstrate your thoughtfulness and courtesy rather than aggressiveness by mentioning that you know he or she is busy. You hope to schedule a mutually convenient time for a brief meeting to discuss your questions and career plans. Most people will be flattered by such a request and happy to talk with you about their work – if they have time and are interested in you.

CLOSINGS

In closing the letter, mention that you will call the person to see if an appointment can be arranged. Be specific by stating the time and day you will call – for example, Thursday at 2pm. You must take initiative to follow up the letter with a definite contact time. If you don't, you cannot expect to hear from the person. It is _your_ responsibility to make the telephone call to schedule a meeting.

ENCLOSURE Dp mpDo **not** enclose your resume with this approach letter. You should take your resume to the interview and present it as a topic of discussion near the end of your meeting. If you send it with the approach letter, you communicate a mixed and contradictory message. Remember your purpose for this interview: to gather information and advice. You are not – and never should be – asking for a job. A resume accompanying a letter appears to be an application or a job request.

Many people will meet with you, assuming you are sincere in your approach. On the other hand, many people also are very busy and simply don't have the time to meet with you. If the person puts you off when you telephone for an appointment, clearly state your purpose and emphasize that you are not looking for a job with this person – only information and advice. If the person insists on putting you off, make the best of the situation: try to conduct the informational interview over the telephone. Alternatively, write a nice thank you letter in which you again state your intended purpose; mention your disappointment in not being able to learn from the person's experience; and ask to be remembered for future reference. Enclose your resume with this letter. As a student, you are in an especially strong position to seek informational interviews. Many people are willing to assist an eager student – more so than an individual who is already in the workforce.

While you are ostensibly seeking information and advice, treat this meeting as an important preliminary interview. You need to communicate your qualifications – that you are competent, intelligent, honest, and likable. These are the same qualities you should communicate in a formal job interview. Hence, follow the same advice given for conducting a formal interview and dressing appropriately for a face-to-face meeting (Chapter 9).

Conduct the Interview Well

An informational interview will be relatively unstructured compared to a formal job interview. Since you want the interviewer to advise you, you reverse roles by asking questions which should give you useful information. You, in effect, become the interviewer. You should structure this interview with a particular sequence of questions. Most questions should be open-ended, requiring the individual to give specific answers based upon his or her experience.

The structure and dialogue for the informational interview might go something like this. You plan to take no more than 45 minutes for this interview. The first three to five minutes will be devoted to small talk – the weather, traffic, the office, mutual acquaintances, or an interesting or humorous observation. Since these are the most critical moments in the interview, be especially careful how you communicate nonverbally. Begin your interview by stating your appreciation for the individual's time:

> *"I want to thank you again for scheduling this meeting with me. I know you're busy. I appreciate the special arrangements you made to see me on a subject which is very important to my future."*

Your next comment should be a statement reiterating your purpose as stated in your letter:

> *"As you know, I am exploring job and career alternatives. I know what I do well and what I want to do. But before I commit myself to a new job, I need to know more about various career options. I thought you would be able to provide me with some insights into career opportunities, job requirements, and possible problems or promising directions in the field of _____."*

This statement normally will get a positive reaction from the individual who may want to know more about what it is you want to do. Be sure to clearly communicate your job objective. If you can't, you may communicate that you are lost, indecisive, or uncertain about yourself. The person may feel you are wasting his or her time.

Your next line of questioning should focus on "how" and "what"questions centering on (1) specific jobs and (2) the job search process. Begin by asking about various aspects of specific jobs:

- Duties and responsibilities
- Knowledge, skills, and abilities required
- Work environment relating to employees, work, deadlines, stress
- Advantages and disadvantages
- Salary ranges and benefits
- Advancement opportunities and outlook

Your informer will probably take a great deal of time talking about his or her experience in each area. Be a good listener, but make sure you move along with the questions.

Your next line of questioning should focus on your job search activities. You need as much information as possible on how to:

- Acquire the necessary skills
- Best find a job in this field
- Overcome any objections employers may have to you
- Uncover job vacancies which may be advertised
- Develop job leads
- Approach prospective employers

Your final line of questioning should focus on your resume. Do not show your resume until you focus on this last set of questions. The purpose of these questions is to: (1) get the individual to read your resume in-depth, (2) acquire useful advice on how to strengthen it, (3) refer you to prospective employers, and (4) be remembered. With the resume in front of you and your interviewee, ask the following questions:

- Is this an appropriate type of resume for the jobs I outlined?

- If an employer received this resume in the mail, how do you think he or she would react to it?

- What do you see as possible weaknesses or areas that need to be improved?

- What about the length, paper quality and color, layout, and type style/size? Are they appropriate?

- What should I do with this resume? Broadcast it to hundreds of employers with a cover letter?

- How might I best improve the form and content of the resume?

- Who might be most interested in receiving this resume?

You should receive useful advice on how to strengthen both the content and use of your resume. Most important, these questions force the individual to **read** your resume which, in turn, may be **remembered** for future reference.

Your last question is especially important. You want to be both **remembered** and **referred**. Some variation of the following question should help:

"I really appreciate all this advice. It is very helpful and it should improve my job search considerably. Could I ask you one more favor? Do you know two or three other people who could help me with my job search? I want to conduct as much research as possible, and their advice might be helpful also."

Before you leave, mention one more important item:

"During the coming weeks, should you hear of any job opportunities for someone with my interests and qualifications, I would appreciate being kept in mind. And please feel free to pass my name on to others."

Send a nice thank you letter – preferably by mail – within 48 hours of completing this informational interview. Express your genuine gratitude for the individual's time and advice. Reiterate your interests, and ask to be remembered and referred.

Be sure to follow up on any useful advice you receive, particularly referrals. Approach referrals in the same manner you approached the person who gave you the referral. Write a letter requesting a meeting. Begin the letter by mentioning:

"Mr./Ms./Dr. _____ suggested that I contact you concerning my research on careers in _____."

If you continue prospecting, networking, and conducting informational interviews, soon you will be busy conducting interviews and receiving job offers. While 100 informational interviews over a two-month period should lead to several formal job interviews and offers, the pay-offs are uncertain because job vacancies are unpredictable. We know cases where the first referral turned into a formal interview and job offer for a student. More typical cases require constant prospecting, networking, and informational interviewing activities. The telephone call or letter inviting you to a job interview can come at any time. While the timing may be unpredictable, your persistent job search activities will be largely responsible for the final outcome.

Telephone for Job Leads

Telephone communication should play an important role in prospecting, networking, and informational interviews. However, controversy centers around how and when to use the telephone for generating job leads and scheduling interviews. Some people recommend writing a letter and waiting for a written or telephone reply. Others suggest writing a letter and following it with a telephone call. Still others argue you should use the telephone exclusively rather than write letters.

How you use the telephone will indicate what type of job search you are conducting. Exclusive reliance on the telephone is a technique used by highly formalized job clubs which operate phone banks for generating job leads. Using the Yellow Pages as the guide to employers, a job club member may call as many as 50 employers a day to schedule job interviews. A rather aggressive yet typical telephone dialogue goes something like this:

"Hello, my name is Tim Jackson. I would like to speak to the head of the communications department. By the way, what is the name of the director?"

"You want to talk to Ms. Quincy. Her number is 141-234-8765 or I can connect you directly."

"Hello, Ms. Quincy. My name is Jim Jackson. I'm graduating from Washington University in June with a degree in communications. During the past

year I worked as an intern in advertising with L.C. Communications. I've developed an extensive portfolio of materials which were used in an innovative environmental protection campaign. I'd like to meet with you to discuss possible openings in your department for someone with my qualifications. Would it be possible to see you on Wednesday at 10am?"

Not surprisingly, this telephone approach generates many "no's." If you have a hard time handling rejections, this telephone approach will help you confront your anxieties. The principle behind this approach is *probability*: for every 25 telephone no's" you receive, you will probably get one or two "yeses." Success is just 25 telephone calls away! If you start calling prospective employers at 9am and finish your 25 calls by 12 noon, you should generate at least one or two interviews. That's not bad for three hours of job search work. It beats a direct-mail approach.

While the telephone is more efficient than writing letters, its effectiveness is questionable. When you use the telephone in this manner, you are basically asking for a job. You are asking the employer: *"Do you have a job for me?"* There is nothing subtle or particularly professional about this approach. It is effective in uncovering particular types of job leads for particular types of individuals. If you need a job – any job – in a hurry, this is one of the most efficient ways of finding employment. However, if you are more concerned with finding a job that is right for you – a job you do well and enjoy doing, one that is fit for you – this telephone approach is inappropriate.

You must use your own judgment in determining when and how to use the telephone in your job search. There are appropriate times and methods for using the telephone, and these should relate to your job search goals and needs. We prefer the more conventional approach of writing a letter requesting an informational interview and following it up with a telephone call. While you take the initiative in scheduling an appointment, you do not put the individual on the spot by asking for a job. You are only seeking information and advice. This low-keyed approach results in numerous acceptances and has a higher probability of paying off with interviews than the aggressive telephone request. You should be trying to uncover jobs that are right for you rather than any job that happens to pop up from a telephoning blitz.

Key Networking Books

Numerous books can assist you in developing effective networking skills. While most such books focus on networking in all types of situations, these three books focus specifically on networking for finding a job:

The Savvy Networker: Building Your Job Net for Success, Ron and Caryl Krannich (Impact Publications, 2001)

A Foot in the Door: Networking Your Way Into the Hidden Job Market, Katharine Hansen (Ten Speed Press, 2000)

Information Interviewing: How to Tap Your Hidden Job Market, Martha Stoodley (Ferguson Publishing, 1996)

Other popular networking books that focus on networking in many different business and social settings include the following:

Golden Rule of Schmoozing, Aye Jaye (Sourcebooks, 1998)

How to Work a Room, 2nd Edition, Susan RoAne (Warner Books, 2000)

Make Your Contacts Count, Anne Baber and Lynne Waymon (AMACOM, 2001)

Masters of Networking, Ivan R. Misner, Don Morgan, et al. (Bard Press, 2000)

Networking Smart, Wayne E. Baker (McGraw-Hill, 1994)

People Power, Donna Fisher (Bard Press, 1995)

Power Networking, Donna and Sandy Vilas (Bard Press, 2000)

Power to Get In, Michael A. Boylan (St. Martin's Press, 1998)

The Secrets of Savvy Networking, Susan RoAne (Warner Books, 1993)

Internet Resources for Networking

While a good book can be a terrific resource for developing networking skills, numerous Internet websites also are wonderful resources for understanding, developing, and practicing networking skills. We recommend visiting the following websites which deal with different aspects of networking, from joining an online career-related network to locating former classmates and friends whom you might want to contact as part of your network building activities.

Usenet newsgroups that offer online networking opportunities include the following websites:

- Cyberfiber   www.cyberfiber.com
- Google   groups.google.com
- JobBankUSA   jobbankusa.com/usejobs.html
- Topica   topica.com
- Usenet Info Center   metalab.unc.edu/usenet-i/
                                    home.html

Sites for finding, or creating, mailing lists related to your career:

- Coollist   coollist.com
- Google   groups.google.com
- Publicly Accessible
  Mailing Lists   paml.net
- Topica   topica.com/dir/cid=561
- Yahoo! Groups   groups.yahoo.com

Mega employment sites with message boards to network for information, advice, and referrals:

- Monster.com   community.monster.com/boards
- Vault.com   vault.com/community/mb/mb_
                                    home.jsp

Sites with useful information and advice on how to sharpen your networking skills:

- WetFeet   wetfeet.com/advice/networking.asp
- Monster.com   content.monster.com/network
- Quintessential Careers   quintcareers.com/
                                    networking.html
- Riley Guide   www.rileyguide.com/netintv.html
- WinningTheJob   www.winningthejob.com
- SchmoozeMonger   www.schmoozemonger.com
- Susan RoAne   susanroane.com/free.html
- Contacts Count   contactscount.com/articles.html

Directories to associations function as key networking sources:

- Associations on the Net   ipl.org/ref/AON
- AssociationCentral   associationcentral.com
- American Society of
  Association Executives   www.asaenet.org
- GuideStar   guidestar.org

Major women's online networking groups:

- Advancing Women   advancingwomen.com
- American Association of
  University Women   aauw.org
- American Business
  Women's Association   abwahq.org
- Business Women's
  Network Interactive   BWNi.com
- Federally Employed Women   few.org
- iVillage   ivillage.com
- Systers   systers.org
- Women.com   women.com

Alumni groups for networking:

- Alumni.net   alumni.net
- Alumniconnections   bcharrispub.com/isd/alumni
                                       connections.html
- Planet Alumni   planetalumni.com

Locators for finding old friends and re-building networks:

- Anywho   anywho.com
- Classmates   classmates.com
- InfoSpace   infospace.com
- KnowX   knowx.com
- Switchboard   switchboard.com
- The Ultimate White Pages   theultimates.com/white
- Whowhere Lycos   whowhere.lycos.com
- WorldPages   worldpages.com
- Yahoo   people.yahoo.com

Military locators and buddy finders:

- GI Search.com   gisearch.com
- Military.com   military.com
- Military Connections   militaryconnections.com
- Military USA   militaryusa.com

Job search clubs and support groups:

- 5 O'Clock Clubs   fiveoclockclub.com
- ExecuNet   execunet.com
- Professionals in Transition   jobsearching.org

Network Your Way to Job Success

Effective job seekers include **both** the advertised and hidden job market in their job search. Whatever you do, make sure you understand how to navigate the hidden job market.

Become proactive by developing the necessary networking skills for acquiring useful information, advice, and referrals. If you launch an effective networking campaign, you should be able to significantly shorten your job search time. You'll meet many helpful individuals who can provide advice on how you can improve your job search. Best of all, these individuals will plug you into the word-of-mouth networks where the good jobs will be found. If you spend most of your time responding to classified ads and online job postings, you may be disappointed and frustrated with the results. You, in effect, are conducting a traditional job search which we outlined on page 12. But if you focus on your networks, especially those with job and career content, you may discover a whole new world of job search success!

9

Interview for Jobs and Get Offers

THE JOB INTERVIEW IS THE MOST IMPORTANT STEP IN THE job search. Everything you do up to this point in your job search should be designed to get the interview. Once you get an interview, which may become a series of three or four interviews with a single employer, your goal should be to learn as much as possible about the job and employer so you can make an informed decision whether or not you want the job. As such, the interview becomes a two-way communication process – you assess the employer and the employer assesses you to decide whether or not you want to work together.

Unfortunately, many job seekers finally get the job interview and then make a series of errors that either knock them out of competition or result in making bad employment decisions. Many of the errors may seem unbelievable, but they occur every day with thousands of candidates.

Stressful Times

Congratulations! You've just been invited to a job interview. Your job search efforts, from self-assessment and research to resume writing and networking, have finally paid off. All you have to do now is go into the job interview and sell yourself. However, that's easier said than done. The very thought of going to a job interview touches on a full range of emotions – joy of getting the interview and some apprehension thinking about what to wear, say, and do during the interview. Like an actor in the theater, you will be onstage facing a critical audience that will ask you many probing questions to determine whether or not to offer you the job. Chances are you are competing with a few other equally qualified candidates, which may string out the hiring decision for two to three weeks.

The job interview is one of the most stressful situations you may encounter, and especially if you really want the job in question. Within the space of a few days, you need to get ready for a major performance. Perhaps you should rehearse the gist of why you are the perfect fit for this job. But the interview is more than just talk centering on a series of questions and answers. It's also about making good impressions, from what you wear and how you smell to the way in which you greet potential employers, maintain eye contact during the interview, and close and follow up the interview. Do you communicate confidence and trustworthiness in your demeanor, or are you that interviewee who has a limp handshake and shifty eyes? How do you dress, what do you say, and how do you handle yourself throughout various phases of the interview process? If lunch or dinner is included in the interview, what should you order and how should you mind your table manners? Again, you're onstage and your audience is judging you with a very critical eye.

What's Your Interview Quotient (I.Q.)?

Just how well prepared are you for the job interview? Respond to the following statements by indicating your degree of agreement with each:

SCALE:	5 = strongly agree	2 = disagree
	4 = agree	1 = strongly disagree
	3 = maybe, not certain	

1. I know what skills I can offer employers.   5 4 3 2 1

2. I know what skills employers most seek
   in candidates.   5 4 3 2 1

3. I can clearly explain to employers what
   I do well and enjoy doing.   5 4 3 2 1

4. I can explain in 60 seconds why an
   employer should hire me.   5 4 3 2 1

5. I can identify and target employers
   I want to get an interview with.   5 4 3 2 1

6. I can develop a job referral network.   5 4 3 2 1

7. I can prospect for job leads.   5 4 3 2 1

8. I can generate at least one job interview
    for every 10 job search contacts I make.   5 4 3 2 1

9. I can follow up on job interviews.   5 4 3 2 1

10. I can persuade an employer to renegotiate
    my salary after six months on the job.   5 4 3 2 1

11. I know which questions interviewers are
    most likely to ask me.   5 4 3 2 1

12. If asked to reveal my weaknesses, I know how
    to respond – answer honestly, but always
    stress my strengths.   5 4 3 2 1

13. I know how to best dress for the interview.   5 4 3 2 1

14. I know the various types of interviews I may
    encounter and how to appropriately respond
    in each situation.   5 4 3 2 1

15. I can easily approach strangers for job
    information and advice.   5 4 3 2 1

16. I know where to find information on
    organizations that are most likely to be
    interested in my skills.   5 4 3 2 1

17. I know how to go beyond vacancy announce-
    ments to locate job opportunities appropriate
    for my qualifications.   5 4 3 2 1

18. I know how to interview appropriate
    people for job information and advice.   5 4 3 2 1

19. I know many people who can refer me to
    others for informational interviews.   5 4 3 2 1

20. I can uncover jobs on the hidden job market.   5 4 3 2 1

21. I know how to prepare and practice for the
    critical job interview.   5 4 3 2 1

22. I know how to stress my positives.   5 4 3 2 1

23. I know how to research the organization and
    individuals who are likely to interview me.   5 4 3 2 1

24. I have considered how I would respond to
    illegal questions posed by prospective employers.   5 4 3 2 1

25. I can telephone effectively for job leads.   5 4 3 2 1

26. I am prepared to conduct an effective
    telephone interview.   5 4 3 2 1

27. I know when and how to deal with salary
    questions.   5 4 3 2 1

28. I know what to read while waiting in the
    outer office prior to the interview.   5 4 3 2 1

29. I can nonverbally communicate my interest
    and enthusiasm for the job.   5 4 3 2 1

30. I know the best time to arrive at the
    interview site.   5 4 3 2 1

31. I know how to respond using positive form
    and content as well as supports when
    responding to interviewers' questions.   5 4 3 2 1

32. I know how to summarize my strengths
    and value at the closing of the interview.   5 4 3 2 1

33. I know what to include in a thank-you letter.   5 4 3 2 1

34. I know when and how to follow up the
    job interview.   5 4 3 2 1

35. I know what do during the 24- to 48-hour
    period following a job offer.   5 4 3 2 1

36. I can clearly explain to interviewers what
    I like and dislike about particular jobs.   5 4 3 2 1

37. I can explain to interviewers why I made
    my particular educational choices, including
    my major and grade point average.   5 4 3 2 1

38. I can clearly explain to interviewers what
    I want to be doing 5 or 10 years from now.   5 4 3 2 1

39. I have a list of references who can speak in
    a positive manner about me and my work
    abilities.   5 4 3 2 1

40. I can clearly state my job and career
    objectives as both skills and outcomes.   5   4   3   2   1

41. I have set aside 20 hours a week to primarily
    conduct informational interviews.   5   4   3   2   1

42. I know what foods and drinks are best to
    select if the interview also includes a
    luncheon or dinner meeting.   5   4   3   2   1

43. I know how to listen effectively.   5   4   3   2   1

44. I can explain why an employer should hire me.   5   4   3   2   1

45. I am prepared to handle the salary question
    at whatever point it may come up.   5   4   3   2   1

46. I know when to use my resume in an
    informational interview.   5   4   3   2   1

47. I can generate three new job leads each day.   5   4   3   2   1

48. I can outline my major achievements in jobs
    I have held and show how they relate to
    the job I am interviewing for.   5   4   3   2   1

49. I know what the interviewer is looking for
    when he or she asks about weaknesses.   5   4   3   2   1

50. I am prepared to handle both serial and
    stress interviews.   5   4   3   2   1

TOTAL I.Q.

Once you have completed this exercise, add your responses to compute a total score. This will comprise your composite I.Q. If your score is between 200 and 250, you seem well prepared to successfully handle the interview. If your score is between 150 and 199, you are heading in the right direction, and many of our recommended resources should help you increase your interview competencies. If your score falls below 150, you have a great deal of work to do in preparation for the job interview.

Interview Sins and Knockouts

Unlike many other job search mistakes, interview errors tend to be unforgiving. This is the time when first impressions count the most.

Employers have both positive and negative goals in mind. On the positive side, they want to hire someone who can do the job and add value or benefits to their organization. On the negative side, they are always looking for clues that tell them why they should **not** hire you. After all, you are probably another stranger who makes inflated claims about your competence in the hope of getting a job offer. It's not until you start performing on the job that the employer gets to see the "real you" and discover your patterns of behavior.

> *Employers also look for clues that tell them why they should _not_ hire you.*

In the meantime, the employer needs to be on his or her guard looking for evidence that you may be the wrong person for the job. Make a mistake during the job interview and you may be instantly eliminated from further consideration. Therefore, you must be on your very best behavior and avoid the many common mistakes interviewees make.

The following mistakes are frequently cited by employers who have interviewed hundreds of applicants:

1. **Arrives late to the interview.** First impressions really do count and they are remembered for a long time. Arrive late and you've made one of the worst impressions possible! Indeed, regardless of what you say or do during the interview, you may never recover from this initial mistake. Employers wonder, *"Will you also come to work late?"*

2. **Makes a bad impression in the waiting area.** Treats receptionists and secretaries as inferiors – individuals who may have important input into the hiring process when later asked by the employer *"What was your impression of this candidate?"* Caught reading frivolous materials – *People Magazine* – in the waiting areas when company reports and related literature were readily available.

3. **Offers stupid excuses for behavior.** Excuses are usually red flags indicating that a person is unwilling to take responsibility and do the work. Here's a killer excuse for arriving late for a job interview: *"I got lost because your directions weren't very clear."* Goodbye! Here are some other classic excuses heard during job interviews:

   - I forgot.
   - It wasn't my fault.
   - It was a bad company.
   - My boss was a real jerk.
   - The college wasn't very good.
   - I can't remember why I did that.

  ■ No one there appreciated my work.
  ■ I didn't have time to visit your website.

4. **Presents a poor appearance and negative image.** Dresses inappropriately for the interview – under-dresses or over-dresses for the position. The interviewee may choose poor quality clothing, select inappropriate colors, or put them together poorly. He or she may need to learn some basic grooming habits, from haircut and style to makeup and nails, or undergo a major makeover.

5. **Expresses bad, negative, and corrosive attitudes.** Tends to be negative, overbearing, extremely aggressive, cynical, and opinionated to the extreme. Expresses intolerance and strong prejudices toward others. Complains a lot about everything and everybody. In Yiddish such chronic complainers are known as *kvetchers*. Indicates a possible caustic personality that will not fit in well with the company. Regardless of how talented this person may be, unless he works in a cell by himself, he'll probably be fired within two months for having a bad attitude that pollutes the office and harms morale.

6. **Engages in inappropriate and unexpected behaviors for an interview situation.** Shows off scars, tattoos, muscles, or pictures of family. Flirts with the interviewer. Possibly an exhibitionist who may also want to date the boss and harass co-workers!

7. **Appears somewhat incoherent and unfocused.** Tends to offer incomplete thoughts, loses focus, and jumps around to unrelated ideas. Hard to keep a focused conversation going. Incoherent thought processes indicate a possible attention problem.

8. **Inarticulate.** Speaks poorly, from sound of voice and diction to grammar, vocalized pauses, and jargon. Uses lots of *"you know," "ah," "like," "okay,"* and *"well"* fillers. Expresses a low-class street language – *"cool," "damn," "man," "wow."* Not a good candidate for using the telephone or interacting with clients. Appears verbally illiterate. Writing is probably similar.

9. **Gives short and incomplete answers to questions.** Tends to respond to most questions with *"Yes," "No," "Maybe,"* or *"I'm not sure"* when the interviewer expects more in-depth answers. Appears shallow and indicates a lack of substance, initiative, interest, and enthusiasm.

10. **Lacks a sense of direction.** Appears to have no goals or apparent objectives. Just looking for a paycheck rather than pursuing a passion.

11. **Appears ill or has a possible undisclosed medical condition.** Looks pale, glassy-eyed, gaunt, or yellow. Coughs, sneezes, and sounds terrible. Talks about her upcoming surgery – within six weeks of starting the job!

12. **Volunteers personal information that normally would be illegal or inappropriate to ask.** Candidate makes interviewer feel uncomfortable by talking about religion, political affiliation, age, family, divorce, sexual orientation, or physical and mental health.

13. **Emits bad or irritating smells.** Reeks of excessive perfume, cologne, or shaving lotion – could kill mosquitos! Can smell smoke or alcohol on breath. Strong body order indicates personal hygiene problems. Has bad breath throughout the interview, which gets cut short for an unexplained reason!

14. **Shows little enthusiasm, drive, or initiative.** Appears to be just looking for a job and a paycheck. Tends to be passive and indifferent. No evidence of being a self-starter who takes initiative and solves problems on his own. Not sure what motivates this person other than close supervision. Indeed, he'll require lots of supervision or we'll have an employee with lots of play-time on his hands or the job will expand to fill the time allotted. He'll become the "job guy" who always says *"I did my job just like you told me."* but not much beyond what's assigned. Don't expect much from this person who will probably be overpaid for what he produces.

15. **Lacks confidence and self-esteem.** Seems unsure of self, nervous, and ill at ease. Lacks decisiveness in making decisions. Communicates uncertainly with such comments as *"I don't know," "Maybe," "I'm not sure," "Hadn't really thought of that," "Interesting question," "I'll have to think about that,"* or redirects with the question *"Well, what do you think?"*

16. **Appears too eager or hungry for the job.** Is overly enthusiastic, engages in extreme flattery, and appears suspiciously nervous. Early in the interview, before learning about the company or job, makes such comments as *"I really like it here," "I need this job," "Is there overtime?," "What are you paying?," "How many vacation days do you give?"*

17. **Communicates dishonesty or deception.** Uses canned interview language, skirts probing questions, and appears disingenuous. Looks like a tricky character who has things to hide and thus will probably be sneaky and deceptive on the job.

18. **Feels too smooth and superficial.** Dresses nicely, has a firm handshake and good eye contact, answers most questions okay, and appears enthusiastic – just like the books tell job seekers to do. When asked more substantive *"What if"* and behavior-based questions, or requested to give examples of specific accomplishments, the candidate seems to be caught off balance and stumbles with incomplete answers. Can't put one's finger on the problem, but the gut reaction is that this role-playing candidate is very superficial and will probably end up being the "dressed for success" and "coached for the interview" employee from hell!

19. **Appears evasive when asked about possible problems with background.** Gives elusive answers to red flag questions about poor grades, changes in major, and excessive number of jobs. Such answers raise questions about the interviewee's honesty, credibility, sense of responsibility, and overall behavior. Indicates a possible negative behavior pattern that needs further investigation. On second thought, don't waste time investigating such candidates, who are more trouble than they are worth.

20. **Speaks negatively of previous employers and co-workers.** When asked why he left previous employers, usually responds by bad-mouthing them. Has little good to say about others who apparently were not as important as this candidate.

21. **Maintains poor eye contact.** At least in North America, eye contact is an indication of trustworthiness and attention. Individuals who fail to maintain an appropriate amount of eye contact are often judged as untrustworthy – have something to hide. Having too little or too much eye contact during the interview gives off mixed messages about what you are saying. Worst of all, it may make the interviewee feel uncomfortable in your presence.

22. **Offers a limp or overly firm handshake.** Interviewers often get two kinds of handshakes from candidates – the wimps and the bone-crushers. Your initial handshake may say something about your personality. Candidates offering a cold, wet, and limp handshake often come across as corpses! Bone-crushers may appear too aggressive.

23. **Shows little interest in the company.** Indicates he didn't do much research, since he knows little about the company and didn't have time to check out the company's website. Asks this killer question: *"What do you do here?"* Goodbye, again!

24. **Talks about salary and benefits early in the interview.** Rather than try to learn more about the company and position as well as demonstrate her value, the candidate seems preoccupied with salary and benefits by bringing them up within the first 15 minutes of the interview. Shows little interest in the job or employer beyond the compensation package. When the interviewee prematurely starts to talk about compensation, red flags go up again – this is a self-centered candidate who is not really interested in doing the job or advancing a career.

25. **Is discourteous, ill-mannered, and disrespectful.** Arrives for the interview a half hour late with no explanation or a phone call indicating a problem en route. Just sits and waits for the interviewer to ask questions. Picks up things on the interviewer's desk. Bites nails and picks nose during the interview. Challenges the interviewer's ideas. Closes the interview without thanking the interviewer for the opportunity to interview for the job. Not even going to charm and etiquette school would help this candidate!

26. **Tells inappropriate jokes and laughs a lot.** Attempts at humor bomb – appears to be a smart ass who likes to laugh at his own jokes. Comes across as an irritating clown who says stupid and silly things. Will need to frequently put this one out to pasture to keep him away from other employees who don't share such humor.

27. **Talks too much.** Can't answer a question without droning on and on with lots of irrelevant talk. Volunteers all kinds of information, including interesting but sensitive personal observations and gossip, the interviewer neither needs nor wants. Doesn't know when to shut up. Would probably waste a lot of valuable work time talking, talking, and talking and thus irritating others at work. Seems to need lots of social strokes through talk which she readily initiates.

28. **Drops names to impress the interviewer.** Thinks the interviewer will be impressed with a verbal Rolodex of who he knows. But interviewers tend to be put off with such candidates who, instead, appear insecure, arrogant, and patronizing – three deadly sins that may shorten your interview from 45 minutes to 15 minutes!

29. **Appears needy and greedy.** Talks a lot about financial needs and compensation. When discussing salary, talks about his personal financial situation, including debts and planned future purchases, rather than what the job is worth and what value he will bring to the job. Seems to expect the employer is interested in supporting his

lifestyle, which may be a combination of irresponsible financial behavior, failing to plan, living beyond his pay grade, and having bad luck. This line of talk indicates he probably has debilitating financial problems that go far beyond the salary level of this job. Not interested in paying for his needs.

30. **Closes the interview by just leaving.** How you close the interview may determine whether or not you will be invited back to another interview or offered the job. Most interviewees fail to properly close interviews. A proper close should include these six elements:

    1. Indicate you are indeed interested in the job – if you are.
    2. Summarize what you see as your major strengths and possible future contributions to the company.
    3. Thank the interviewer for his or her time.
    4. Ask when they plan to make the final hiring decision.
    5. Shake hands and say *"I hope to hear from you soon. Would it be okay to call you next week?"*
    6. Leave with a smile on your face and a spring to your step – positive body language as you exit.

    Never ever close the interview with this rather stupid and presumptuous closing prior to being offered the job: *"So when can I start?"* This question will finish off the interview and your candidacy – you're back to being needy and greedy! Also, don't play the hard-to-get pressure game, even if it's true, by stating *"I have another interview this week. When can I expect to hear from you?"* One other critical element to this close: send a nice thank you letter within 24 hours in which you again express your appreciation for the interview and your interest in the job.

31. **Fails to talk about accomplishments.** Candidate concentrates on explaining work history as primarily consisting of assigned duties and responsibilities. When asked to give examples of her five major accomplishments in her last jobs, doesn't seem to understand the question, gives little evidence of performance, or reverts once again to discussing formal duties and responsibilities. When probed further for accomplishments, can't really say much and feels uncomfortable about this line of questioning.

32. **Does not ask questions about the job or employer.** When asked *"Do you have any questions?,"* replies *"No"* or *"You've covered everything."* Asking questions is often more important than answering questions. When you ask thoughtful questions, you emphasize your interest in

the employer and job as well as indicate your intelligence – qualities employers look for in candidates.

33. **Appears self-centered rather than employer-centered.** This will become immediately apparent by the direction of the answers and questions coming from the interviewee. If they primarily focus on benefits to the interviewee, the candidate will tend to be self-centered. For example, a candidate who frequently uses "I" when talking about himself and the job may be very self-centered. On the other hand, the candidate who talks about "we" and "you" is usually more employer-oriented. Contrast these paired statements about the job and compensation:

> *"What would I be doing in this position?"*

> *"What do you see us achieving over the next six months?"*

> or

> *"What would I be making on this job?"*

> *"What do you normally pay for someone with my qualifications?"*

34. **Demonstrates poor listening skills.** Doesn't listen carefully to questions or seems to have her own agenda that overrides the interviewer's interest. Tends to go off in different directions from the questions being asked. Not a very empathetic listener both verbally and nonverbally. Seems to be more interested in talking about own agenda than focusing on the issues at hand. Apparently wants to take charge of the interview and be the Lone Ranger. The job really does require good listening skills!

35. **Seems not too bright for the job.** Answering simple interview questions is like giving an intelligence test. Has difficulty talking about past accomplishments. Doesn't seem to grasp what the job is all about or the skills required. Seems confused and lacks focus. Should never have gotten to the job interview but had a terrific looking resume which was probably written by a professional resume writer!

36. **Fails to know his/her worth and negotiate properly when it comes time to talk about compensation.** Job seekers are well advised to only talk about salary and benefits **after** being offered the job. If you prematurely talk about compensation, you may diminish

your value as well as appear self-centered. Be sure to research salary comparables so you know what you are worth in today's job market (start with www.salary.com). Listen carefully throughout the interview and ask questions which would give you a better idea of what the job is actually worth. Stress throughout the interview your skills and accomplishments – those things that are most valued by employers who are willing to pay what's necessary for top talent. When you do start negotiating, let the employer state a salary figure first and then negotiate using salary ranges to reach common ground. These and other salary negotiation techniques are outlined in several books on salary negotiations as well as on several websites (see the list of resources at the end of this chapter).

37. **Fails to properly prepare for the interview.** This is the most important mistake of all. It affects all the other mistakes. Indeed, failing to prepare will immediately show when the candidate makes a bad first impression, fails to indicate knowledge about the company and job, poorly answers standard interview questions, and does not ask questions. In other words, the candidate makes many of the mistakes outlined above because he or she failed to anticipate what goes into a winning interview. Since you should be communicating your very best self during the interview, failing to prepare for it says something about how you deal with important things in your life and work. In this case, the employer and job were not important enough for you to prepare properly. That's okay. The employer now knows the real you.

Behavioral and Internet Trends

Within the past few years, the job interview – as well as the whole hiring process – has changed in several important ways. These changes require both interviewees and interviewers to better prepare for the job interview. Most changes reflect the need of employers to better define their hiring needs and then make more intelligent and cost-effective hiring decisions. While employers used to hire fast and fire slow, more and more employers see the wisdom of doing things differently: hire slow and fire fast. This means more extensive screening of candidates and focusing on **patterns of accomplishments** in order to best **predict** employee behavior. Employers want a perfect "fit." This also means conducting a different style of interviewing. Rather than call a candidate in for two interviews, an employer may interview a single candidate four to seven times before making a job offer. So, how do you handle your fifth interview? Not surprisingly, many candidates have difficulty remaining buoyant after the third interview!

At the same time, employers are taking more time to screen candidates with everything from drug, skills, and psychological testing to in-depth background checks. Within the interview itself, more and more employers are asking behavior-based questions to ascertain a candidate's ability to make decisions and solve problems relevant to their organization. Consequently, candidates who prepare for interviews with memorized or canned answers to anticipated interview questions do not do well in such interviews; they appear coached and thus lack authenticity. Going beyond behavior-based questions, many employers also seek better indicators of a candidate's decision-making style and pattern of performance. They want to know more about your motivated skills and abilities (Chapter 3) and whether or not your MAS is a good fit for their organization.

Within the very near future, the Internet may play a key role in screening candidates, from doing background checks and administering skills and psychological tests to conducting interviews via a video link. Indeed, the Internet is proving to be the perfect medium for improving both the job search and the hiring processes. For employers, new Internet-based hiring software will enable them to eliminate many of the costly face-to-face steps currently involved in interviewing candidates. In so doing, interviews will be more employer-centered with greater emphasis placed on what you can do for the employer.

> *Employers are taking more time to screen candidates these days.*

The overall trend is simple: no more hiring surprises due to poor hiring skills! Employers want to better predict individual performance within their organizations. They can no longer make costly hiring mistakes that are often attributed to their own lack of good screening and interview skills. They want to take the guesswork out of hiring. They want the perfect skills set for the perfect fit.

Interview for the Job

Nearly 95 percent of all organizations require job interviews prior to hiring employees. In fact, employers consider an effective interview to be the most important hiring criteria – outranking grade point average, related work experience, and recommendations.

While the job interview is the most important job search activity, it also is the most stressful job search experience. Your application, resume, and letters may get you to the interview, but you must perform well in person in order to get a job offer. Knowing the stakes are high, most people face interviews with dry throats and lots of butterflies; it is a time of great stress. You will be onstage, and you are expected to perform well.

How do you prepare for the interview? First, you need to understand the nature and purpose of the interview. Second, you must prepare to respond to the interview situation and the interviewer. Make sure whomever assists you in preparing for the interview evaluates your performance. Practice the whole interviewing scenario, from the time you enter the door until you leave. You should sharpen your nonverbal communication skills and be prepared to give positive answers to questions as well as ask intelligent questions. The more you practice, the better prepared you will be for the real job interview.

A Communication Focus

An interview is a two-way communication exchange between an interviewer and interviewee. It involves both verbal and nonverbal communication. While we tend to concentrate on the content of what we say, research shows that approximately 65 percent of all communication is nonverbal. Furthermore, we tend to give more credibility to nonverbal than to verbal messages. Regardless of what you say, how you dress, sit, stand, use your hands, move your head and eyes, and listen communicates both positive and negative messages.

Job interviews can occur in many different settings and under various circumstances. You may write job interview letters, schedule interviews by telephone, be interviewed over the phone, and encounter one-on-one as well as panel, group, and serial interviews. Each situation requires a different set of communication behaviors. For example, while telephone communication is efficient, it may be ineffective for interview purposes. Only certain types of information can be effectively communicated over the telephone because this medium is primarily verbal. Honesty, intelligence, and likability – three of the most important values you want to communicate to employers – are primarily communicated nonverbally. Although your enthusiasm can be communicated vocally on the telephone, many other nonverbal aspects, such as facial expression and gestures, are absent. Therefore, you should be very careful of telephone interviews – whether giving or receiving them.

Job interviews have different purposes and can be negative in many ways. From your perspective, the purpose of an initial job interview is to get a second interview, and the purpose of the second interview is to get a job offer. However, for many employers, the purpose of the interview is to eliminate you from a second interview or job offer. The interviewer wants to know why he or she should *not* hire you. The interviewer tries to do this by identifying your weaknesses. These differing purposes can create an adversarial relationship and contribute to the overall interviewing stress experienced by both the applicant and the interviewer.

Since the interviewer wants to identify your weaknesses, you must counter by **communicating your strengths** to lessen the interviewer's fears of hiring you. Recognizing that you are an unknown quantity to the employer, you must raise the interviewer's expectations of you.

Answer Questions

Hopefully your prospecting, networking, informational interviewing, and resume and letter writing activities result in several invitations to interview for jobs appropriate to your objective. Once you receive an invitation to interview, you should prepare for the interview as if it were a $1,000,000 prize. After all, that may be what you earn during your employment.

The invitation to interview will most likely come by telephone. In some cases, a preliminary interview will be conducted by telephone. The employer may want to shorten the list of eligible candidates from 10 to three. By calling each individual, the employer can quickly eliminate marginal candidates as well as update the job status of each individual. When you get such a telephone call, you have no time to prepare. You may be dripping wet as you step from the shower or you may have a splitting headache as you pick up the phone. Telephone interviews always seem to occur at bad times. Whatever your situation, put your best foot forward based upon your thorough preparation for an interview. You may want to keep a list of questions near the telephone just in case you receive such a telephone call.

Telephone interviews often result in a face-to-face interview at the employer's office. Once you confirm an interview time and place, you should do as much research on the organization and employer as possible as well as learn to lessen your anxiety and stress levels by practicing the interview situation. **Preparation and practice** are the keys to doing your best.

During the interview, you want to impress upon the interviewer your knowledge of the organization by asking insightful questions and giving intelligent answers. Your library, Internet, and networking research should yield useful information on the organization and employer. Be sure you know something about the organization. Interviewers are normally impressed by interviewees who demonstrate knowledge and interest in their organization.

You should practice the actual interview by mentally addressing several questions most interviewers ask. Most of these questions will relate to your educational background, work experience, career goals, personality, and related concerns. The most frequently asked questions include:

Education

- Describe your educational background.
- Why did you attend _____ University (College or School)?
- Why did you major in _____?
- What was your grade point average?
- What subjects did you enjoy the most? The least? Why?
- What leadership positions did you hold?
- How did you finance your education?
- If you could, what would you change about your education?

- Why were your grades so low? So high?
- Did you do the best you could in school? If not, why not?
- What type of specialized training have you received?
- How do you plan to keep up in your field?

Work Experience

- What were your major achievements in each of your past jobs?
- Why did you leave these jobs?
- What is your typical workday like?
- What functions do you enjoy doing the most?
- What did you like about your boss? Dislike?
- Which job did you enjoy the most? Why? Which job did you enjoy the least? Why?
- Have you ever been fired? Why?
- What did you especially like about your present or last job?

Career Goals

- Why do you want to join our organization?
- Why do you think you are qualified for this position?
- Why are you looking for another job?
- Why do you want to make a career change?
- What ideally would you like to do?
- Why should we hire you?
- How would you improve our operations?
- What do you want to be doing five years from now?
- How much do you want to be making five years from now?
- What are your short-range and long-range career goals?
- If you were free to choose your job and employer, where would you go?
- What other types of jobs are you considering? Companies?
- When will you be ready to begin work?
- How do you feel about relocating, traveling, working overtime, and spending weekends in the office?
- What attracted you to our organization?

Personality and Other Concerns

- Tell me about yourself.
- What are your major weaknesses? Your major strengths?
- What causes you to lose your temper?
- What do you do in your spare time? Any hobbies?
- What types of books do you read?
- What role does your family play in your career?

Take Your Briefcase With You to the Interview
Phil Hey, Director, Career Services, Briar Cliff University

Here's a story with a happy ending: a former student of mine was using a selective placement agency that handled only high-tech jobseekers. He asked me if I would be a reference, which I was happy to be. Two days later he emailed me that he got the job. Then the next day I got a call from his placement agency, which was checking on his references. I asked the placement officer how my student had done in the interview; though he is an excellent writer and worker, he is not a particularly fluent speaker. The officer said, *"He beat out two of our other applicants for the job, and in fact he got offered more money than they had advertised as the top of the range."* *"Do you know what he did to get that offer?"* I asked. *"Yes,"* said the man, *"he was the only candidate who brought in work samples."*

I shouldn't have been surprised. I told the officer what I recommend to all my students: to take a briefcase with them to the interview (and if they don't have a professional-looking one, I'd lend them mine). Think of it this way: going into an interview is making an expedition into an unexplored territory, and a job candidate can't stop the interview while he or she makes a run home to get some necessary supply. In a real sense, if it isn't in the briefcase, it doesn't exist.

The first essential category to pack for the expedition is job- and career-related stuff:

- Another set of pre-interview instructions and communications: how to get to the interview site, when it starts, interviewer's name, and so on.
- Business cards, in addition to those the applicant carries on his or her person.
- Extra copies of the resume, application letter, list of references (and/or reference letters).
- Work samples, ready for professional presentation; maybe a college research paper is genuinely good enough to share, but if it looks marked-up and ratty, it will only hurt. Many professions have formatting standards for work, and in samples they should be followed to the letter.
- Credentialing that relies on organizations. I don't think a diploma would be useful, but a transcript might well be. Likewise for such certification as teaching credentials or competency in a particular software (such as Microsoft)
- Materials related to the company, perhaps already flagged and marginal-noted for questions and comments. "I noticed in your last annual report that your cost of sales increased significantly, and I have some ideas about how to bring it down." Companies care a great deal that applicants know them thoroughly.
- Scheduling aids, whether a PDA, a Dayrunner, or a vest-pocket calendar. If they make an offer, when can it be accepted? And what else is going on in the meantime? Being organized and aware of scheduling is a great career asset.
- Writing and note-taking materials: several pens or pencils and a pad of scratch paper. It is completely permissible to take notes in an interview; the interviewer will certainly be taking notes on the applicant.

They should be well enough organized that the applicant doesn't have to go into a scramble to find the relevant document. A few file folders or accordion folders can do nicely.

The second essential category is quality-of-life materials:

- A little pack of facial tissues.
- A reliable painkiller.
- Any medicine to treat a recurring condition.
- Feminine protection as apt.
- Binaca or breath mints.
- Emergency and convenience phone numbers.

If you don't get a second chance to make a good first impression, then neither do you have a very good chance to correct a bad one!

- How well do you work under pressure? In meeting deadlines?
- Tell me about your management philosophy.
- How much initiative do you take?
- What types of people do you prefer working with?
- How _____ (creative, analytical, tactful, etc.) are you?
- If you could change your life, what would you do differently?

Prepare for Objections and Negatives

Interviewers must have a healthy skepticism of job candidates. They expect people to exaggerate their competencies and overstate what they will do for the employer. They sometimes encounter dishonest applicants, and some people they hire fail to meet their expectations. Being realists who have made poor hiring decisions before, they want to know why they should **not** hire you. Although they do not always ask you these questions, they think about them nonetheless:

- Why should I hire you?
- What do you really want?
- What can you really do for me?
- What are your weaknesses?
- What problems will I have with you?

Underlying these questions are specific employers' objections to hiring you:

- You're not as good as you say you are; you probably hyped your resume or lied about yourself.
- All you want is a job and security.
- You have weaknesses like the rest of us. Is it alcohol, sex, drugs, finances, shiftlessness, petty politics?
- You'll probably want my job in another five months.
- You won't stay long with us. Ambitious people like you join the competition or **become** the competition.

Employers raise such suspicions and objections because it is difficult to trust strangers in the employment game and they may have been "burned" before. Indeed, there is an alarming rise in the number of individuals lying on their resumes or falsifying their credentials.

How can you best handle employers' objections? You must first recognize their biases and stereotypes and then **raise** their expectations. You do this by stressing your strengths and avoiding your weaknesses. You must be impeccably honest in doing so.

Your answers to employers' questions should be positive and emphasize your **strengths**. Remember, the interviewer wants to know what's wrong with you – your **weaknesses**. When answering questions, both the **substance** and **form** of your answers should be positive. For example, such words as *"couldn't," "can't," "won't,"* and *"don't"* may create a negative tone and distract from the positive and enthusiastic image you are trying to create. While you cannot eliminate all negative words, at least recognize that the type of words you use makes a difference; try to better manage your word choice. Compare your reactions to the following interview answers:

QUESTION: **You've worked part-time for XYZ company for the past two years. What have you liked the best about working for XYZ and what have liked the least?**

ANSWER 1:   *The best thing about working for XYZ is that the pay for a part-timer like me is pretty good. What I've liked least is having to work on weekends.*

ANSWER 2:   *XYZ has given me a lot of responsibility as a part-time employee. After training of course, I supervised a crew of 5 employees on weekends. That experience taught me a lot about leading employees and seeing to it the job is done right and on time. I will be able to use these skills on my next job.*

Which one has the greatest impact in terms of projecting positives and strengths? The first answer communicates too many negatives and is completely self-centered. The second answer is positive and upbeat in its orientation toward skills, accomplishments, and the future.

In addition to choosing positive words, select **content information** which is positive and **adds** to the interviewer's knowledge about you. Avoid simplistic "yes/no" answers; they say nothing about you. Instead, provide information which explains your reasons and motivations behind specific events or activities. For example, how do you react to these two factual answers?

QUESTION: **I see from your resume that you've been working during your junior and senior years. Why aren't you planning to work full-time for Company X once you graduate?**

ANSWER 1:   *There are a lot of internal political problems at Company X. Everyone is ready to stab a co-worker in the ack just to get ahead. Believe me, two years working there is enough.*

ANSWER 2:   *I have gained experience and learned a lot during the two years I worked at Company X. I know this experience and my skills can be useful in a number of settings. I am particularly interested in the work your (department or company).*

Let's try another question reflecting possible objections to hiring you:

QUESTION: **Your background bothers me somewhat. You took six years to earn your bachelor's degree and your work experience has been in a different industry.**

ANSWER 1:   *I understand your concern.*

ANSWER 2:   *I spent six years earning my bachelor's degree because I was working full-time or very nearly full-time hours during the years I was in college. I supported myself and paid for all my college expenses. I understand your concern about my work being in a different industry, but the basic work skills I developed will transfer readily to this industry and my college course work is closely aligned with the job opening here. I am a quick learner and am open to the training I would receive here.*

The first answer is incomplete. It misses an important opportunity to explain this issue in a positive manner which is clearly reflected in the second response.

The most difficult challenge to your positive strategy comes when the interviewer asks you to describe your negatives or weaknesses. Be careful in how you answer this sensitive question:

QUESTION: **We all have our negatives and weaknesses. What are some of yours?**

You can handle this question in any of five different ways, yet still give positive information on yourself:

1.   **Discuss a negative which is not related to the job:**

     I don't enjoy accounting. I know it's important, but I find it boring. Even at home my wife takes care of our books. Marketing is what I really like to do. I'm glad this job doesn't involve any accounting!

2. **Discuss a negative which the interviewer already knows:**

I spent a great deal of time working on advanced degrees, as indicated in my resume, and thus I lack extensive work experience. However, I believe my education has prepared me well for this job. My leadership experience in college taught me how to work with people, organize, and solve problems. I write well and quickly. My research experience helped me analyze, synthesize, and develop strategies.

3. **Discuss a negative which you have improved upon:**

I used to get over-committed and miss important deadlines. But then I read a book on time management and learned what I was doing wrong. Within three weeks I reorganized my use of time and found I could meet my deadlines with little difficulty. The quality of my work also improved. Now I have time to work out at the gym each day. I'm doing more and feeling better at the same time.

4. **Discuss a "negative" which can also be a positive:**

I'm somewhat of a workaholic. I love my work, but I sometime neglect my family because of it. I've been going into the office seven days a week, and I often put in 12-hour days. I'm now learning to better manage my time.

5. **Discuss a negative outside yourself:**

I don't feel that there is anything seriously wrong with me. Like most people, I have my ups and downs. But overall I have a positive outlook, feel good about myself and what I've accomplished so far in my life. However, I am somewhat concerned how you might view my wanting to change occupations. I want to assure you that I'm not making this change on a whim. I've thought the issues and took a hard look at what I do well and enjoy doing. Like many young people, I guess I didn't have much life experience when I started my college major four years ago, and I got into communication because I enjoyed that kind of environment. As I took more classes and had opportunities to become involved in different areas, my interest in management training developed. I found that I not only enjoyed those activities, but that I had some natural talent for them. I am committed to finding work that allows me to conduct training. I believe my earlier work in communication actually supports that goal.

All of these examples stress the basic point about effective interviewing. Your single best strategy for managing the interview is to **emphasize your strengths and positives**. Questions come in several forms. Anticipate these questions, especially the negative ones, and practice positive responses in order to project your best self in an interview situation.

Encounter Behavior-Based Questions

More and more employers are conducting a different type of interview than
they did five or 10 years ago. Known as "behavior-based interviews," these
interviews are filled with behavior-based questions designed to elicit clear
patterns of behavior, which are primarily sets of accomplishments, relevant
to the employer's situation. They are specific. and challenge interviewees to
provide concrete examples of their achievements in different types of
situations. Such interviews are based on the simple belief that how a job
candidate has responded to certain types of situations in the past is a good
predictor of how that person will behave in a similar future situation. Their
behavioral "stories" provide clues on how they will solve future problems.
Behavior-based questions are likely to begin with some variation of:

- *Give me an example of a time when you . . .*
- *Give me an example of how you . . .*
- *Tell me about how you . . .*

Because you may not have a lot of work experience, you are likely to
encounter more of the *"what would you do if . . ."* variety of questions. This is
an opportunity for you to sell your positives with an example or two of what
you actually did if you have such an experience or what you (hypothetically)
might do. Take, for example, the following question:

*"This job requires good people management skills. How would you resolve a
conflict between two employees in your department?"*

If true, the applicant might respond:

*"I avoid being authoritarian or confrontational in my dealing with people. I
try to help the individuals involved arrive at a solution they will support. Let
me give you an example that happened recently. I am president of the Business
Management Club at EZ University. Recently two factions developed within
the organization. Each faction was passionate in their support of different
directions they thought the club should take. I discussed their views with the
leaders of each faction and tried to really listen to what they were saying and
where they were coming from. Then I brought the two leaders together and
facilitated a discussion until the three of us reached a consensus.*

Obviously you want to select examples that promote your skills and have
a positive outcome. Even if the interviewer asks about a time when something
negative happened, try to select an example where you were able to turn the
situation around and something positive came out of it. For example, if asked,
"Tell me about a time you made a bad decision," try to identify an occasion where:

- Even though it wasn't the best decision, you were able to pull something positive out of the situation.

- Though it was a poor decision, you learned from it, and in the next similar situation you made a good decision or know how you will handle it differently the next time a similar situation arises.

- It was a bad decision but the negative outcome had only minimal impact.

In other words, try to pull something positive – either that you did or that you learned – out of even a negative experience you are asked to relate. As you prepare for your interview, consider situations where you:

- demonstrated leadership
- solved a problem
- increased company profits or organizational funds
- made a good decision/made a poor decision
- handled change (not money, but changing events)
- handled criticism
- met a deadline/missed a deadline
- worked as part of a team

Think hard, and you should be able to come up with examples from your participation in campus organizations or your part-time work experience. Add to this list other behavioral questions you think of that pertain to the job for which you are applying. For example, if the job includes making presentations, expect questions about a speech where you achieved your goal or conversely about a time when your speech failed miserably.

Ask others who have interviewed with the company, if possible, to find out the types of questions to expect. You may encounter hypothetical questions in which you are asked not what you did, but what you would do *if* something occurred. With hypothetical questions, the interviewer is less interested in your actual answer – often there is no correct or incorrect response – than in your thought process. The information is in how you would solve a problem or respond to a particular type of situation.

Develop Strong Storytelling Skills

Individuals who do well in behavior-based interviews are those who have a rich background of accomplishments as well as are good storytellers. Indeed, **storytelling** is one of the key communication skills involved in conducting effective interviews. If you want to do well in this type of interview, be sure to **anticipate questions** you might be asked so you can prepare a well thought-out response – a set of revealing stories about your performance – prior to the interview. It is far easier to formulate positive responses to questions in the relaxed setting of your living room than in the stressful and time-constrained setting of the job interview. Prepare the 'gist' or general strategy of your response. **Do not** memorize word for word responses. You will either forget your word for word response or it will sound 'canned.' Know the thrust of your response and you should do fine.

> *Good storytellers tend to do well in job interviews. They give examples of their performance*

Face Illegal Questions

Many questions are illegal, but some employers ask them nonetheless. Consider how you would respond to these questions:

- Are you married, divorced, separated, or single?
- How old are you?
- Do you go to church regularly?
- Do you have many debts?
- Do you own or rent your home?
- What social and political organizations do you belong to?
- Are you living with anyone?
- Are you practicing birth control?
- Were you ever arrested?
- How much insurance do you have?
- How much do you weigh?
- How tall are you?

Don't get upset and say *"That's an illegal question...I refuse to answer it!"* While you may be perfectly right in saying so, this response lacks tact, which may be what the employer is looking for. For example, if you are divorced and the interviewer asks about your divorce, you might respond with *"Does a divorce have a direct bearing on the responsibilities of this position?"* Some employers may ask such questions just to see how you answer or react under stress. Others may do so out of ignorance of the law. Whatever the case, be prepared to handle such questions with tact.

Ask Questions

Interviewers expect candidates to ask intelligent questions concerning the organization and the nature of the work. Moreover, you need information and should indicate your interest in the employer by asking questions. Consider asking some of these questions if they haven't been answered early in the interview:

- Tell me about the duties and responsibilities of this job.
- How does this position relate to other positions within this organization?
- How long has this position been in the organization?
- What would be the ideal type of person for this position? Skills? Personality? Working style? Background?
- Can you tell me about the people who have been in this position before? Backgrounds? Promotions? Terminations?
- Whom would I be working with in this position?
- Tell me something about these people? Their strengths? Their weaknesses? Their performance expectations?
- What am I expected to accomplish during the first year?
- How will I be evaluated?
- Are promotions and raises tied to performance criteria?
- Tell me how this operates?
- What is the normal salary range for such a position?
- Based on your experience, what type of problems would someone new in this position likely encounter?
- I'm interested in your career with this organization. When did you start? What are your plans for the future?
- I would like to know how people get promoted and advance in this organization?
- What is particularly unique about working in this organization?
- What does the future look like for this organization?

You may want to write your questions on a 3x5 card and take them with you to the interview. While it is fine if you can recall these questions, you may need to refer to your list when the interviewer asks you if you have any questions. You might do this by saying: *"Yes, I jotted down a few questions which I want to make sure I ask you before leaving."* Then pull out your card(s) and refer to the questions.

Appear Likable

Remember, most people invited to a job interview have already been "screened in." They supposedly possess the basic qualifications for the job, such as education and work experience. At this point employers will look for several qualities in the candidates, such as honesty, credibility, intelligence, competence, enthusiasm, spontaneity, friendliness, and likability. Much of the message communicating these qualities will be conveyed through your attire as well as through other nonverbal behaviors.

In the end, employers hire people they **like** and who will interact well on an interpersonal basis with the rest of the staff. Therefore, you should communicate that you are a likable candidate who can get along well with others. You can communicate these messages by engaging in several nonverbal behaviors. Four of the most important ones include:

1. **Sit with a very slight forward lean toward the interviewer.** It should be so slight as to be almost imperceptible. If not overdone, it communicates your interest in what the interviewer is saying.

2. **Make eye contact frequently, but don't overdo it.** Good eye contact establishes rapport with the interviewer. You will be perceived as more trustworthy if you will look at the interviewer as you ask and answer questions. To say someone has "shifty eyes" or cannot "look us in the eye" is to imply they may not be completely honest. To have a direct, though moderate eye gaze conveys interest, as well as trustworthiness.

3. **A moderate amount of smiling will also help reinforce your positive image.** You should smile enough to convey your positive attitude, but not so much that you will not be taken seriously. Some people naturally smile often and others hardly ever smile. Monitor your behavior or ask a friend to give you frank feedback.

4. **Try to convey interest and enthusiasm through your vocal inflections.** Your tone of voice can say a lot about you and how interested you are in the interviewer and organization.

Close the Interview

Be prepared to end the interview. Many people don't know when or how to close interviews. They go on and on until someone breaks an uneasy moment of silence with an indication that it is time to go.

Interviewers normally will initiate the close by standing, shaking hands, and thanking you for coming to the interview. Don't end by saying *"Goodbye and thank you."* As this stage, you should summarize the interview in terms of your interests, strengths, and goals. Briefly restate your qualifications and continuing interest in working with the employer. At this point it is proper to ask the interviewer about selection plans:

"When do you anticipate making your final decision?"

Follow this question with your final one:

"May I call you next week (or whenever is appropriate in response to your question about timing of the final decision) to inquire about my status?"

By taking the initiative in this manner, the employer will be prompted to clarify your status soon, and you will have an opportunity to talk to him or her further.

Many interviewers will ask you for a list of references. Be sure to prepare such a list **prior to** the interview. Include the names, addresses, phone numbers, and emails of four individuals who will give you positive professional and personal recommendations. If asked for references, you will appear well prepared by presenting a list in this manner. If you fail to prepare this information ahead of time, you may appear at best disorganized and at worst lacking good references. Always anticipate being asked for specific names, addresses, and phone numbers of your references.

Always Remember to Follow Up

Once you have been interviewed, be sure to follow through to get nearer to the job offer. One of the best follow-up methods is the thank you letter; you will find examples of these letters at the end of Chapter 7. After talking to the employer over the telephone or in a face-to-face interview, send a thank you letter by email, if appropriate, and/or by mail. If mailed, this letter should be typed – not handwritten – on good quality bond paper. In this letter express your gratitude for the opportunity to interview. Re-state your interest in the position and highlight any particularly noteworthy points made in your conversation or anything you wish to further clarify. Close the letter by mentioning that you will call in a few days to inquire about the employer's decision. When you do this, the employer should remember you as a thoughtful person.

> *One of the best follow-up methods is the thank you letter. Email and/or mail a typed letter.*

If you call and the employer has not yet made a decision, follow through with another phone call in a few days. Send any additional information to the employer which may enhance your application. You might also want to ask one of your references to call the employer to further recommend you for the position – especially if this individual knows the employer well. However, don't engage in overkill by making a pest of yourself. You want to tactfully communicate two things to the employer at this point: (1) you are interested in the job, and (2) you will do a good job.

References: What You Need to Know
Thomas J. Denham, Director of the Career Center, Siena College

What's a "Credentials File"?

Your college career center may have a fee or free service that allows you to maintain a "Credentials File" for your reference letters and other official documents. Once established, you may request that the File be reproduced and sent to potential companies or graduate schools that review recommendations for a candidate's academic performance, experience, skills, and personal character.

Employers in a few fields, such as education and human services, expect the Credentials File as part of the hiring process. Recruiters are interested in knowing about your intellectual capabilities, principal achievements, potential for success, and your personal dimensions, i.e., what kind of a colleague you would make, how well you get along with others, and your level of reliability and responsibility. Generally your File is not requested by employers in business and industry.

Should Letters Be "Confidential" or "Non-Confidential"?

This is a difficult question that requires some background information in order for you to make a wise decision. The Family Educational Rights and Privacy Act of 1974 states that you may have access to any documents in your Credentials File which were submitted after January 1, 1975 unless you voluntarily waive your right in writing for access to such information.

If you waive your right of access, your File will be considered confidential, i.e., you will not have access to its contents. Some employers and graduate schools believe confidential letters are more valid, frank, and thus more weighted. If you do not waive your right of access, your File will be considered non-confidential, i.e., you will have access to its contents.

Choose your references carefully. Consider which faculty members and professional supervisors know your work well enough to be able to describe your capabilities in an articulate and credible way. Academic and professional competence and potential are the most appropriate areas fo them to address. Do not seek out writers who do not know your work, i.e., avoid letters that are only character references. Ask quite frankly if the person can give you a positive reference.

Reference Letter Do's and Don'ts

- Don't wait until the final hour to request your letters; give your writers plenty of time (several weeks).
- Do arrange to meet with each of your potential references to discuss your background and future goals.
- Do explain the purpose of the letter, i.e., employment or graduate study.
- Do provide your resume, a list of your courses, and other accomplishments for the writer to review.
- Do ask your reference to write factually and specifically with examples.
- Do have your reference writer address the letter to a particular person.
- Do request that they shape the letter to the type of position or graduate school you are applying to.
- Do clarify the nature of your relationship to the reference writer (professional, personal, or academic).
- Do have work supervisors indicate your job title and the time period involved.
- Do make sure your writer comments on your career potential and commitment.
- Do request a closing paragraph summarizing your major strengths and abilities.
- Do thank each person who writes a letter for you with a note of appreciation.

Useful Interviewing Resources

Interview preparation is essential for conducting a winning interview. Fortunately, numerous books and websites are available to help job seekers improve their interview skills.

Books on Job Interviewing

101 Dynamite Answers to Interview Questions, Caryl and Ron Krannich (Impact Publications, 2000)

101 Dynamite Questions to Ask at Your Job Interview, Richard Fein (Impact Publications, 2001)

101 Great Answers to the Toughest Interview Questions, 4th Edition, Ron Fry (Career Press, 2000)

250 Job Interview Questions You'll Most Likely Be Asked, Peter Veruki (Adams Media, 1999)

Haldane's Best Answers to Tough Interview Questions, Bernard Haldane Associates (Impact Publications, 2000)

Interview for Success, 8th Edition, Caryl and Ron Krannich (Impact Publications, 2003)

Interview Rehearsal Book, Deb Gottesman and Buzz Mauro (Berkley Publishing Group, 1999)

Job Interviews for Dummies, 2nd Edition, Joyce Lain Kennedy (John Wiley & Sons, 2000)

Naked at the Interview, Burton Jay Nadler (John Wiley & Sons, 1994)

The Perfect Interview, 2nd Edition, John Drake (AMACOM, 1997)

Power Interviews, Revised Edition, Neil M. Yeager and Lee Hough (John Wiley & Sons, 1998)

Savvy Interviewing: The Nonverbal Advantage, Caryl and Ron Krannich (Impact Publications, 2000)

Sweaty Palms, H. Anthony Medley (Ten Speed Press, 1992)

Interview-Related Websites

- Monster.com   interview.monster.com
                              content.monster.com/jobinfo/
                                 interview
- CollegeGrad.com   collegegrad.com/intv
- JobInterview.net   job-interview.net
- Interview Coach   interviewcoach.com
- Quintessential Careers   quintcareers.com/intvres.html
- Riley Guide   rileyguide.com/netintv.html
- WinningTheJob   winningthejob.com

Several additional books and websites focus on salary negotiations – which should occur **after** receiving a job offer, either at the very end of the interview or in a separate interview session. We summarize these related resources at the end of Chapter 10.

The Face-to-Face Encounter

While much of the job search can be conducted in isolation of people, the job interview puts you face-to-face with potential employers. As such, it requires important communication and social skills – both verbal and nonverbal – that determine whether or not you will be offered the job. If you develop an effective networking campaign (Chapter 8) that connects you to lots of people with whom you conduct informational interviews, you should be well prepared to handle the face-to-face job interview.

10

Negotiate Your Best Salary and Benefits

Y OU WILL EVENTUALLY NEED TO FACE KEY MONEY QUES-
tions: What are you worth in today's job market? What are your
salary expectations? How can you best demonstrate your value to an
employer? What dollar value will the employer assign to you? What
compensation are you willing to accept?

You may think you are worth a lot. After impressing upon the employer
that you are the right person for the job, the bottom line becomes money –
your talent and labor in exchange for the employer's cash and benefits. How,
then, are you going to deal with these questions in order to get more than the
employer may initially be willing to offer?

Most Salaries Are Negotiable

Salary is one of the most important yet least understood considerations in the
job search. Many individuals do very well in handling all interview questions
except the salary question. They are either too shy to talk about money or
they believe they must take what they are offered – because salary is predetermined by employers. As a result, many applicants may be paid much less
than they are worth. Over the years, they will lose thousands of dollars by
having failed to properly negotiate their salaries. Indeed, many employees are
probably underpaid by hundreds of dollars because they failed to properly
negotiate their salaries.

Salary is seldom predetermined. Most employers have some flexibility to negotiate salary. Indeed, they usually have a specific **salary range**, rather than salary figure, in mind when recruiting for a position. Accordingly, they can hire you at the bottom of the range but they also can hire you at the top of the range or even extend the range should you exceed their expectations. While most employers do not try to exploit applicants, neither do they want to pay applicants more than what they must for the applicant to accept the position.

Salaries are usually assigned to positions or jobs rather than to individuals. But not everyone is of equal value in performing the job; some are more productive than others. Since individual performance differs, you should attempt to establish your value in the eyes of the employer rather than accept a salary figure for the job. The art of salary negotiation will help you do this.

Consider Your Financial Future

We all have financial needs which our salary helps to meet. But salary has other significance too. It is an indicator of our worth to others. It also influences our future income. Therefore, it should be treated as one of the most serious considerations in the job interview.

> *The salary you receive today will influence your future earnings.*

The salary you receive today will influence your future earnings. Yearly salary increments will most likely be figured as a percentage of your base salary rather than reflect your actual job performance. When changing jobs, expect employers to offer you a salary similar to the one you earned in your last job. Once they learn what you made in your previous job, they will probably offer you no more than a 10% to 15% increase, regardless of your productivity. If you hope to improve your income in the long run, you must negotiate the best possible salary today by communicating your value to employers.

Prepare for the Salary Question

You should be well prepared to deal with the question of salary anytime during your job search but especially during the job interview. Based on your research (Chapter 6) as well as salary information gained from your networking activities (Chapter 8), you should know the approximate salary range for the position you are seeking. If you fail to gather this salary information **prior to** the screening or job interview, you may do yourself a disservice by accepting too low a figure or pricing yourself out of consideration. It is always best to be informed so you will be in better control to negotiate salary and benefits.

One of the best ways to prepare for the salary question is to practice a mock interview session with a friend. Ask him or her to raise the question and observe your response.

Time the Salary Question Well

The question of salary may be raised anytime during the job search. Employers may want you to state an expected salary figure on an application form, in a cover letter, or over the telephone. Most frequently, however, employers will talk about salary during the employment interview. If at all possible, keep the salary question open until the very last. Even with application forms, cover letters, and telephone screening interviews, try to delay the discussion of salary by stating "open" or "negotiable." After all, the ultimate purpose of your job search activities is to demonstrate your **value** to employers. You should not attempt to translate your value into dollar figures until you have had a chance to convince the employer of your worth. This is best done near the end of the job interview.

Although employers will have a salary figure or range in mind when they interview you, they still want to know your salary expectations. How much will you cost them? Will it be more or less than the job is worth and their budgeted salary range? Employers prefer hiring individuals for the least amount possible. You, on the other hand, want to be hired for as much as possible. Obviously, this is a situation where there is room for disagreement and unhappiness as well as negotiation and compromise.

> *Salary should be the last major item you discuss with the employer.*

One easy way employers screen you in or out of consideration is to raise the salary question early in the interview. A standard question is: *"What are your salary requirements?"* When asked, don't answer with a specific dollar figure. You should aim at establishing your value in the eyes of the employer prior to talking about a figure. If you give the employer a salary figure at this stage, you are likely to lock yourself into it, regardless of how much you impress the employer or what you find out about the duties and responsibilities of the job. Therefore, salary should be the **last** major item you discuss.

You should never ask about salary prior to being offered the job, even though it is one of your major concerns. Try to let the employer initiate the salary question. And when he or she does, take your time. Don't appear too anxious. While you may know – based on your previous research – approximately what the employer will offer, try to get the employer to state a figure first. If you do this, you should be in a stronger negotiating position.

Handle the Salary Question With Tact

When the salary question arises, assuming you do not want to put it off, your first step should be to clearly summarize the job responsibilities/duties as you understand them. At this point you are attempting to do three things:

1. Seek clarification from the interviewer as to the actual job and all it involves.

2. Emphasize the level of skills required in the most positive way. In other words, you emphasize the value and worth of this position to the organization and subtly this may help support the actual salary figure that the interviewer or you later provide.

3. Focus attention on your value in relation to the requirements of the position – the critical linkage for negotiating salary from a position of strength.

You might do this, for example, by saying:

> *"As I understand it, I would report directly to the vice-president in charge of marketing and I would have full authority for marketing decisions that involve expenditures of up to $50,000. I would have a staff of five people – a secretary, two copywriters, and two marketing assistants."*

Such a summary statement establishes for both you and the interviewer that (1) this position reports to the highest levels of authority; (2) this position is responsible for decision-making involving fairly large sums of money; and (3) this position involves supervision of staff.

Although you may not explicitly draw the connection, you are emphasizing the value of this position to the organization. This position should be worth a lot more than one in which the hiree will report to the marketing manager, be required to get approval for all expenditures over $100, and has no staff – just access to the secretarial pool! By doing this you will focus the salary question (which you have not yet responded to) around the exact work you must perform on the job in exchange for salary and benefits. You have also seized the opportunity to focus on the value of the person who will be selected to fill this vacancy.

Your conversation might go something like this. The employer poses the question:

> *"What are your salary requirements?"*

Your first response should be to summarize the responsibilities of the position. You might begin with a summary statement followed by a question:

> *"Let me see if I understand all that is involved with this position and job. I would be expected to _____. Have I covered everything or are there some other responsibilities I should know about?"*

This response focuses the salary question around the **value** of the position in relation to you. After the interviewer responds to your final question, answer the initial salary expectation question in this manner:

> *"What is the normal salary range in your company for a position such as this?"*

This question establishes the value, as well as the range, for the position or job – two important pieces of information you need before proceeding further into the salary negotiation stage. The employer normally will give you the requested salary range. Once he or she does, depending on how you feel about the figure, you can follow up with one more question.

> *"What is the normal salary range for someone with my qualifications?"*

This question further establishes the value for the individual versus the position. This line of questioning will yield the salary expectations of the employer without revealing your desired salary figure or range. It also will indicate whether the employer distinguishes between individuals and positions when establishing salary figures.

Reach Common Ground and Agreement

After finding out what the employer is prepared to offer, you have several choices. First, you can indicate that his or her figure is acceptable to you and thus conclude your final interview. Second, you can haggle for more money in the hope of reaching an acceptable compromise. Third, you can delay final action by asking for more time to consider the figure. Finally, you can tell the employer the figure is unacceptable and leave.

The first and the last options indicate you are either too eager or playing hard-to-get. We recommend the second and third options. If you decide to reach agreement on salary in this time, haggle in a professional manner. Do this best by establishing a salary range from which to bargain in relation to the employer's salary range. For example, if the employer indicates that he or she is prepared to offer $30,000 to $35,000, you should establish common ground for negotiation by placing your salary range into the employer's range. Your response to the employer's $30,000 to $35,000 range might be:

"Yes, that does come near what I was expecting. I was thinking more in terms of $34,000 to $39,000."

You, in effect, place the top of the employer's range into the bottom of your range. At this point you should be able to negotiate a salary of $35,000 to $37,000, depending on how much flexibility the employer has with salaries. Most employers have more flexibility than they are willing to admit.

Once you have placed your expectations at the top of the employer's salary range, you need to emphasize your value with **supports**, such as examples, illustrations, descriptions, definitions, statistics, comparisons, or testimonials. It is not enough to simply state you were "thinking" in a certain range; you must state why you believe you are worth what you want. Using statistics and comparisons as your supports, you might say, for example:

"The salary surveys I have read indicate that for the position of _____ in this industry and region the salary is between $34,000 and $39,000. Since, as we have discussed, I have extensive experience in all the areas you outlined, I would not need training in the job duties themselves – just a brief orientation to the operating procedures you use here at _____. I'm sure I could be up and running in this job within a week or two. Taking everything into consideration – especially my skills and experience and what I see as my future contributions here – I really feel a salary of $38,000 is fair compensation. Is this possible here at _____?"

Another option is to ask the employer for time to think about the salary offer. You want to sleep on it for a day or two. A common professional courtesy is to give you at least 48 hours to consider an offer. During this time, you may want to carefully examine the job. Is it worth what you are being offered? Can you do better? What are other employers offering for comparable positions? If one or two other employers are considering you

> How you negotiate your salary will affect your future relations with the employer.

for a job, let this employer know his or her job is not the only one under consideration. Let the employer know you may be in demand elsewhere. This should give you a better bargaining position. Contact the other employers and tell them you have a job offer and that you would like to have your application status with them clarified before you make any decisions with the other employer. Depending on how much flexibility an employer may have to accelerate a hiring decision, you may be able to go back to the first employer with another job offer. With a second job offer in hand, you should greatly enhance your bargaining position.

In both recommended options, you need to keep in mind that you should always negotiate from a position of knowledge and strength – not because of need or greed. Research salaries for your occupation, establish your value, discover what the employer is willing to pay, and negotiate in a professional manner. For how you negotiate your salary will affect your future relations with the employer. In general, applicants who negotiate well will be treated well on the job.

Consider Benefits With Care

Many employers will try to impress candidates with the benefits offered by the company. These might include retirement, bonuses, stock options, medical and life insurance, and cost of living adjustments. If the employer includes these benefits in the salary negotiations, do not be overly impressed. Most benefits are standard – they come with the job. When negotiating salary, it is best to talk about specific dollar figures. But don't neglect to both calculate and negotiate benefits. Benefits can translate into a significant portion of one's compensation, especially if you are offered stock options, profit sharing, pensions, insurance, and reimbursement accounts. Indeed, a few years ago many individuals who have taken stock options in lieu of high salaries with start-up high-tech firms discovered the importance of benefits when their benefits far outweighed their salaries; making only $25,000 a year, some of them became instant millionaires when their companies went public! A few years later many of the stock options were worthless. However the benefits package should be looked at carefully. The U.S. Department of Labor estimates that benefits now constitute 43 percent of total compensation for the average worker. For example, a $50,000 offer with Company X may translate into a compensation package worth $60,000; but a $40,000 offer with Company Y may actually be worth more than $70,000 when you examine their different benefits.

If the salary offered by the employer does not meet your expectations, but you still want the job, you might try to negotiate for some benefits which are not considered standard. These might include longer paid vacations, some flextime, and profit sharing.

Offer a Renegotiation Option

You should make sure your future salary reflects your value. One approach to doing this is to reach an agreement to renegotiate your salary at a later date, perhaps in another six to eight months. Use this technique especially when you feel the final salary offer is less than what you are worth, but you want to accept the job. Employers often will agree to this provision since they have nothing to lose and much to gain if you are as productive as you tell them.

However, be prepared to renegotiate in both directions – up and down. If the employer does not want to give you the salary figure you want, you can create good will by proposing to negotiate the higher salary figure down after six months if your performance does not meet the employer's expectations. On the other hand, you may accept this lower figure with the provision that the two of you will negotiate your salary up after six months if you exceed the employer's expectations. It is preferable to start out high and negotiate down rather than start low and negotiate up.

Renegotiation provisions stress one very important point: you want to be paid on the basis of your performance. You demonstrate your professionalism, self-confidence, and competence by negotiating in this manner. More important, you ensure that the question of your monetary value will not be closed in the future. As you negotiate the present, you also negotiate your future with this as well as other employers.

Take Time Before Accepting

You should accept an offer only after reaching a salary agreement. If you jump at an offer, you may appear needy. Take time to consider your options. Remember, you are committing your time and effort in exchange for money and status. Is this the job you really want? Take some time to think about the offer before giving the employer a definite answer. But don't play hard-to-get and thereby create ill will with your new employer.

While considering the offer, ask yourself several of the same questions you asked at the beginning of your job search:

- What do I want to be doing five years from now?

- How will this job affect my personal life?

- Do I want to travel?

- Do I know enough about the employer and the future of this organization?

- How have previous occupants of this position fared? Why did they have problems?

- Are there other opportunities that would better meet my goals?

Accepting a job is serious business. If you make a mistake, you could be locked into a very unhappy situation for a long time.

If you receive one job offer while considering another, you will be able to compare relative advantages and disadvantages. You also will have some external leverage for negotiating salary and benefits. While you should not play games, let the employer know you have alternative job offers. This communicates that you are in demand, others also know your value, and the employer's price is not the only one in town. Use this leverage to negotiate your salary, benefits, and job responsibilities.

If you get a job offer but you are considering other employers, let the others know you have a job offer. Telephone them to inquire about your status as well as inform them of the job offer. Sometimes this will prompt employers to make a hiring decision sooner than anticipated. In addition you will be informing them that you are in demand; they should seriously consider you before you get away!

Some job seekers play a bluffing game by telling employers they have alternative job offers even though they don't. Some candidates do this and get away with it. We don't recommend this approach. Not only is it dishonest, it will work to your disadvantage if the employer learns that you were lying. But more important, you should be selling yourself on the basis of your strengths rather than your deceit and greed. If you can't sell yourself honestly, don't expect to get along well on the job. When you compromise your integrity, you demean your value to others and yourself.

Your job search is not over with the job offer and acceptance. You need to set the stage. Be thoughtful by sending your new employer a nice thank-you letter. As outlined at the end of Chapter 7, this is one of the most effective letters to write for getting your new job off on the right foot. The employer will remember you as a thoughtful individual whom he looks forward to working with.

The whole point of our job search methods is to clearly communicate to employers that you are competent and worthy of being paid top dollar. If you follow our advice, you should do very well with employers in interviews and negotiating your salary as well as working on the job.

Know and Stress Your Value

One final word of advice. Many job seekers have unrealistic salary expectations and exaggerated notions of their worth to potential employers. Given the greater emphasis on productivity and performance in the workplace, many employers are reluctant to negotiate salaries upwards prior to seeing you perform in their organization. Make sure you make a case for justifying your salary expectations. Do you know, for example, what you're really worth in today's job market? Have you researched salary comparables by examining salary surveys found through your professional association, employment firms, and government studies, or revealed on several key websites, such as salary. com and jobstar.org? In a full employment economy, where your skills and experience are in high demand, you should be better able to negotiate compensation. During recessions, salaries may actually decline. Some employers may ask for give-backs from highly-paid employees. A recent example involves airline pilots and flight attendants at near bankrupt United Airlines in 2002.

Your ability to negotiate will in part be a function of such supply and demand factors in the labor market.

You will need to stress your **value** more than ever in employer-centered terms. Your value primarily comes in two forms: income and savings for the organization. For example, if you think you are worth $50,000 a year in salary, will you be productive enough to generate $300,000 of business for the company to justify that amount? Alternatively, are you prepared to save the company $50,000 next year? If you can't translate your salary expectations into dollars and cents profits or savings for the employer, perhaps you should not be negotiating at all!

Use the Right Resources

Several books and websites will help you conduct research on salary comparables as well as develop effective negotiation strategies for getting what you believe you and the position are really worth:

Books on Salary Negotiations

101 Salary Secrets: How to Negotiate Like a Pro, Daniel Porot (Ten Speed Press, 2001)

Are You Paid What You're Worth?, Michael F. O'Malley and Suzanne Oaks (Broadway Books, 1998)

Better Than Money, David E. Gumpert (Lauson Publishing Co., 2000)

Dynamite Salary Negotiations: Know What You're Worth, and Get It, 4th Edition, Ron and Caryl Krannich (Impact Publications, 2001)

Get More Money On Your Next Job, Lee E. Miller (McGraw-Hill, 1997)

Get Paid What You're Worth: The Expert Negotiator's Guide to Salary and Compensation, Robin Pinkley and Gregory Northcraft (St. Martin's Press, 2000)

Get a Raise in 7 Days, Ron and Caryl Krannich (Impact Publications, 1999)

Haldane's Best Salary Tips for Professionals, Bernard Haldane Associates (Impact Publications, 2001)

Interviewing and Salary Negotiation, Kate Wendleton (Career Press, 1999)

Negotiating Your Salary: How to Make $1000 a Minute, Jack Chapman (Ten Speed Press, 2001)

Salary-Related Websites

▪ Salary.com	salary.com
▪ JobStar.org	jobstar.org
▪ Wageweb	www.wageweb.com
▪ Abbott-Langer	abbott-langer.com
▪ Robert Half International	www.rhii.com
▪ Monster.com	salary.monster.com
▪ SalarySource.com	salarysource.com
▪ Quintessential Careers	quintcareers.com/salary_negotiation.html
▪ Riley Guide	rileyguide.com/offers.html
▪ WinningTheJob	winningthejob.com

11

Turn Your Job Into a Great Career

AFTER NEGOTIATING THE JOB OFFER, SHAKING HANDS, and feeling great for having succeeded in getting a job that seems right for you, what's next? How do you get started on the right foot and continue to advance your career? What's the best way to handle the critical first 90 days on the job? What does it take to become a successful employee? What behaviors do you need to acquire as well as change?

Neither a Student Nor a Professional

If you've just graduated and this is your first full-time job, you are truly in transition. Lacking a track record of performance, your most important assets may be your enthusiasm, attitude, and willingness to learn and develop on the job. Neither a student nor a professional, you need to immediately prove your worth so the employer feels confident he or she made the right hiring decision. You'll need to be patient and driven to achieve goals. How you manage the critical first 90 days on the job can have an important impact on your future professional development with this or other employers.

Take More Positive Actions

If you managed your interviews and salary negotiations in a professional manner, your new employer should view you in a positive light. Once you've

211

completed the interviews, reached agreement on compensation, and accepted the offer, you should do two things:

1. **Send your new employer a nice thank you letter.**

   Never underestimate the power of a simple thank you letter. It may be the single most important action you take. Mention your appreciation for the professional manner in which you were hired and how pleased you are to be joining the organization. Reaffirm your goals and your commitment to producing results. This letter should be well received. After all, employers seldom receive such thoughtful letters, and your reaffirmation helps ease the employer's fears of hiring an untested quantity. It's best to type rather than handwrite this letter – this is professional business communication that should represent your best professional effort.

2. **Send thank you letters to those individuals who assisted you with your job search, especially those with whom you conducted informational and referral interviews.**

   Tell them of your new position, thank them for their assistance, and offer your assistance in the future. Not only is this a nice and thoughtful thing to do, it also is a wise thing to do for your future. As we noted in Chapter 8, successful individuals continually nurture their network. Type these letters unless the recipient is a close personal friend – in which case a handwritten note is appropriate.

Always remember to build and nurture your network. You work with people who can help you in many ways. Take good care of your network by sending a thank you letter and keeping in contact. In another few years you may be looking for another position. In addition, people in your network may later want to hire you away from your present employer. Since they know what you can do and they like you, they may want to keep you informed of new opportunities. While you will be developing new contacts and expanding your network in your new job, your former contacts should be remembered for future reference. An occasional letter, New Year's card, or telephone call are thoughtful things to do.

You also should read these three books on how to succeed in today's workplace, with special emphasis on developing positive workplace behaviors:

Maximum Success: Changing the 12 Behavior Patterns That Keep You From Getting Ahead, James Waldroop and Timothy Butler (Doubleday, 2000)

How to Be a Star at Work: 9 Breakthrough Strategies You Need to Succeed, Robert E. Kelley (Time Books, 1999)

What Your Boss Doesn't Tell You Until It's Too Late: How to Correct Behavior That is Holding You Back, Robert Bramson (Fireside, 1996)

Tales and Lessons From the Working World

Many former students who work for employers who recruit through Campus CareerCenter (Chapter 13) share their stories about what it's really like in the working world. They identify challenges faced and lessons learned as well as offer useful tips for others who may follow in their footsteps. While each organization has its own unique culture, new employees share similar experiences about the realities of work. Frequent advice given by these former students concerns the following on-the-job orientations and skills for success:

- Be patient
- Get organized
- Set priorities
- Listen, listen, and listen
- Ask lots of questions
- Become a team player
- Network, network, network
- Respect others and their ideas
- Associate with energetic and positive people
- Keep focused on goals
- Pursue your passions
- Plan your career development

As during the job search in general, **networking** appears to be critical for surviving and prospering on the job. Indeed, it will later play an important role as you advance on the job and change jobs. As we outlined in Chapter 8, how you connect, build, and nurture your networks will be key to determining your future success with this or other employers.

Several recently hired students and graduates share their "Day-in-the-Life" profiles and observations. Telling us what it's really like working in these new jobs, they provide revealing insights about their first few months on the job including the many trials, challenges, and rewards they encountered:

Operations Manager, Staples, Inc. store (see Staples profile on page 258)

> **Cheri** attended a career fair at her school where she learned about career opportunities with Staples. She was especially attracted to the values of this dynamic company. Accepted into the Manager in Training program,

she soon became a store Operations Manager. The training program was at first overwhelming, but she learned the importance of organization and asking questions. "I really had to stay organized! I turned to my management team and the associates for help. They were amazing and so patient with me. The best advice they gave me was to 'just jump in and do it,' and ask questions when I wasn't sure." As a new Operations Manager, "I learned the importance of prioritizing what needs to be done and making an action plan to achieve it. This includes getting the most important duties done first and delegating responsibility for projects to associates. Everyday I learn something new, which makes my job exciting and I look forward to coming to work. What I like best about my job is interacting with the associates and customers. I also like the open communication among all parts of the company. If I have a problem, I can turn to my management team, another store, or someone in a corporate position, and know that I will get treated with respect and my concern will be addressed immediately. Staples is committed to developing talent for the future success of the company. That's why I feel confident that no matter what direction my career path takes me, I have the support to succeed."

Personnel Management Trainee, Morale, Welfare and Recreation (MWR), U.S. Army (see organizational profile on pages 258-259)

After three months as a trainee, **Jennifer** has settled into a comfortable work schedule, knowing exactly what she can accomplish in a day. Her advice for on-the-job success is very simple: "Network, network, network! Bear in mind that you are working toward a long-term goal. Take advantage of every opportunity, and never forget that you are always representing yourself, your trainer and your supervisor." She also offers these important words of wisdom for students and graduates starting out on a new job: "Patience. Keep your cool. Develop a strong support network. Always carry a notebook and pen. Don't be afraid to ask questions and do research!"

Wilderness Youth Counselor, Eckerd Youth Alternatives, Inc. (see organizational profile on page 251)

Jason heard about this job by attending a career fair at his school. The recruiter outlined in great detail what appeared to be a fascinating job working with at-risk youth. It seemed to be a perfect fit given Jason's values: "I knew I would be in for a challenge, but I'd have the opportunity to make a difference in kids' lives, which to me was the ultimate reward. Before graduation I applied for the Wilderness Youth Counselor and was thrilled to be offered the position." After a month-long training program known as "Catatogas" – which Jason called an "amazing experience" – he began loving a job that fulfilled his personal goals. "The Pow Wow is a great way to finish our days. We sit around a fire at our campsite and congratulate each other on reaching our individual and group goals. It's a great way to reflect on all the things that we accomplished and some of the things that we can work towards improving. This is what it is all about. This is my reward right in front of my eyes. I am making a difference. We can all turn out the lights now as we walk to our tents and end our day on a positive note. There is no other job like it, ever!"

Revenue Officer, Internal Revenue Service (see IRS profile on page 254)

Amy has found the interesting and rewarding work at the IRS a terrific learning experience and a real boost to her career development: "As a Revenue Officer, every day is different, which makes it really interesting. After extensive training, I was assigned a variety of cases to handle at one time, and often spend a lot of time out of the office. Aside from the highly technical aspects of the job, interpersonal and organizational skills are key to my success. I mainly resolve tax collection issues for individuals or businesses. Believe it or not, quite a few taxpayers are actually happy to see me. I am their first face-to-face contact and I help them solve whatever the problem is – usually filing tax returns, paying overdue taxes, and setting up systems for future compliance. I get to learn a lot about all different kinds of businesses and how they operate, just by doing my job. This job allows me to work independently on cases and arrange a flexible work schedule. It gives me an opportunity to interact with people from all walks of life and all types of businesses, which is extremely rewarding. One day I may deal with a small business owner and the next day I may deal with a CPA representing a large business. I also get to work with all parts of the IRS organization, which helps me with my professional development."

Assistant Producer, Electronic Arts (EA) (see company profile on page 251)

Ashley accepted an internship in game development and was immediately attached to a mentor. Every day brought her new challenges. She quickly learned the importance of thinking fast on her feet and finding simple direct solutions to complex problems. Key skills for success included the ability to analyze, critical thinking, communication, and teamwork. Both the job (making games) and fellow employees were great fun. Best of all, she went from intern to a full-time employee at EA. "Making games is a dream come true. Working on a team, working with the team leads, working together to build pipelines and processes that will culminate in the genesis of a game . . . that is an awesome experience! My internship at EA taught me what it means to be a professional game developer, and showed me the commitment and teamwork needed to make a great game. I look forward to becoming a great producer one day and leading a team of talented developers to make a great game. The challenges I face will be to pioneer forward and find working solutions that enable the team to produce results. It's hard to make a game. It's even harder to make a great game. My challenge is to learn how to do both."

Quality Associate, Convergys Corporation (see profile on pages 251)

Shawn started with the company as an intern and then was offered a full-time job as a Quality Associate. He tests applications before they go into production. He really enjoys being exposed to new technologies and seeing how his work fits into the overall business objective. Meeting deadlines and assuring quality at the same time can be challenging. He quickly learned the skills and characteristics of a good Quality Associate: analysis, timeliness, and preciseness. The ability to effectively communicate between technical and non-technical people is especially important: "It requires networking with people inside and outside of my organization." He finds the responsibilities particularly rewarding. "I am the last line of defense between Convergys and our clients. Once the product leaves my hands, I am approving that everything works according to our standards." He's looking forward to a great future with this company: "Once I graduated from college, I thought I knew a whole lot about this career field. In college you only scratch the surface of Information Technology. I feel privileged to be an employee of Convergys. I see growth in myself as well as my career path. The next step in my career path is to become an applications developer. I would like to become well rounded. I believe the technology and opportunity exists at Convergys."

Priority Accounts Underwriter, Hartford Life (see profile on page 253)

Meghan started with Hartford Life one month after graduating with a BS in Finance. After a two-month intensive training program, she began working in the Group Benefits Division, which insures companies whose employees receive employer-provided benefits. We provide coverages such as Life, Long Term Disability, and Short Term Disability. I am in the Priority Accounts New Business side of the division, which involves companies that have fewer than 500 employees and are not currently covered by The Hartford. I work very closely with my sales rep. All of the underwriters on the floor interact throughout the day to discuss plan options, potential risks, and business decisions. I have an opportunity to work independently, while having access to an immense support staff. As a newly graduated businessperson, I do not feel that there could have been a better career for me. Here I have the opportunity to learn about so many different industries, areas of the country, and different careers through my research and my interaction with others. I see a lot of opportunity Insurance, so I plan to remain in the business of Group Benefits. Eventually I can see myself venturing out into a sales role, once I feel I have learned as much as I can in underwriting."

Field Engineer, Siemens Westinghouse Power Corporation (see company profile on pages 257–258)

Charles had several summer internships with a Chicago utility company. He became fascinated with the work of the Field Engineer and decided to contact Siemens upon graduation. Landing a job as Field Engineer has been wonderful. He loves the unpredictable and global nature of the job. "Each job is a whole new set of challenges and lessons to be learned. As a single person, I embrace the opportunity to travel the world, while making a handsome living and providing a vital industrial resource. I am able to save more money than most of my friends net in a year. The thing I like most about my job is the fact that I cannot tell you what a 'typical' day of my life is like – the unpredictability is the very aspect that I relish most. I hate to wake up any given day and not learn or experience something different. One job might be a Voltage Regulator checkout where I might get sent to South America for three days, or maybe a Generator Overhaul in Puerto Rico lasting nearly three months. Tomorrow I could be sent to a steam turbine plant in Montana or a Gas Turbine in Texas. You just never know for sure until you're on the plane! I am pleased with my choice to become a Field Engineer. I know there will probably come a day when I will want to 'settle down' and have a family, but for the foreseeable future, I will continue to enjoy the plethora of challenges, diverse experiences, and tangible rewards which are associated with this line of work. This job is pretty much devoid of any office politics and 'cliques'. The field is the great equalizer and is very results-oriented. Siemens is one of a very few companies whose motto is followed – 'you can do that' is Siemens' motto, and their philosophy."

From Intern to Desk Assistant, ABC News (see ABC profile on page 250)

Navneet initially served as an edit/production intern with World News Today. Upon graduation he landed a full-time job as desk assistant. "The best part of my job is the fact that I come into work in the morning and never am sure how things are going to turn out by the end of the day. Because the broadcast has to go on at 6:30 each night, most of my tasks are deadline-oriented. For example, it's important that the correspondents' scripts are distributed promptly to senior producers and writers so that they can be edited and revised in time to make air. Other tasks include researching, gathering footage for the opening headlines of the show, and building the script pack that the anchor, director, writers, and producers work off of during the live evening broadcast. More often than not, you end up juggling several assignments at a time, so it's important to be aware of your priorities and also be organized enough to get everything done in a timely manner. I feel very fortunate to be at ABC. I think the key to making the transition from college life to career life is remaining open to all possibilities while keeping your goals in sight."

Business Development, The Gallup Organization (see profile on pages 252)

Matt is proud of the fact that he was the youngest employee ever hired in a business development role at Gallup. He soon began working closely with major clients and interacting with top managers at Gallup. "One of the great things about development at Gallup is that it is all about learning by action. From Day 1, I had opportunities to research and give advice to multi-billion dollar organizations. One of the most exciting things about working for Gallup is that it is easy to see what impact we have on our clients. We are able to show the changes we have helped our clients make in bottom line profitability, sales growth, customer retention, and ultimately market capitalization."

College Program Internship, Walt Disney World® (see profile on page 259)

Bridget responded to an ad on her campus bulletin board. After visiting The Walt Disney World College Program website and meeting with a College Program recruiter, she was offered an internship as a Camp Counselor at Disney's Animal Kingdom (Camp Minnie/Mickey). "My job was fantastic! I was responsible for guide activity, guest safety, and, most of all, guest interaction on a daily basis. I communicated with people from around the world, finding ways to talk with them even if I did not know their language. The most challenging aspect of this job was maintaining patience and understanding. After three months of the Animal Kingdom, and Walt Disney World, I went back to school a new person. My level of patience was much higher than it had been in the past. I was more apt to working with people and accepting others' different personalities. I was more wise and understanding of cultures and foreign languages and more open to trying new things." After graduation, Bridget applied for a College Recruiting Advanced Internship with Disney and became a recruiter.

Retail Management Trainee, Hannaford Brothers, Inc. (profile on page 253)

Jerod was hired as a Retail Management Trainee (RMT) with this supermarket chain. "Looking back at the last year, I had a great deal of fun and learned so much about the retail industry and Hannaford Brothers. To be in this industry you have to genuinely like people. If you have that trait, like to work hard, and enjoy never being bored, then this is a great environment to be in. After successfully completing my RMT program, I became an assistant store manage in one year. I truly do enjoy my job, working with such great people, and learning something new every day."

Special Agent, Office of Special Investigations, U.S. Air Force (page 258)

Christie was training to become Special Agent when a unique event changed her whole outlook on her job, career, and life. "Learning the techniques and skills used by Air Force Office of Special Investigations (AFOSI) agents while at the AFOSI Academy was an exciting 11 weeks. The defining moment for me was getting the news of the terrorist attacks, and realizing that I was learning the necessary skills to help America fight the war on terrorism. It was very eerie because from where we were training, we could see the smoke from the Pentagon. At that moment, every person in the class knew their job was going to be different. Right then, it all changed. A new outlook was placed on everything. I was not just learning 'how' to do things but 'why' they needed to be done. Being a part of the first AFOSI class to graduate after 9-11 means more than having the title Special Agent. It showed me what it means to be a part of an organization that holds freedom in its highest regard. While at the AFOSI Academy after the 9-11 attacks, I became acutely aware of the importance of this job and the awesome responsibilities I was about to undertake. The pride I felt at graduation was like no other, knowing that I was about to become one of the men and women trusted to ensure the safety and security of this nation. I knew upon my return to my AFOSI detachment that I would have to put all of the Academy's counterintelligence and force protection training to immediate use!"

Quality Engineer, GAF Materials Corporation (see profile on page 252)

Craig completed his degree in chemical engineering and began exploring job opportunities on the Internet. After visiting several companies, he decided GAF Materials was for him. "When I interviewed, I was shocked to see the vice-presidents of the company conducting the interviews. It impressed me that these important people took the time to carefully question and choose the future leaders of their company. I started as a Quality Engineer and for the first few months I LEARNED. I found it to be absolutely critical to ask questions, and then ask some more. After working just six months, I was promoted to Quality Engineering Manager. My job poses new challenges everyday and it's rewarding to be able to apply my problem-solving skills to real world, practical problems. I have learned three important lessons during my first two years in the workforce. You should ask probing questions, be confident of your abilities, and respect each and every person you work with. This advice can be helpful for anyone making the transition from college to their professional career. Listen to other people's ideas and feelings. Respect your co-workers' opinions and in turn they will respect yours. If you remember to ask questions, to believe in yourself, and to respect others, YOU WILL SUCCEED."

Industrial Operations Associate, Aventis Pasteur (see profile on page 250)

Bryan met an Aventis Pasteur representative at a career fair. During their meeting, he learned about a new start-up program for recent college graduates and was shortly hired. Working in teams, he is involved in validating the influenza, diphtheria, and tetanus vaccine production processes. He learned how important problem-solving and communication skills are to success on the job. He is especially committed to the life-saving mission of this company which has an illustrious heritage dating back to Louis Pasteur. "I am proud to be part of Aventis Pasteur's vision for the future and commitment to protecting life. My job is important to me because our products ensure the health of many people worldwide. We are the leading manufacturer of vaccines in the United States and are counted on heavily to supply people with safe, effective methods to prevent disease. We certainly take that charge seriously and work very hard to eliminate disease and sickness worldwide."

Summer Intern, Cargill, Inc. (see profile on page 250)

Sarah attended an IT career fair at her school during her sophomore year. She really didn't know what she wanted to do. Overwhelmed by so many huge companies and students, after only five minutes she tried to sneak out of the building. However, a Cargill representative spotted her and for 20 minutes discussed the company and her potential as an intern. She gave him her resume and shortly thereafter Cargill offered her a summer internship. It was a very challenging experience. She acquired a great deal of knowledge and worked with a wonderful group of people. "In addition to learning, there were several opportunities to have fun with the other interns. Together, we had lunches, a picnic, and an evening cruise on the St. Croix river. I know that all of us left with many new friends. The most encouraging piece of knowledge that I took away from the summer came from my mentor: Acquiring the technical knowledge will come with time. What is more important is your ability to communicate with people, collaborate in a group, and maintain honest, ethical business relationships. In hindsight, he couldn't have been more right! The two pieces of advice that I can pass on is to, one, be patient with yourself. There were many days when I felt way out of my league. There was seemingly so much that I didn't know. Ask questions! You won't know if you don't ask! Two, you have to be your own advocate. Having self-respect and confidence will bring success." Sarah was offered another internship the following summer. She looks forward to continuing with Cargill in the future.

Summer Intern, Boston Scientific Corporation

Patricia attended a mock interview session which also involved meeting industry representatives. After attending a company presentation, she was offered a summer internship in the Imaging and Sensing Lab of Boston Scientific Corporation. Working closely with a mentor, she acquired a great deal of hands-on research experience. She also had an opportunity to interact with other interns and engage in several fun activities as a group. "My internship has given me a great perspective on what it is like working in the 'real world.' It has shown me that the exchange of ideas, time management, and teamwork are integral parts of any job. Most importantly, I found it is common to be overwhelmed and not understand something in a new environment. Asking questions is the best way to learn."

Be Alert to Changing Job Requirements

In today's highly competitive and fast-paced work environments, the skills required for the job you have today may change tomorrow. The job you were initially hired to do will often expand into many different directions that can result in a substantial raise or promotion; be open to such changes. Always make sure your on-the-job skills are up-to-date and that you are doing more than what you consider to be "your job." This may mean acquiring new skills and redefining your job in reference to changing organizational requirements. Take initiative and demonstrate your entrepreneurial skills. Individuals who unexpectedly become victims of downsizing are often ones who did a particular job well but suddenly discover they have the wrong set of skills for an organization undergoing transformation as it attempts to become more competitive. Never assume the skills and experience you have today will be sufficient for the job tomorrow. Always define what you are doing today in terms of the larger organization. Ask yourself, for example, "*Am I a continuing asset to what may be a rapidly changing organization? Will I be needed as much tomorrow as I am today?"*

Beware of Office Politics

After three months on the job, you should know who's who, who has clout, whom to avoid, and how to get things done in spite of people, their positions, and their personal agendas. In other words, you will become inducted into the informal structure of the organization. You should become aware of this structure and use it to your advantage.

While it goes without saying that you should perform in your job, you need more than just performance. You should understand the informal organization, develop new networks, and use them to advance your career. This means conducting an internal career advancement campaign as well as an annual career check-up.

Don't expect to advance by sitting around and just doing your job, however good you may be. Power is distributed in organizations, and politics is often ubiquitous. Learn the power structure as well as how to play positive politics. For sound advice on this subject, see Karen Ginsburg Wood's *Don't Sabotage Your Success! Make Office Politics Work* (Enlightened Concepts Publishing, 2000); Michael and Deborah Dobson's *Enlightened Office Politics* (AMACOM, 2001); Alan R. Schonbuerg's *169 Ways to Score Points With Your Boss* (McGraw-Hill, 1998); Andrew J. DuBrin's *Winning Office Politics* (Prentice-Hall Press, 1990); Phil Porter's *Eat or Be Eaten!* (Prentice-Hall Press, 2000); Casey Fitts Hawley's *100+ Tactics for Office Politics* (Barrons Educational Series, 2001); and Kathleen Kelley Reardon's *The Secret Handshake* (Doubleday, 2000).

After a while many organizations appear to be similar in terms of the quality and quantity of politics. Intensely interpersonal jobs are the most political. Indeed, people are normally fired because of politics – not gross incompetence. What do you do, for example, if you find yourself working for a tyrannical or incompetent boss, a jealous co-worker is out to get you, or you find yourself in compromising ethical situations, such as you are expected to lie or cheat? Some organizational environments can be unhealthy for your professional development.

Conduct an Annual Career Check-Up

We recommend an annual career check-up. Take out your resume and review it. Ask yourself several questions:

- Am I achieving my objective?
- Has my objective changed?
- Is this job meeting my expectations?

- Am I doing what I'm good at and enjoy doing?
- Are my skills up-to-date for this job and organization?
- Am I able to fully use my skills as well as acquire new skills?
- Does this company fully value my contributions?
- Is this job worth keeping?
- How can I best achieve career satisfaction either on this job or in another job or career?
- What other opportunities elsewhere might be better than this job?

Perhaps changing jobs is not the best alternative for you. If you encounter difficulties with your job, you should first assess the nature of the problem. Perhaps the problem can be resolved by working with your present employer. Many employers prefer this approach. They are learning that increased job satisfaction translates into less job stress and absenteeism as well as more profits for the company. Progressive employers want happy workers because they are productive employees. They view job-keeping and job-revitalization as excellent investments in their futures.

Alternatively, you may want to enter your resume into various online resume databases where you can literally keep yourself in the job market 24 hours a day, 365 days a year. Whether you are actively looking for a job or just keeping in touch with potential opportunities, putting your resume online may be a good way to conduct a career check-up on a regular basis. Indeed, we expect more and more individuals will use the Internet in this manner. Putting your resume online allows you to remain constantly active in the job market. In so doing, new and unexpected job opportunities may come your way even though you are perfectly happy with your current job. In other words, participation in such resume databases may result in employers coming to you rather than you seeking out employers by using the job search strategies and techniques outlined in this book.

The concept of an annual career check-up may be replaced with the concept of a lifetime membership in a career health or fitness club. You keep your career healthy and fit by always keeping yourself on the job market.

Use Job-Keeping and Advancement Strategies

Assuming you enjoy your work, how can you best ensure keeping your job as well as advancing your career in the future? What job-keeping skills should you possess for the career environments of today and tomorrow? How can you best avoid becoming a victim of cutbacks, politics, and terminations?

Most employers want their employees to perform according to certain expectations associated with today's changing workplace. Hecklinger and Curtin in *Training for Life* (Kendall/Hunt) define these expectations as a set of 13 basic job-keeping skills:

1. **Ability to do the job well:** develop your competence.

2. **Initiative:** work on your own without constant direction.

3. **Dependability:** being there when you are needed.

4. **Reliability:** getting the job done.

5. **Efficiency:** being accurate and capable.

6. **Loyalty:** being faithful.

7. **Maturity:** handling problems well.

8. **Cheerfulness:** being pleasant to be with.

9. **Helpfulness:** willing to pitch in and help out.

10. **Unselfishness:** helping in a bind even though it is not your responsibility.

11. **Perseverance:** carrying on with a tedious project.

12. **Responsibility:** taking care of your duties.

13. **Creativity:** finding new ways to solve the employer's problems.

While using these skills will not ensure job security, they will most likely enhance your security and potential for advancement.

A fourteenth job-keeping skill – **managing your political environment** – is one employers don't like to talk about. It may well be more important than all the other job-keeping skills. Many people who get fired are victims of political assassinations rather than failures at meeting the boss's job performance expectations or scoring well on the annual performance appraisal.

You must become savvy at the game of office politics in order to survive in many jobs. For example, what might happen if the boss you have a good working relationship with today is replaced tomorrow by someone you don't know or by someone you know but don't like? Through no fault of your own – except having been associated with a particular mentor or patron – you may become a victim of the new boss's housecleaning. Accordingly, you get a two-hour notice to clean out your desk and get out. Such political assassinations are common occurrences in the publishing, advertising, and media businesses.

These 14 basic job-keeping strategies should be linked to eight survival tactics that can be used to minimize the uncertainty and instability surrounding many jobs today:

1. **Learn to read danger signals.** Beware of cutbacks, layoffs, and firings before they occur. Adjust to the danger signals by securing your job or by looking for another job.

2. **Document your achievements.** Keep a record of what you accomplish – problems you solve, contributions you make to improving productivity and profits.

3. **Expand your horizons.** Become more aware of other areas in the company and acquire skills for performing other jobs. The more skills you have, the more valuable you should be to the company.

4. **Prepare for your next job.** Seek more training through:

    ▪ apprenticeships
    ▪ community colleges
    ▪ weekend colleges
    ▪ private, trade, or technical schools
    ▪ Internet and correspondence courses
    ▪ industrial training programs
    ▪ government training programs – U.S. Department of Agriculture, for example
    ▪ military training
    ▪ cooperative education
    ▪ four-year college or university

5. **Promote yourself.** Talk about your accomplishments with co-workers and supervisors – but don't boast. Keep them informed about your work; let them know you are available for promotion. Check out our related on-the-job advancement tips in *Get a Raise in 7 Days: 10 Salary Savvy Steps to Success* (Impact Publications, 1999).

6. **Attach yourself to a mentor or sponsor.** Find someone in a position of influence and power whom you admire and who can help you acquire more responsibilities, skills, and advancement. Avoid currying favor.

7. **Continue informational interviewing.** Educate yourself as well as expand your interpersonal network of job contacts by regularly talking to people about their jobs and careers. As noted in Chapter 8, whether on or off the job, continue to connect, build, and nurture your networks.

8. **Use your motivated abilities and skills.** Success tends to attract more success. Regularly use the abilities and skills you enjoy in different everyday settings.

The most important thing you can do now is to assess your present situation as well as identify what you want to do in the future with your career and life. Perhaps you have new goals related to family and lifestyle which are not compatible with the demands of your current job. You may conclude that your job is not worth keeping. Indeed, one of the most important issues you may need to face concerns your career development – deciding when to stay and when to go.

Assess and Change When Necessary

We are not proposing disloyalty to employers or regular job-hopping. Hopefully you will land a terrific job that leads to a long-term commitment on the part of both you and the employer. Rather, we believe in the great American principle of "self-interest rightly understood"; your first obligation is to yourself. No one owes you a job, and neither should you feel you owe someone your career and life. Jobs and careers should not be life sentences. Periodically assess your career health and feel free to make changes when necessary. You owe it to yourself and others around you to be your very best self.

Since many jobs change for the worse, it may not be worth staying around for the resulting stress, headaches, and ulcers normally associated with unhappy work situations. Indeed, many people stay around too long; they fail to read signs that say it's time to go. If the organization does not meet your career expectations, use the same job search methods that got you into the organization. Be prepared to bail out for greener pastures by doing your job research and conducting informational and referral interviews. While the grass may not always be greener on the other side, many times it is; you will know by conducting another job search. For advice on this increasingly important subject, especially recognizing the signs and taking action for changing jobs and careers, see Gary Rubin's *Quit Your Job and Grow Some Hair: Know When to Go, When to Stay* (Impact Publications, 2003).

Revitalize Your Job

Assuming you know how to survive on your job, what do you do if you experience burnout and high levels of job stress, or are just plain bored with your job? A job change, rather than resolving these problems, may lead to a repetition of the same patterns elsewhere. Techniques for changing the nature of your present job may prove to be your best option.

Most people will sometime experience what Marilyn Moats Kennedy

(*Career Knockouts*, Follett) calls the "Killer Bs": blockage, boredom, and burnout. What can individuals do to make their jobs less stressful, more interesting, and more rewarding? One answer is found in techniques collectively referred to as "job revitalization."

Job revitalization involves changing work patterns. It requires you to take risks. Again, you need to evaluate your present situation, outline your career and life goals, and develop and implement a plan of action. A job-revitalization campaign may include meeting with your superior to develop an on-the-job career development plan. Set goals with your boss and discuss with him or her how you can best meet these goals on the job. If your boss is not familiar with career development and job-revitalization alternatives, suggest some of these options:

- Rotating jobs
- Redesigning your job
- Creating a new position
- Promotions
- Enlarging your job duties and responsibilities
- Sabbatical or leave of absence
- Part-time work
- Flextime scheduling
- Job sharing
- Retraining or educational programs
- Internship

Perhaps your supervisor can think of other options which would be acceptable to company policy as well as productive for both you and the organization.

More and more companies are recognizing the value of introducing career development programs and encouraging job-revitalization among their employees. They are learning it is more cost-effective to retain good employees by offering them new job options for career growth within the organization than to see them go. They are especially protective of their star employees, trying to find new ways to keep them happy and productive! Such programs and policies are congruent with the productivity and profit goals of organizations. They are good management practices. As organizations in the coming decade stress greater productivity, hiring right, and retaining star performers, they will place more emphasis on career development and job revitalization. For extended treatments of these subjects within the context of today's changing workplace, see Dr. Beverly Kaye's and Sharon Jordan-Evans' *Love 'Em or Lose 'Em: Getting Good People to Stay* (Berrett-Koehler, 2002); Dr. Jim Harris' and Joan Brannick's, *Finding and Keeping Great Employees* (AMACOM, 1999); and Robert E. Kelley's *How to Be a Star At Work* (Time Books, 1999).

12

Government, Nonprofit, and International Jobs

MOST OF THE JOB SEARCH STRATEGIES OUTLINED IN previous chapters are applicable for finding jobs and launching careers in the private sector within North America. However, another 30 million jobs are available in the public sector, which encompasses both government agencies and nonprofit organizations. For individuals interested in working abroad or landing a job without borders, the international arena offers millions of additional jobs. Finding jobs in these sectors requires modification of our strategies, especially when faced with formalized application procedures in government and the important role of networking and personal contacts with nonprofit and international employers.

Public and International Arenas

Some of today's most interesting and rewarding entry-level jobs for college graduates are found with government and nonprofit organizations as well as in the international arena. If you are interested in pursuing such jobs, you should find this special chapter especially useful because of its focus on key resources. Our basic goal here is to briefly introduce you to jobs in these fascinating arenas and then point you to the best resources, from books and software to subscriptions and websites, for organizing a job search responsive to these specialty arenas.

At the same time, you should check out the many employers and jobs featured on www.campuscareercenter.com. Several government agencies, non-profit organizations, and international employers regularly announce opportunities for college students and graduates on this website. As noted in Chapters 11 and 13, these employers offer many exciting entry-level jobs that can lead to long-term career opportunities.

Government and Law Enforcement Jobs

Nearly 20 million people work for government at all levels in the United States. While the federal government employs nearly 2.7 million people, state governments employ 4.8 million, and local governments (counties, school districts, townships, municipalities, special districts) nearly 12 million people.

Within the federal government, the six largest agencies in terms of employees consist of the following:

1. U.S. Postal Service
2. Department of Defense
3. Department of Veterans Affairs
4. Department of Treasury
5. Department of Justice
6. Department of Agriculture

The soon to be formed Department of Homeland Security, with an estimated 170,000 employees, should become the fourth largest federal agency.

While governments at all levels periodically go through hiring freezes, cutbacks, and expansions due to changing political and economic conditions, in general government employment remains one of the most stable and secure arenas for jobs and careers. It's especially attractive to recent college graduates who can find many attractive entry-level opportunities with some of the most highly respected federal agencies, such as the National Security Council (NSC), Federal Reserve, National Institutes of Health (NIH), Defense Advanced Research Projects Agency (DARPA), Federal Bureau of Investigation (FBI), Central Intelligence Agency (CIA), and the Securities and Exchange Commission (SEC). Indeed, many agencies offer special internship and management training programs for recent college graduates.

Take, for example, the federal government opportunities for college graduates. During the next two years (2003-2004), federal agencies will hire more than 250,000 employees to replace the large number of individuals retiring and resigning as well as for recruiting individuals for new homeland security responsibilities. At the same time, each year federal government agencies employ over 50,000 students who work in a variety of federal-sponsored student employment or internship programs.

Government agencies hire for almost every conceivable position found in the private sector as well as for many positions that are unique to the functions of government, especially in the law enforcement and security areas. But unlike the private sector, government agencies have highly formalized application procedures which include specific eligibility requirements. In the case of the federal government, the formal application procedure for most GS (General Schedule) positions involves acquiring vacancy announcements and submitting either an OF-612 or Federal Resume directly to a hiring agency. Within the past few years, the federal hiring process has increasingly been decentralized to the agency level. As a result, applicants need to research agencies and follow the specific application procedures outlined by each agency. At the same time, the federal hiring process has increasingly moved online. Accordingly, you are well advised to access agency websites, research opportunities, download vacancy announcements, and apply online with an electronic resume which must meet specific agency screening requirements. In some cases, such as Foreign Service positions with the U.S. Department of State, the hiring process may take several months. In other cases, such as Border Patrol positions with the U.S. Department of Treasury, the time frame from submitting an application to being interviewed and offered a job may only take a few days or weeks. Understanding individual agency hiring practices is essential for anyone applying for a government job.

The subject of government employment can easily occupy separate books which indeed it does. If you are interested in pursuing a job or career with government, we highly recommend the following resources.

Useful Books, Software, Subscriptions

The following books, software, and subscriptions provide a wealth of information on how to find jobs in government. While most resources focus on the federal government, others also include state and local government opportunities with special emphasis on jobs in law enforcement and security:

Book of U.S. Government Jobs, 8th Edition, Dennis Damp (Bookhaven Press, 2002)

The Complete Guide to Public Employment, 3rd Edition, Ron and Caryl Krannich (Impact Publications, 1995)

Directory of Federal Jobs and Employers, Ron and Caryl Krannich (Impact Publications, 1996)

FBI Careers, Thomas H. Ackerman (JIST Works, 2002)

Federal Application Kit (Federal Research Service)

Federal Applications That Get Results, Russ Smith (Impact Publications, 1996)

Federal Career Opportunities (Federal Research Service, biweekly job listings)

Federal Employment From A to Z (Federal Research Service, 2002)

Federal Jobs in Law Enforcement, Russ Smith (Impact Publications, 1996)

Federal Resume Guidebook, Kathryn Kraemer Troutman (JIST Works, 1999)

Find a Federal Job Fast: How to Cut the Red Tape and Get Hired, 4th Edition, Ron and Caryl Krannich (Impact Publications, 1999)

Government Job Applications and Federal Resumes, Anne McKinney (Prep Publishing, 1999)

Government Job Finder, 4th Edition, Daniel Lauber (Planning/Communication, 2003)

Guide to America's Federal Jobs, 2nd Edition (JIST Works, 2000)

Guide to Careers in Federal Law Enforcement, Thomas H. Ackerman (Hamilton Burrows Press, 2000)

Quick and Easy Federal Jobs Kit, CD-ROM Version 6.5 (Data Tech, 2001)

Ten Steps to a Federal Job: Navigating the Federal Job System, Kathryn Kraemer Troutman (JIST Works, 2002)

Relevant Websites

A great deal of government employment information can be found online. While most federal, state, and local government agencies have their own websites, other websites function as gateways to numerous government agencies. Several websites also focus on specialty areas, such as law enforcement, within government at all levels. The following websites should prove especially useful in your government job search:

❑ USA Jobs: <u>www.usajobs.opm.gov</u>

This is the federal government's (Office of Personnel Management) gateway site to federal employment. Functions as a job board for vacancies with various federal agencies. Includes information on the application process, Senior Executive Service, student employment, veterans preference, and online applications.

❑ Federal Jobs Central: <u>fedjobs.com</u>

Publishers of the popular *Federal Jobs Digest*, which lists vacancies with most federal agencies, this site includes one of the most comprehensive databases of current federal job openings. Includes featured agencies, pay scales, application tools, tips, and links to other resources.

❑ Federal Jobs Digest: <u>jobsfed.com</u>

Publishers of the long-running *Federal Jobs Digest*, this site includes a huge database of agency vacancies along with a job matching service, federal benefits, hiring news, federal resume advice, and a bookstore (includes only two of their own titles).

❑ Lawenforcementjob.com: <u>lawenforcementjob.com</u>

Offers a wealth of information on law enforcement careers. Includes job postings, message boards, online tests, linkages to other relevant sites, and bookstore.

Numerous other websites also focus on government and law enforcement jobs:

▪ Careers in Government	<u>careersingovernment.com</u>
▪ Careers in Law Enforcement	<u>lejobs.com</u>
▪ Classified Employment Web Site	<u>yourinfosource.com/CLEWS</u>
▪ Cop Career.com	<u>copcareer.com</u>
▪ Corrections.com	<u>database.corrections.com/ career</u>
▪ Federal Jobs Net	<u>federaljobs.net</u>
▪ FederalJobSearch	<u>federaljobsearch.com</u>
▪ Federal Times	<u>federaltimes.com</u>
▪ FedGate	<u>fedgate.org</u>
▪ FedWorld.gov	<u>www.fedworld.gov</u>
▪ FirstGov	<u>firstgov.gov</u>

- GovernmentJobs.com   governmentjobs.com
- Govjobs.com   govjobs.com
                              govtjob.net
- Law Enforcement Jobs   lawenforcementjobs.com
- Officer.com   officer.com
- PoliceCareer.com   policecareer.com
- Police Employment   policeemployment.com
- PSE-NET.com   PSE-NET.com
- StateJobs.com   statejobs.com
- United Nations   unsystem.org
- US Government Jobs.com   usgovernmentjobs.com
- Whitehouse   whitehouse.gov

If you're interested in working for the federal government, you may want to explore employment opportunities with these major federal agencies:

- African Development
  Foundation   www.adf.gov
- Agency for International
  Development (USAID)   www.usaid.gov
- Central Intelligence Agency www.cia.gov
- Consumer Product Safety
  Commission   www.cpsc.gov
- Department of Agriculture   www.usda.gov
- Department of Commerce   www.commerce.gov
- Department of Defense   www.dtic.mil
- Department of Energy   www.energy.gov
- Department of Health
  and Human Services   www.os.dhhs.gov
- Department of Justice   www.usdoj.gov
- Department of State   www.state.gov
- Department of
  Transportation   www.dot.gov
- Environmental Protection
  Agency   www.epa.gov
- Export-Import Bank   www.exim.gov
- Federal Communications
  Commission   www.fcc.gov
- Federal Emergency
  Management Agency   www.fema.gov
- General Services
  Administration   www.gsa.gov
- Immigration and
  Naturalization Service   www.ins.usdoj.gov

- Inter-American Foundation   www.iaf.gov
- Internal Revenue Service   www.irs.ustreas.gov
- Peace Corps   www.peacecorps.com
- Smithsonian Institution   www.si.edu
- U.S. Postal Service   www.usps.gov

Nonprofit Opportunities

The U.S. nonprofit sector consists of nearly 1 million organizations that employ over 10 million people in the United States and abroad. For many job seekers, this is a hidden job market consisting of trade and professional associations, educational groups, charitable organizations, foundations, research organizations, public policy groups, and related organizations that claim nonprofit tax status. Many of them operate in a single community or at the state and national levels. Others have an international presence. They operate in a wide variety of fascinating fields: arts, entertainment, child welfare, civil liberties, consumer advocacy, economic development, education, environment, food and nutrition, housing, homeless, medical and health care, politics, and relief assistance.

The nonprofit sector offers numerous opportunities for people interested in pursuing a cause, helping people, acquiring knowledge, and promoting interests of specialty groups. Many of these organizations are at the forefront of major policy issues, such as child labor, auto safety, hunger, homelessness, AIDS, civil rights, nuclear power, cancer, and environmental degradation. They conduct research, sponsor educational programs, extend technical assistance, and engage in lobbying activities.

For college students and graduates, nonprofit organizations are excellent places to find entry-level jobs which can lead to rapid advancement. If you are especially interested and skilled in fundraising, conducting research, organizing meetings, and recruiting members, the nonprofit sector may be the ideal employment arena for you. For information on the organizations that comprise the nonprofit sector as well as how to land a job with these organizations, be sure to consult the following resources:

Useful Books

100 Best Nonprofits to Work For, Leslie Hamilton (Arco Publishing, 1998)

Education Job Finder, Daniel Lauber (Planning/Communications, 2003)

From Making a Profit to Making a Difference, Richard M. King (Planning/Communications, 2000)

Harvard Business School Guide to Careers in the Nonprofit Sector, Stephanie Lowell (Harvard Business School Press, 2000)

Jobs and Careers With Nonprofit Organizations, Ron and Caryl Krannich (Impact Publications, 1999)

Nonprofits Job Finder, 5th Edition, Daniel Lauber (Planning/Communications, 2003)

Relevant Websites

Most nonprofit organizations maintain their own websites which include information on opportunities. The following sites function as gateways to the employment world of the nonprofit sector:

❏ **GuideStar: guidestar.org**

This is the ultimate gateway site for researching the nonprofit sector. Includes a database of more than 700,000 U.S. nonprofit organizations. Use the search engine to find a nonprofit that fits your particular interests. The site also includes an annual nonprofit compensation report, articles, news, conferences, and links to other related sites.

❏ **Action Without Borders: idealist.org**

If you are interested in international nonprofit organizations, it doesn't get any better than this gateway site to jobs with international nonprofits. The site includes links to thousands of job resources in 153 countries. Offers job postings, a "push" email service, and newsletter. Resources cover organizations, jobs, volunteering, services, campaigns, events, internships, career affairs, career information, and tools for organizations.

❏ **Access: www.accessjobs.org**

Access operates as an employment clearinghouse for the nonprofit sector. Includes a database of jobs with the nonprofit sector. Job seekers can post their resumes online. Regularly sponsors job fairs for nonprofit organizations. Includes an internship and volunteer section, career counseling services, links to partner sites, and a bookstore.

Several of the following websites function as gateways to thousands of nonprofit organizations:

- **Charity Village**
- **Council on Foundations**
- **Foundation Center**
- **Impact Online**
- **Independent Sector**
- **Internet Nonprofit Center**

charityvillage.com
cof.org
fdncenter.org
impactonline.org
indepsec.org
nonprofits.org

If you are interested in working with international nonprofit organizations, begin by exploring the gateway website, Action Without Borders site (idealist.org). Also, include in your research the following websites:

- **AIESEC**
- **Global Health Council**
- **IAESTE**
- **InterAction**
- **Intercristo**
- **International Service Agencies**
- **JustAct (Youth Action for Global Justice)**
- **PACT**
- **Volunteers for Peace**
- **World Learning**

aiesec.org
www.globalhealth.org
iaeste.org
interaction.org
jobleads.org

charity.org

justact.org
pactworld.com
www.vfp.org
worldlearning.org

Some of the major nonprofit organizations that also maintain informative websites include:

- **Academy for Educational Development**
- **ACCION International**
- **Adventist Development and Relief Agency International**
- **Africare, Inc.**
- **Agricultural Co-op Development International**
- **Air Serv International**
- **American Friends Service Committee**
- **American Jewish Joint Distribution Committee**

aed.org
accion.org

www.adra.org
africare.org

www.acdivoca.org
airserv.org

www.afsc.org

www.ajc.org

- American Red Cross
  International Services   redcross.org/services/intl
- AmeriCares Foundation   www.americares.org
- Amnesty International (USA)   amnesty-usa.org
- Asia Foundation   www.asiafoundation.org
- Battelle Memorial Institute   www.battelle.org
- Bread for the World   www.bread.org
- Brother's Brother Foundation   www.brothersbrother.org
- CARE   www.care.org
- Catholic Relief Services   www.catholicrelief.org
- Centre for Development
  and Population Activities   www.cedpa.org
- Childreach   www.childreach.org
- Christian Children's Fund   christianchildrensfund.org
- Church World Service   churchworldservice.org
- Compassion International   compassion.org
- Direct Relief International   directrelief.org
- Doctors Without Borders   dwb.org
- Educational Development
  Center   www.edc.org
- Family Health International   www.fhi.org
- Food for the Hungry, Inc.   fh.org
- Greenpeace   greenpeaceusa.org
- Habitat for Humanity
  International   habitat.org
- Heifer Project International   heifer.org
- Helen Keller International   hki.org
- The Hunger Project   www.thp.org
- Institute of International
  Education   www.iie.org
- InterExchange   interexchange.org
- International Aid, Inc.   internationalaid.org
- International Catholic
  Migration Commission   www.icmc.net
- International Development
  Enterprises   ideorg.org
- International Executive
  Service Corps   www.iesc.org
- International Eye Foundation   iefusa.org
- International Institute of
  Rural Reconstruction   panasia.org.sg/iirr
- International Rescue
  Committee   www.intrescom.org

- LASPAU – Academic and
  Professional Programs
  for the Americas　　　www.laspau.harvard.edu
- Laubach Literacy
  International　　　laubach.org
- Lutheran Immigration
  and Refugee Service　　　www.lirs.org
- Lutheran World Relief　　　www.lwr.org
- MAP International　　　www.map.org
- Mennonite Central
  Committee　　　www.mcc.org
- Mercy Corps International　　　mercycorps.org
- MidAmerica International
  Agricultural Consortium　　　miac.org
- National Cooperative
  Business Association　　　www.cooperative.org
- National Widelife Federation　　　nwf.org
- The Nature Conservancy　　　tnc.org
- OIC (Opportunities Industrial
  Centers) International　　　www.oicinternational.org
- Operation USA　　　opusa.org
- Opportunity International　　　www.opportunity.org
- Oxfam America　　　www.oxfamamerica.org
- PACT (Private Agencies
  Collaborating Together)　　　pactworld.org
- Partners of the Americas　　　www.partners.net
- Pathfinder International　　　www.pathfind.org
- People to People Health
  Foundation (Project HOPE)　　　projhope.org
- PLAN International　　　www.plan-international.org
- Planned Parenthood
  Federation　　　plannedparenthood.org
- Population Action
  International　　　populationaction.org
- Population Council　　　www.popcouncil.org
- Population Reference Bureau　　　www.prb.org
- Population Services
  International　　　www.psi.org
- Program for Appropriate
  Technology in Health　　　path.org
- Project Concern International　　　projectconcern.org
- Research Triangle Institute　　　www.rti.org
- Salvation Army World
  Service Office　　　www.salvationarmy.org

- Save the Children
  Foundation, Inc.   savethechildren.org
- The Sierra Club   sierraclub.org
- TechnoServe   technoserve.org
- U.S. Catholic Conference
  Office of Migration
  and Refugee Services   www.nccbuscc.org/mrs
- U.S. Committee for UNICEF   www.unicefusa.org
- Unitarian Universalist
  Service Committee   www.uusc.org
- Volunteers in Overseas
  Cooperative Assistance   www.acdivoca.org
- Volunteers in Technical
  Assistance   www.vita.org
- Winrock International
  Institute for Agricultural
  Development   winrock.org
- World Concern   worldconcern.org
- World Council of
  Credit Unions   woccu.org
- World Education   www.worlded.org
- World Relief Corporation   worldrelief.org
- World Resources Institute   www.wri.org
- World SHARE, Inc.   www.worldshare.org
- World Vision Relief and
  Development, Inc.   worldvision.org
- World Wildlife Fund   wwf.org
- Worldteach   worldteach.org
- Worldwatch Institute   www.worldwatch.org
- Y.M.C.A.   ymca.org
- Y.W.C.A.   www.ywca.org
- Zero Population Growth   zpg.org

The following nonprofit research, educational, and trade organizations and associations variously function as think tanks, lobbying groups, and training organizations. Most do a great deal of international work:

- American Enterprise
  Institute (AEI)   www.aei.org
- Brookings Institution   brook.edu
- CATO Institute   cato.org
- Center for Strategic and
  International Studies   www.csis.org
- Chamber of Commerce   www.uschamber.org

- Council for International
  Exchange of Scholars   www.cies.org
- Council of the Americas   counciloftheamericas.org
- Council on Foreign Relations   cfr.org
- Council on International
  Educational Exchange   www.ciee.org
- Earthwatch Institute   earthwatch.org
- Foreign Policy Association   fpa.org
- Freedom House   freedomhouse.org
- Heritage Foundation   heritage.org
- Hoover Institute on War,
  Revolution, and Peace   hoover.org
- Human Rights Watch   hrw.org
- The International Center   www.internationalcenter.com
- International Food Policy
  Research Institute   www.cgiar.org
- International Schools
  Services   iss.edu
- Meridian International Ctr.   www.meridian.org
- NAFSA/Association of
  International Educators   nafsa.org
- Near East Foundation   neareast.org
- Network for Change   library.envirolink.org
- RAND Corporation   www.rand.org
- U.S.-China Business Council   www.uschina.org
- United States Olympic Com.   www.usoc.org
- The Urban Institute   urban.org
- World Learning   www.worldlearning.org
- World Neighbors   www.wn.org
- Youth for Understanding
  International Exchange   www.yfu.org

International Jobs and Careers

Individuals interested in international jobs tend to have a passion for working in the international arena. This passion is usually related to a particular region, country, or culture they came into contact with as students. Some took foreign language courses that led to a summer or semester abroad program. Others, with a serious case of wanderlust, may just enjoy traveling the globe. In the end, many share the same goal – find a job that will enable them to travel and/or live abroad.

Finding an international job is easier said than done. Indeed, it can be a daunting task for individuals unfamiliar with this unique employment arena. It's especially frustrating for students at colleges and universities that provide little international employment assistance. Since most college career service offices primarily focus on helping students find jobs in the U.S., many international-oriented students feel they are on their own trying to locate international opportunities.

The good news is that the Internet has become the international job seeker's best friend. Numerous websites provide international employment assistance. If you are interested in finding an international job, you are well advised to use the following print and electronic resources.

Useful Books

The following books should prove especially useful in navigating this fascinating job arena. You may want to start by exploring summer abroad programs and international internships with these resources:

> *Directory of International Internships*, 5th Edition, Charles A. Gliozzo and Vernicka K. Tyson (Michigan State University, 2003)

> *Peterson's Internships 2003* (Peterson's, 2002)

> *Peterson's Study Abroad 2002* (Peterson's, 2002)

> *Summer Study Abroad 2002* (Peterson's, 2002)

For short-term and volunteer international job opportunities, check out these key resources:

> *Back Door Guide to Short-Term Job Opportunities*, 3rd Edition, Michael Landes (Ten Speed Press, 2002)

> *How to Live Your Dream of Volunteering Overseas*, Joseph Collins et al. (Penguin, 2002)

> *Overseas Summer Jobs*, 32rd Edition, David Woodworth and Ian Collier, eds. (Vacation Work, 2002)

> *Work Your Way Around the World*, 10th Edition, Susan Griffith (Vacation Works, 2001)

If you are primarily interested in teaching English abroad, which is one of the easiest ways to break into the international job market, be sure to review these two key resources:

Teaching English Abroad, 4ᵗʰ Edition, Susan Griffin (Vacation Works, 2001)

Teaching English Overseas: A Job Guide for Canadians and Americans, Jeff Mohamed (English International, 2000)

If you are interested in more long-term international job and career opportunities, these resources should prove useful:

Best Resumes and CVs for International Jobs: Your Passport to the Global Job Market, Ronald L. Krannich and Wendy S. Enelow (Impact Publications, 2002)

Careers in International Affairs, 6ᵗʰ Edition, Maria Pinto Carland and Michael Trucano, eds. (Georgetown University Press, 1997)

Directory of American Firms Operating in Foreign Countries, 17ᵗʰ Edition (World Trade Academy Press, 2002)

Directory of Jobs and Careers Abroad, 10ᵗʰ Edition, Elisabeth Roberts, ed. (Vacation Work, 2000)

The Directory of Websites for International Jobs, Ron and Caryl Krannich (Impact Publications, 2002)

The Global Citizen: A Guide to Creating an International Life and Career, Elizabeth Kruempelmann (Ten Speed Press, 2002)

The Global Resume and CV Guide, Mary Anne Thompson (John Wiley & Sons, 2000)

How to Get a Job in Europe, 5ᵗʰ Edition, Robert Sanborn and Cheryl Matherly (Planning/Communications, 2003)

Inside Secrets to Finding a Career in Travel, Karen Rubin (JIST Works, 2001)

International Job Finder, Daniel Lauber (Planning/Communications, 2002)

International Jobs: Where They Are, How to Get Them, 5ᵗʰ Edition, Eric Kocher and Nina Segal (Perseus Publishing, 1999)

International Jobs Directory: A Guide to Over 1001 Employers, Ron and Caryl Krannich (Impact Publications, 1999)

Jobs for Travel Lovers: Opportunities At Home and Abroad, 4th Edition, Ron and Caryl Krannich (Impact Publications, 2003)

Work Abroad: The Complete Guide to Finding a Job Overseas, 4th Edition, Clay Hubbs, Susan Griffin, and William Nolting, eds. (Transitions Abroad, 2002)

Work Worldwide: International Job Strategies for the Adventuresome Job Seeker, Nancy Mueller (Avalon Travel Publishing, 2000)

Working Abroad: Using the Internet to Find a Job and Get Hired, Erik Olson and Jim Blau (Princeton Review, 2002)

For a complete directory of the latest international job and career resources, see Impact's latest edition of the authoritative *Global Work, Travel, and Study* catalog which can be requested in paper form or downloaded electronically from the publisher's website: www.impactpublications.com.

Relevant Websites

Given the seeming difficulty in locating and communicating with international employers, the Internet plays an increasingly important role in an international job search. Job seekers and employers can now quickly connect with each other and communicate by email and conduct online interviews. In addition to the many nonprofit international sites identified in the previous section, the websites below primarily focus on international jobs. Students and others interested in finding short-term employment abroad, opportunities for teaching English abroad, or starting an international career should check out the first four websites. They tend to function as key student-oriented gateway work, study, and travel abroad resources:

❑ **University of Michigan International Center:**
   umich.edu/~icenter/overseas/work/index.html

Regularly updated by international resource guru Bill Nolting, who is the Director of the International Center, this is one of the most authoritative resources for keeping abreast of international resources relating to work abroad. It covers everything someone just starting out will find useful – international internships, short-term paid work opportunities, volunteering abroad, and teaching abroad (with or without certification). It also includes opportunities for students interested in government, engineering, science, law, and social work. Special sections offer information on working abroad in Spanish-, German-, and French-speaking countries as well as tips for minorities and women. You'll also find job search advice, linkages to work abroad programs, and linkages to its study and travel abroad programs and resources. If you want to know who is doing what and where, be sure to visit this rich website, which will quickly get you up and running with the right international resources.

❑ **Transitions Abroad: transitionsabroad.com**

This is the website of the publisher of *Transitions Abroad*, the most authoritative magazine on alternative study, travel, and work abroad. The site includes an excellent collection of international resources for students, graduates, experienced professionals, and seniors. It offers a comprehensive list of programs with ESL, special interest vacations, student overseas programs, language schools, teen study and travel, senior travel, disability travel, volunteering abroad, internships abroad, and responsible adventure travel. It includes another section with online work, study, and travel abroad resources. If you're not sure whether you want to travel, study, or work aboard – or do all three – be sure to survey the rich collection of resources available on this site.

❑ **iAgora.com: iagora.com**

This is one of the most dedicated and enthusiastic groups of international-oriented students and professionals. It's literally an international community of individuals all over the world who are interested in work and study abroad. It's a great place to access resources as well as network with individuals in other countries. It includes separate sections on work abroad (entry-level and internships), study abroad, international travel, and networking groups (Forums, iClubs, iNotes, and chat). It also includes a classified section with ads from over 1,000 cities in 197 countries. Young people with a passion for international work and study will find this innovative site especially useful.

❑ **JobWeb: www.jobweb.com/catapult/interntl.htm**

This section of JobWeb's site for college students includes numerous resources for international students in the U.S. and for U.S. students going abroad. It also includes a searchable database of employers who hire college graduates.

Some of our favorite international gateway and employment sites include the following.

❏ **EscapeArtist.com: <u>escapeartist.com</u>**

This is the ultimate gateway site to the international arena. It's jam-packed with just about everything you ever wanted to know about moving, living, working, investing, and retiring abroad. It is a no-nonsense site that delivers lots of great content. Indeed, it prides itself in having attitude: *"We don't have a lot of nonsense about culture shock and 'how to keep in contact with home' chat-baloney. If you want to go, go; if you want to whimper, stay home. Home is where the heart's on fire."* The site includes extensive sections on international jobs. You can easily spend hours getting lost and found on this site. If there only is one international website you use, make sure it's this one.

❏ **Overseas Jobs: <u>overseasjobs.com</u>**

This well organized site includes numerous international job listings as well as a resume database (through <u>AboutJobs.com</u> database). Offers company profiles, job search tips, mailing list, and links to related sites in its network.

❏ **Monster Work Abroad: <u>international.monster.com</u>**

This website includes a large database of international jobs, a huge resume database, expert advice, chats, boards, and articles. Includes job search tips and resources for improving an international job search. One of the best international job sites on the Web. This site appeals to a wide range of international job seekers, from entry-level to senior-level and consultants. Also check out these special international sections:

<u>forums.monster.com/forum.asp?forum=119</u>

<u>international.monster.com/workabroad/articles</u>

Individuals from abroad interested in finding a job in the United States should visit this section of the site:

<u>forums.globalgateway.monster.com/forumasp?forum=120</u>

❑ **International Job Links:**
www.joblinks.f2Scom/index_eng.htm

This is a useful gateway site designed to assist both job seekers and employers in locating relevant international employment sites. It starts with a world map from which users can select particular regions for identifying job boards, job agents, recruiters, headhunters, and related sites. Sites are classified as to whether or not they offer job postings and resume databases.

❑ **About.com:**
jobsearch.about.com/cs/internationaljobs1

This is the international employment directory section within the larger About.com site. It includes many useful resources to help individuals conduct an effective international job search. It covers such topics as international jobs, country information, etiquette abroad, international internships, international interviewing skills, international volunteer opportunities, online work abroad resources, international salary information, seniors living and working abroad, travel resources for global workers.

❑ **Going Global: www.goinglobal.com**

This relatively new site is operated by Mary Anne Thompson, author of the popular *The Global Resume and CV Guide*. The site extends the baseline work she did in the book on individual country employment profiles. Users can preview more than 25 country guides online – each of which run 50 to 75 pages when printed out – as well as purchase them in the form of e-books. Individual country profiles examine key employment issues as well as cover work permits, visa regulations, key employers, employment websites, local recruitment firms, and more. The site also includes tips on writing resumes and CVs, links to career professionals in each country (local advisor teams of career management professionals), a newsletter, hot topics, and a global forum (message board). Primarily focusing on offering international job information, advice, consultation, and contacts on specific countries, the site does not include a job board nor a resume database. You'll need to click on to partner sites in order to access such functions. Plan to use this site for organizing a job search targeted on specific countries. You can also access this site through www.campuscareercenter.com and www.impactpublications.com.

❏ JobsAbroad.com: **jobsabroad.com**

This site should be of special interest to students and recent graduates who are interested in acquiring work experience abroad as
volunteers, interns, teachers, or in other types of paid positions.
Individuals can search for job postings by job type and country. The
site also includes information on study abroad, language schools, and
budget travel as well as links to its other international study and
travel site, GoAbroad.com (www.goabroad.com).

❏ Job Pilot International: **jobpilot.com**

While this international employment website primarily covers 15
European countries, it also includes the Middle East, Thailand,
Australia, the United States, and a few other countries. The site
allows job seekers to browse job postings for each country, submit a
resume/CV to country-specific JobPilot sites, and acquire job search
resources and information on work permits and visas. It includes a
"Career Journal" section with tips on writing CVs, interviewing,
negotiating salary, and resigning.

❏ TopJobs.net: **topjobs.net**

This employment website specializes in management, professional,
technical, and graduate positions. It primarily covers most of the key
European markets (Ireland, Sweden, Switzerland, Norway, and the
United Kingdom) and maintains affiliate relations with sites in
Spain, Poland, and Thailand. Job seekers can search job postings by
job category, industry sector, geographical region, and date. Job
seekers also can browse company profiles and receive job opportunities via email. Its WAP service allows individuals to access the
TopJobs site at any time and place by using a WAP-enabled mobile
phone. Country sites have their own URLs:

▪ **United Kingdom**	www.topjobs.co.uk
▪ **Ireland**	www.topjobs.ie
▪ **Norway**	www.topjobs.no
▪ **Sweden**	www.topjobs.se
▪ **Switzerland**	www.topjobs.ch
▪ **Spain**	www.topjobs.es
▪ **Poland**	www.topjobs.pl
▪ **Thailand**	www.topjobs.co.th
▪ **International**	www.international.topjobs.net

❑ JobsBazaar.com: **jobsbazaar.com**

This site includes over 12,000 jobs available in the United States, Singapore, Australia, United Kingdom, Canada, and India. Job seekers can research over 1,800 companies, post their resume online, blast their resume to over 4,100 recruiters, browse job postings, subscribe to a newsletter, join chat groups and a discussion forum, and use several useful tools and resources for calculating salary, relocating, and more. The site also includes information on visas and immigration and trips on departing for abroad and returning home.

❑ International Career Employment Center: **internationaljobs.org**

This is primarily an international job listing newspaper. Individuals can subscribe online to two versions. The _International Career Employment Weekly_ includes over 500 job vacancies each week. If you're not ready to apply for a job but want to observe what's available, you should subscribe to the monthly job listing newspaper, _International Employment Hotline_. The site includes a free job listing section called "Hot Jobs This Week." Many of the positions listed are with nonprofits, NGOs, and consulting firms engaged in development and relief work. Subscription rates for individuals range from $26 for 6 issues (6 weeks) to $280 for 98 issues (2 years). The site offers a half price special on these rates for students, recent graduates, and volunteers ($13 for 6 issues to $140 for 98 issues).

❑ Expatica: **www.expatica.com/jobs**

Designed for expatriates in search of jobs in Belgium, France, Germany, and the Netherlands, this site includes a handy search engine for finding jobs by keywords, job category, country, salary level, and date of listing. The site also includes job search advice and numerous interesting articles on various aspects of living, working, and job hunting abroad.

❑ Expat Exchange: **www.expatexchange.com**

This is one of the most comprehensive websites designed to assist expats with every aspect of living and working abroad. It includes an international job and career section which has a pull-down search engine for specifying individual countries. A search results in a linkage to an employment website that should have job listings related to the particular country. While this site does not operate its own job postings and resume database, it's worth visiting simply because of the larger international context within which it represents jobs.

Other useful international employment-related sites include the following:

- About.com   intljobs.about.com
- AboutJobs.com   aboutjobs.com
- ActiJob.com   actijob.com
- Alliances Abroad   alliancesabroad.com
- Dave's ESL Café   eslcafe.com
- Employment Guide   employmentguide.com
- Expat Exchange   expatexchange.com
- Global Career Center   globalcareercenter.com
- Heidrick & Struggles   heidrick.com
- International Staffing
  Consultants   www.iscworld.com
- International Resources   umich.edu/%7Eicenter/
- Job Monkey.com   jobmonkey.com
- Jobshark.com   jobshark.com
- Jobs.Net   jobs.net
- JobsDB.com   jobsdb.com
- Jobware International   jobware.com
- Korn/Ferry International   ekornferry.com
- Nicholson International   nicholsonintl.com
- Management Recruiters
  International   brilliantpeople.com
- PlanetRecruit   planetrecruit.com
- PricewaterhouseCoopers   pwcglobal.com
- Spencer Stuart   spencerstuart.com
- Teaching Jobs Overseas   joyjobs.com
- Top Jobs   topjobs.net
- WorldWorkz   worldworkz.com

The largest number of websites for international job seekers are regional or country-specific, such as www.africajobs.net, asia-net.com, asiadragons. com, careerone.com.au (Australia), jobscanada.com, eurojobs.com, www. southamericajobs.net, www.arabiajobs.com, and Monster. com's 15 country-specific websites. We outline hundreds of these and other international-related sites, including several international headhunter sites, in a separate companion volume, *The Directory of Websites for International Jobs* (Impact Publications).

13

CampusCareerCenter's Employer Network

NUMEROUS EMPLOYERS RECRUIT COLLEGE STUDENTS
and graduates online through CampusCareerCenter.com. If you
register with this website – free to students and graduates – you
can join this unique community of students, employers, and university administrators in developing a well-targeted job search. You can enter
your resume online, browse job listings, explore company profiles, acquire
career advice, and share information about internships, jobs, and employers.

While Chapter 11 included first-person insights from students and graduates working in several companies featured in the following pages, this final
chapter presents profiles of 53 employers who recruit interns and part-time
and full-time employees through CampusCareerCenter. Representing a rich
collection of employers, they include businesses, nonprofits, and government
agencies. You can explore these and dozens of other employers, including job
listings, by going directly to the "Research Companies" section of www.
campuscareercenter.com. All of these companies also have their own websites
from which you can acquire in-depth information on their operations, view
job listings, and apply for jobs online. The Campus CareerCenter site includes
current job listings and position descriptions for these same companies. By
exploring this site and its student-friendly companies, you'll learn a great deal
about opportunities relevant to your interests, skills, and experience. Best of
all, you'll come into contact with some of the world's best companies and
organizations that want to hire college students and graduates for hundreds
of internships and entry-level positions.

ABC News
abcnews.com

Headquartered in New York City, ABC News has over 1,000 employees worldwide, with bureaus in 10 cities in the U.S. and over 20 in foreign countries. It includes the acclaimed news programs *World News Tonight, Nightline, Good Morning America, 20/20,* and *This Week.* ABC News offers internship and entry-level opportunities to qualified students and graduates interested in pursuing a career in broadcast journalism and who have a genuine interest in current events and a strong desire to become a journalist. See employee insights on page 217.

American Management Systems (AMS)
ams.com/career

AMS is a $1 billion international business and information technology consulting firm whose customers include 43 state and provincial governments, most federal agencies, and hundreds of companies in the Fortune 500. Founded in 1970, AMS is headquartered in Fairfax, Virginia, with 49 offices worldwide. The company is traded on the NASDAQ under the symbol AMSY.

Aventis Pasteur
www.us.aventispasteur.com

With a mission to protect and improve human health, Aventis Pasteur annually sells over 1 billion doses of vaccines used to immunize 400 million people around the world. "In the future we must meet ever more stringent economic demands while remaining true to our primary vocation of providing effective responses for the vaccination needs of both industrialized and developing nations. We are pursuing an ongoing strategy of innovation through major research and development programs." See employee insights on page 219.

Black & Decker
www.bdk.com/sales

Black & Decker is a global manufacturer and marketer of quality power tools and accessories, hardware and home improve-ment products, and technology-based fastening systems. Its products and services are marketed in more than 100 countries, and it has manufacturing operations in 10 countries. Noted for product innovation, quality, design, and value, it offers strong brand names and new-product development capabilities.

The Boston Beer Company
www.bostonbeer.com

The Boston Beer Company is the leader among craft beers, outselling the next five competitors combined. Samuel Adams brands have won top honors at The Great American Beer Festival for 14 consecutive years. Producing more than 1,270,000 barrels of beer every year, it employer over 350 people throughout the country, with Breweries located in Boston and Cincinnati. Employees enjoy both professional and personal growth within the company and take pride in our products . They also receive two free cases of product each month!

Cargill, Inc.
www.cargill.com

Employing over 90,000 people in 57 countries, Cargill is one of the largest food companies in the world. It is an international marketer, processor, and distributor of agricultural, food, financial, and industrial products, working with products ranging from flour and chocolate to fertilizer and steel. The company provides distinctive customer solutions in supply chain management, food applications, and health and nutrition. Cargill especially values people with high ethical standards and integrity who like to be challenged, providing them with a demanding and highly fulfilling work environment starting with immediate responsibility for decisions affecting the business. See employee insights on pages 219-220.

Christian Hospital
www.bjc.org

Christian Hospital Northeast-Northwest is a 698-bed, two-division facility located in northwest St. Louis County, Missouri. The nonprofit hospital offers a full range of health care services and an array of medical and surgical specialties. Christian Hospital's medical staff comprises more than 600 area physicians. It currently has a diverse workforce of 3,000+ healthcare professionals.

Convergys Corporation
convergys.com

Convergys Corporation (NYSE: CVG), a member of the S&P 500 and the Forbes' Platinum 400, provides award-winning billing and customer care products and services to leading companies in telecommunications, cable and broadband, technology, financial services and next-generation services in more than 40 countries around the world. Headquartered in Cincinnati, Convergys employs more than 45,000 people in its integrated contact centers, data centers, and other offices in the U.S., Europe, Asia/Pacific, Canada, Latin America and Israel. The company offers both Co-op and Internship opportunities for full-time college students. See employee insights on page 216.

Crawford & Company
crawfordandcompany.com

Crawford & Company is the world's largest independent provider of diversified services to insurance companies, self-insured corporations, and government entities. Its many services include claims management, loss adjustment, healthcare management, risk management services, investigation services, class action administration, and risk information services. Based in Atlanta, the company employs nearly 10,000 employees worldwide and operates over 700 offices in 65 countries. The corporation's shares are traded publicly on the New York Stock Exchange under the symbols CRD.A and CRD.B.

Eckerd Youth Alternatives
eckerd.org

Looking for a nonprofit opportunity that makes a difference in the lives of others? Eckerd Youth Alternatives was founded by Jack and Ruth Eckerd in 1968 with a vision to create a small wilderness program for troubled youth in the woodlands near Brooksville, FL. That single

wilderness camp for 40 youth has grown into a multi-faceted, not-for-profit organization that offers 39 distinct and diverse youth programs in seven states, and has served more than 50,000 young people over the past three decades. With a focus on the power of early intervention and the value of personal relationships in helping troubled youth, the EYA programs have earned national recognition and have consistently ranked among the best for their effectiveness and success. See employee insights on page 214.

Edward Jones
edwardjones.com/careers

Ranked as No.1 in *Fortune* magazine's 2002 list of the "100 Best Companies to Work For" and recognized by *Working Mother* magazine as one of the "100 Best Companies for Working Mothers," Edward Jones is the perfect place to begin a career. It provides rewarding careers for associates who help individual investors and small business owners achieve their long-term financial goals. It currently employs more than 27,000 associates and has more than 8,000 branch offices throughout the U.S. and through affiliates in Canada and the United Kingdom. With 10,000 branch offices to open in 2003, Edward Jones has become one of the fastest growing and most unique financial services firms in the world.

Electronic Arts
jobs.ea.com

Are you into games? Ever think of turning a hobby into a fun vocation? Electronic Arts is the leading developer, publisher, and distributor of interactive software products otherwise known as videogames. EA makes the best heart pounding, fist-pumping, mind bending, breath-catching interactive entertainment software. They currently create best-selling titles for the PC, Playstation 2, GameCube and Xbox. EA's recruitment focuses on maintaining a dedicated team of pioneers with vision, a passion for quality, and a desire to achieve greatness using innovation and creativity for defining the next interactive experience. See employee insights on page 215.

ENSCO, Inc.
ensco.com

ENSCO, Inc. is a high tech Research & Development firm. Employing over 700 people, the company has enjoyed better than 16% annual growth since 1994, with sales topping $81 million dollars in 2001. Typical skills sought by ENSCO, Inc. for intern/co-op, part-time, and full-time opportunities include: electrical and mechanical engineering, real-time programming, digital signal processing, data acquisition, machine vision, calibration and instrumentation experience, and strong math and electronics aptitudes. Languages include: C/C++, MFC, Visual Basic, and Visual C++. Other skills desired are: GUI knowledge, Win NT, Unix, GIS/GPS, OOD/OOA/OOP, and Web Development.

Enterprise Rent-A-Car
enterprise.com

Enterprise Rent-A-Car, a $6 billion company, is the largest rental car company in the U.S. in fleet size and locations, with more than 4,400 offices in the U.S., Canada, the United Kingdom, Ireland, and Germany. Management Trainees typically receive one or more promotions within their first year, and many double their salaries upon becoming branch managers. Ideal candidates should have a background in sales, management, marketing, retail, hotel, restaurant, tourism, or customer service. They must have the motivation to excel within a busy sales and customer driven environment.

Farmers Insurance
farmersinsurance.com

Farmers is one of the largest auto and homeowners insurance companies in the United States with over 30,000 professionals nationwide. It's a leader in the business insurance market and it provides valuable life insurance protection to millions of Americans. Farmers offers career opportunities for professionals in information technology, accounting, actuarial, claims, marketing, communications, auditing, legal, administration, human resources, and underwriting.

GAF Materials Corporation
gaf.com

GAF Materials Corporation is America's oldest (since 1886) and largest manufacturer of roofing products. With sales in excess of $1 billion, GAFMC currently has 3,300 employees in 26 manufacturing locations nationwide. Through the GAFMC's Leadership Development Program, entry-level employees participate in a leadership focused training and development curriculum during the first 12-24 months. Upon successful job performance and program completion, they move to more responsible assignments, promotions, and relocation and a career path to manufacturing management. See insights from three GAF Materials employees on pages 216-217.

Gallup Organization
gallup.com

The Gallup Organization is one of the world's premier research-based management consulting firms. Working primarily with Fortune 500 companies, Gallup helps companies improve their business performance. Gallup also conducts The Gallup Poll, the world's leading source of public opinion since 1935. Gallup has wholly- owned or majority-owned subsidiaries in more than 25 countries. Worldwide, more than 3,000 research, consulting, and training professionals provide clients with comparable practices, procedures, and standards across national, cultural, and linguistic boundaries. An employee-owned firm, Gallup has experienced revenue grown averaging 25% annually over the past decade. See employee insights on page 217.

General Motors
gm.com/careers

General Motors has a global presence in over 200 countries and worldwide employment of 394,000 people. In 2000, GM's market share was 27.8% of the total U.S. vehicle market and 15.1% of the worldwide vehicle market. GM also has other major business interests, including General Motors Acceptance Corporation (GMAC), Hughes Electronics Corp, GM Locomotive Group, and

Allison Transmission. GM's 2000 worldwide net sales and revenues were $184.6 billion. You may submit an online resume or apply via e-mail at GMJobs@saztec1.com. GM also offers Intern and Cooperative Education Programs. See the CampusCareerCenter website for more information.

Genzyme Biosurgery
genzymebiosurgery.com

Genzyme Biosurgery specializes in bringing biotechnology to surgery through the research and development of biomaterials and biologically based products. Its more than 1,300 employees include over 450 scientists. Genzyme Biosurgery has one of the most aggressive sales forces in the industry with over 165 sales representatives reaching 70 countries. "Join us in celebrating our position as the foremost organization in the rapidly emerging market of biomaterials and biotherapeutic surgical products."

The Gillette Company
gillette.com/careers

The Gillette Company is one of the leading consumer products companies in the world. It hires individuals who want to become part of a dynamic organization, driven by world-class brands, innovative marketing and cutting edge technology. The Gillette Company's Vision is to build Total Brand Value by innovating to deliver consumer value and customer leadership faster, better and more completely than our competition. This Vision is supported by two fundamental principles that provide the foundation for all of our activities: Organizational Excellence and Core Values (Achievement, Integrity, and Collaboration).

Hannaford Brothers Co.
www.hannaford.com

Founded in 1883, Hannaford Brothers is among the most respected names in the grocery business. "To ensure our long-term growth and success, we recruit and develop high-potential individuals to be our leaders of tomorrow. Our Retail Management Training Program offers hands-on experience in operating a finan-cially successful supermarket. By working side by side with associates and managers in all departments within a store, individuals develop the managerial skills they'll need to assume a significant leadership position within our company." See employee insights on p. 218.

Harris Corporation
harris.com

Harris Corporation is an international communications equipment company focused on microwave and broadcast communications, government communication systems, secure tactical radios, and network support. The company provides a wide range of products and services for commercial and government communications markets and has sales and service facilities in more than 90 countries. The company uses advanced technologies to provide innovative and cost-effective solutions for commercial and government customers, and is committed to providing products, systems, and services of the highest quality. Strategic acquisitions and alliances, along with a commitment to research and development, have positioned Harris for profitable growth.

Hartford Life
thehartford.com

The Hartford Financial Services Group, Inc. (NYSE: HIG) is one of the nation's largest insurance and financial services companies. It's a leading seller of investment products, life insurance, group and employee benefits, automobile and homeowner's products, business insurance, and reinsurance. With over 6,000 employees in Connecticut and many other locations around the world, Hartford Life offers a challenging, fast-paced environment where creativity, drive and commitment are rewarded. They recruit candidates who can demonstrate initiative, ownership, leadership, and teamwork. See employee insights on pages 217-218.

Houston's Restaurants, Inc.
houstons.com

For over 20 years Houston's has used a simple formula: to consistently serve genuinely great-tasting food with style.

In 1977, George Biel and his partners opened the very first Houston's Restaurant. Since then Houston's has found its place in the most vibrant cities in America – 40+ locations from San Francisco to Manhattan, and Chicago to Miami. Houston's attracts people dedicated to quality. "We look for people with a real desire to achieve. In other words, we're looking for people who know what it means to be a verb."

Internal Revenue Service
jobs.irs.gov

Who is one of the largest financial institutions on Earth, reinvests some $1 trillion every year back into the U.S. economy, serves as the financial guru to Fortune 500 companies, and has a repeat customer base of some 250 million? It's the IRS, "a highly energetic organization whose services and operations contribute to the American landscape in ways you may not even imagine. When you join the IRS you will excel among the most well trained and dedicated workforces anywhere. At the IRS, you will find an environment that is the very definition of modern thinking. Modernization drives everything we do." Discover the many opportunities at this newly transformed government agency that may indeed surprise you! See employee insights on pages 214-215.

JCPenney, Inc.
jcpenney.com

JCPenney is one of the largest and most trusted retailers in the industry, generating billions of dollars in sales annually. Headquartered in Legacy Corporate Park in Plano, Texas, the JCPenney Company operates more than 1,100 department stores in the nation's leading malls, one of the world's most sophisticated catalog networks, a leading Internet shopping site, Eckerd drugstores, and more. It offers career opportunities for bright, energetic and talented individuals in a stimulating, fast-paced and team-oriented culture. It is committed to the development of each associate's career while supporting the individual's need for a healthy, productive work/lifestyle balance.

Johnson & Johnson
jnj.com

Johnson & Johnson is the world's most comprehensive and broadly based manufacturer of health care products. It includes 37 affiliate companies and more than 195 autonomous operating units in 51 countries with more than 100,000 employees. Its decentralized structure provides many autonomous and entrepreneurial environments that feel more like those of a small company. It is dedicated to giving employees personalized attention in their career planning and development. Johnson & Johnson employees experience a greater range of career path opportunities than found in other big companies.

JP Morgan Chase
careers.jpmorganchase.com

JPMorgan Chase is a leading wholesale financial services firm, complemented by a strong and profitable U.S. consumer business. The firm has five business segments: Investment Banking, Investment Management & Private Banking, Treasury & Securities Services, JPMorgan Partners, and Retail & Middle Market Financial Services. The wholesale businesses operate globally under the JPMorgan brand. Their clients include many of the world's most prominent corporations, governments, wealthy individuals and institutional investors. The retail financial services franchise operates under the Chase brand. Customers include more than 30 million individuals and small businesses across the U.S. Chase products and services encompass: Consumer Banking, Investments, Insurance, Small Business Services, Credit Cards, Home Finance, Auto Finance, Education Finance.

Lexmark International
lexmark.com

Lexmark is a fast-growing, integrated global developer, manufacturer, and supplier of printing solutions and products, including laser, inkjet and dot matrix printers and associated consumable supplies for the office and home markets. Once part of IBM, it became an independent global company in 1991 with its own line of branded products. Lexmark posted revenues of more than $3 billion in fiscal 1998. Its products are sold in nearly 150 countries. With more than 50 sales offices globally, seven manufacturing centers on three continents and more than 8,000 employees, Lexmark's financial success and rapid growth is a result of its unique focus on customer value, customer relationships, service and responsiveness.

M&T Bank Corporation
www.mandtbank.com

M&T Bank Corporation's story reflects well-managed growth (from a $5.2 billion organization in 1987 to pro forma assets of $49 billion in 2002), an extremely high caliber workforce, a strong presence/reputation in the industry, and an exciting future for the corporation and its employees. Headquartered in Buffalo, NY, M&T Bank is a strong regional bank with branches in New York, Pennsylvania, Maryland, Virginia, Delaware, and Washington, DC. Its Management Development Program develops new managers. for the M&T of tomorrow. Over the course of an aggressive one-year training program, participants learn sales, accounting, project management, and leadership skills for opportunities in branch management, commercial lending, business banking, commercial real estate, marketing, technology & banking operations, human resources, risk management, and the M&T Investment Group.

NBA
nba.com

The NBA is a fully integrated global sports marketing and entertainment organization that utilizes broadcasting, sponsorships, new business ventures, special events, grassroots programs, public relations, community relations programs, and consumer products to reach fans around the world. The NBA League Office seeks highly talented individuals with a passion for developing a career in the sports entertainment industry. It offers internships and positions in administration, basketball operations, business development, finance, creative services, events and attractions, global merchandising, information technology, public relations, and several other fields.

Nokia Inc.
nokia.com

Nokia is the recognized world leader in mobile communications and the leading supplier of mobile phones and mobile fixed and IP networks. It employs more than 50,000 people in over 130 countries. With production facilities in 10 countries and research and development operations in 14 countries, Nokia is a broadly held company with listings on six major exchanges. In 2001, Nokia's sales totaled over $28 billion. Nokia is continuously staffed with the best people who come from a variety of backgrounds. Their strategy is to create an inclusive environment that benefits from diversity at all levels, values individual differences, and enables all employees to develop and contribute to their full potential while meeting work-life demands.

Northrop Grumman IT
northropgrummanit.com

Northrop Grumman's Information Technology sector is a premier provider of advanced information technology solutions, engineering and business services for government and commercial clients. Headquartered in Herndon, VA, in 2001 the sector had sales of nearly $4 billion and more than 22,000 employees worldwide. The Information Technology sector supports a wide range of information technology (IT) services for government, commercial and international customers. In the federal IT market, the sector is a leading provider of IT services to the Department of Defense (DoD) including such areas as battle management, mission planning, modeling and simulation, information assurance, software engineering, intelligence, surveillance, space systems, base and range support.

Northwestern Mutual Financial Network
careers.nmfn.com

The Northwestern Mutual Financial Network recruits Financial Representatives who offer clients a variety of world-class solutions and services from life insurance, disability income protection and education funding alternatives, to retirement, estate and business planning expertise. With 145 years of industry experience, the company has been voted the "Most Admired" company in the industry 18 times by *Fortune* magazine. It always receives the highest ratings from the four major rating services: Standard and Poor's (AAA); Moody's (AAA); Fitch (AAA); A.M. Best (A++). Their Financial Representatives were ranked the "Best Sales Force in the Industry" by *Sales & Marketing Management* magazine in the year 2000.

Nova Group USA
TeachinJapan.com

Operating in Japan since 1981, the Nova Group has revolutionized language study with its small, friendly classrooms and affordable programs. Offering exciting life experiences, the Nova Group "provides incomparable support, from initial preparation for departure, to transitional help upon arrival in Japan, to ongoing assistance throughout your time with us. You'll discover a proven teaching system that will challenge and reward you. You'll find our students energetic and eager to learn, our staff professional and helpful. And you'll also work in an active, culturally stimulating environment."

Owens Corning
owenscorning.com

Owens Corning is a world leader in systems solutions in composites, building material systems, and service businesses. Since pioneering the science of glass fiberization, it has become increasingly diversified, with sales from businesses serving the worldwide composites, home improvement, new construction and related markets. Headquartered in Toledo, OH, Owens Corning employs more than 20,000 employees in over 30 countries. It offers numerous entry-level professional opportunities for new graduates. Openings are most commonly found in Corporate Development, Customer Service, Engineering, Finance/Accounting, Human Resources, Information Systems, Internship Opportunities, Manufacturing Technology, Marketing and Sales, Pro-

curement, Production Management, Research and Development, and Supply Chain Management.

Peace Corps
peacecorps.gov

The opportunity to use your skills to benefit a developing country, to assist Volunteers, and to work with professionals make this "the toughest job you'll ever love." More than 6,000 Peace Corps Volunteers are supported by a staff of nearly 500 professionals headquartered in Washington, DC who provide program support, medical support, and administrative services. More than 100 employees operate 11 recruiting offices in the United States who identify new volunteers. Another 200 employees at overseas offices manage the volunteer programs in approximately 90 countries. The Peace Corps employs accountants, managers, administrative assistants, recruiters, computer programmers, overseas program directors, country directors, medical officers, and a variety of other professionals to staff its offices.

Pitney Bowes
Mailing Systems
pb.com

Pitney Bowes is about a lot more than postal machines for businesses. It's a global organization, managing change and positioning customers for both tactical and long-term success with innovative, cost-effective, end-to-end messaging solutions. These are exciting times at Pitney Bowes. The world of business communications is dramatically expanding, and it's creating a whole new world of opportunity. Businesses want integrated solutions for their increasingly complex messaging needs. With this company's unique knowledge of mail, facsimile, copier, software, financing and messaging overall, Pitney Bowes is singularly well positioned to respond – and to build its business – in a dramatic new ways.

PricewaterhouseCoopers LLP
pwcglobal.com

PricewaterhouseCoopers is the world's largest professional services organization.

It employs 120,000 people in more than 150 countries. It offers six lines of services and 22 industry-specialized practices. It helps clients anticipate business trends and solve complex business problems to measurably enhance their ability to build value, manage risk, and improve performance.

RadioShack
radioshackcorporation.com/careers/retail_ccc_rd.html

With over 7,000 stores and dealers offering a wide selection of consumer products, RadioShack Corporation is one of the nation's largest and most trusted consumer electronics retailers. It is estimated that 94 percent of Americans live or work within five minutes of a Radio Shack store. Their objective is to be the best company for high performing people who demonstrate RadioShack's core corporate values: teamwork, pride, trust and integrity. For information on job opportunities, visit the company website or call 1-800-THE-SHACK to locate the nearest hiring office in your area.

Rolls-Royce North America
rolls-royce.com/careers/northamerica

Rolls-Royce employs over 8,500 individuals in more than 65 locations within the U.S. and Canada, generating combined annual revenues in excess of $2 billion. The company is a leader in civil aerospace, defense, marine and energy markets. Its core gas turbine technology has created one of the broadest product ranges of aero engines in the world, with 55,000 engines in service in over 150 countries. Customers include more than 500 airlines, 2,400 corporate and utility operators and 160 armed forces. The company is investing in new products and capabilities for energy markets, which include the oil and gas industry and power generation, and new propulsion technologies to further enhance military capability and effectiveness.

SBC Communications, Inc.
collegejobs.sbc.com

SBC Communications, operating under the Southwestern Bell, Pacific Bell, Nevada Bell, Ameritech, SNET, SBC Telecom, and SBC Technology Resources brands, is one of the world's largest communications companies. It offers communications products and services including local and long distance telephone service, Internet access, high-tech network solutions, and data communications. Employing more than 230,000 people and invested is invested in several countries including China, Japan, Mexico, South Korea, France, South Africa, Switzerland, Israel, and Taiwan. SBC Communications ranks in the top 50 on the Fortune 500 list of America's largest corporations. For three consecutive years, *Fortune* magazine has recognized SBC as the "world's most admired telecommunications company." The company is looking for highly qualified professionals in Information technology, computer science, engineering, finance, marketing, and sales.

Seagate Technology
seagate.com

Seagate is a leading provider of storage technology for Internet, Business and Consumer Applications. Its products include disc drives for Enterprise applications, PCs and Consumer Electronics and Storage Area Network (SAN) solutions. Seagate's market leadership is based on delivering award-winning products, customer support and reliability to meet the world's growing demands for storage. Seagate offers excellent training programs and rewarding career opportunities for undergraduate and graduate students, as well as recent college graduates. For more information on Seagate, please visit sea gate.com/jobs/university.

Siemens-Westinghouse Power Corporation
siemenswestinghouse.com/jobs

Siemens-Westinghouse is an international technology-based company with headquarters in Orlando, Florida. It employs approximately 8,000 people who provide the world's most comprehensive offering of electrical products and services for industrial, commercial, and electric utility applications. The company is especially seeking entry-level candidates with the following majors: Mechanical Engineering, Mechanical Engineering

Technology, Electrical Engineering, Electrical Engineering Technology, Industrial Engineering, Metallurgy, Materials Science, Computer Science, Technical Sales and Marketing, and Supply Management/Logistics. Siemens-Westinghouse offers professional development programs to help new graduates gain valuable skills through a combination of classroom and on-the job training. See employee insights on pages 216-217.

Staples, Inc.
staples.com

Founded in 1986, Staples is an $11 billion retailer of office supplies, business services, furniture and technology to consumers and businesses from home-based businesses to Fortune 500 companies in North America and throughout Europe. Staples.com is the e-commerce business of Staples Inc. that sells office products and services online to businesses of all sizes. Staples offers very competitive benefits including: Casual Work Environment, Annual Stock Options, Annual Bonus Programs, "Work/Life" Initiatives, Staples University Training and Development Programs, Employee Discount Days, and much more. See employee insights on pages 215-216.

State Farm Insurance
statefarm.com

Founded in 1922, State Farm is one of the world's largest and most respected insurers. Since 1942, it has been the #1 auto insurer in the United States – protecting 38 million autos, or about one out of every five cars on the road. Over 16,300 State Farm agents have offices across the United States and Canada. State Farm also boasts more than 1,600 claim service offices as well as 27 regional offices, four insurance support centers, and four dedicated call centers. State Farm is a mutual company – no stockholders to pay. Their first and foremost obligation is to the 27 million households it protects. State Farm has received the highest possible ratings from AM Best, Standard & Poor's, Moody's, and other independent rating organizations that measure financial strength and stability.

Toyota Motor Sales, Inc.
toyota.com

Toyota Motor Sales, U.S.A (TMS) is the marketing, distribution, and sales/service organization for Toyota and Lexus in the United States, which is headquartered in Torrance, CA. The TMS team is comprised of highly accomplished individuals. They recruit students whose extracurricular achievements and scholastic records reflect drive and creativity. They seek those with natural leadership abilities, maturing management skills, and a passion for the automotive industry. "Our objective is to attract the top students from top colleges and universities across the country to assist us in our mission of being 'the most successful and respected car company in America'."

U.S. Air Force - Civilian Careers
www.afpc.randolph.af.mil/cp/recruit/paq.htm

The U.S. Air Force offers civilian employment opportunities for personal and professional growth in over 20 career fields including: Civil Engineering; Human Resources; Communications and Information; Criminal Investigation; Education Services; Family Matters; Financial Management; Historian; Intelligence; Logistics; Manpower; Museum; Public Affairs; Safety and Occupational Health Specialists and Safety Engineers; Scientist and Engineer; Security; Services (child development, youth, recreation, fitness/sports); and Training Instructors. All academic majors may apply. Send your resume to: Civilian Careers with the U.S. Air Force, HQ AFPC/DPKR, 550 E. Street West, Suite 1, Randolph AFB, TX 78150-4530, Phone: 1-800-558-1404, Fax: (210) 565-2565. See insights from three employees on pages 218-219.

U.S. Army (Morale, Welfare and Recreation)
armymwr.com

The U.S. Army's Morale, Welfare and Recreation (MWR) program supports active duty soldiers and their families through a worldwide system of services and activities. Its global network of nearly 34,000 civilian employees operates more than 50 adult and youth recreation programs as well as soldier and family services. MWR hires for a wide range of positions, including executive chefs, golf pros, childcare providers, marketing specialists, and financial managers. The NAF Management Trainee Program hires college graduates with degrees in certain MWR specialties (hospitality, hotel and restaurant management, marketing, HR/personnel, and recreation). The Management Trainee Program offers opportunities to develop a career in several disciplines. For more information of such opportunities, see the CampusCareerCenter website. See insights from two employees on page on pages 213-214.

U.S. Customs Service
customs.treas.gov

Do you want to make a positive difference in the life, security and economy of our nation? If your answer is yes, then consider an exciting career with the U.S. Customs Service. In addition to interdicting and seizing illegal drugs, Customs enforces more than 600 other provisions of law for at least 60 other U.S. agencies. These include statutes that affect the quality of life for every American, including environmental protection, wildlife preservation, safeguarding agriculture, public health, consumer safety and many others. The agency is a vital part of U.S. trade and commerce and an important conduit of revenue to the Treasury.

U.S. Secret Service
www.secretservice.gov

The Secret Service recruits highly qualified men and women who desire a fast paced, exciting, and challenging career. Headquartered in Washington, D.C., and with over 125 offices throughout the U.S. and abroad, the Secret Service is charged with the protection of the nation's leaders and criminal investigations. Its protective mission includes protection of the President and Vice President; their immediate families; former Presidents and their spouses; widows and minor children of former Presidents; major Presidential and Vice Presidential candidates and their spouses; and visiting foreign heads of state. Its investigative

responsibilities cover counterfeiting of currency and securities; forgery and altering of government checks and bonds; thefts and fraud relating to electronic funds transfer, financial access devices, identity, telecommunications, computer, telemarketing, and federally insured financial institutions.

Walt Disney World® Resort
wdwcollegeprogram.com

From world-famous Theme Parks and Resorts to award-winning feature films and Broadway productions, The Walt Disney Company is the world's leader in the entertainment and hospitality industries. The Walt Disney World® Resort is one of this company's major business units. Located on 47 square miles near Orlando, Florida – the most popular vacation spot in the world – the Resort offers 17 world-class hotels. It also features Downtown Disney; Disney's Wide World of Sports; the most well-rounded recreational facilities (golf, tennis, water sports) in the country; and complete convention and banquet facilities tailored for business and leisure groups. It offers a variety of internships through its Walt Disney World College Program. See employee insights on page 259.

Wells Fargo Financial
wellsfargofinancial.com

Wells Fargo Financial provides millions of customers with the financial resources to meet and manage their credit needs and to achieve their financial goals. Headquartered in Des Moines, Iowa, its 12,000 team members serve consumers, businesses and industries, and government entities through more than 1,300 stores and affiliated companies in the United States, Canada, Latin America, and the Pacific Islands. The company is part of the Fortune 100 Wells Fargo & Company, a $298 billion diversified financial services company that has its headquarters in San Francisco.

Indexes

Employers

A-E
ABC News, 217, 250
American Management Systems, 250
Aventis Pasteur, 219, 250
Black & Decker, 250
Boston Beer Company, 250
Boston Scientific Corporation, 220
Cargill, Inc., 219-220, 250
Christian Hospital, 250-251
Convergys Corporation, 215-216, 251
Crawford & Company, 251
Eckerd Youth Alternatives, 214-215, 251
Edward Jones, 251
Electonic Arts, 215, 251
ENSCO, Inc., 252
Enterprise Rent-A-Car, 252

F-J
Farmers Insurance, 252
GAF Materials Corporation, 219, 252
Gallup Organization, 217, 252
General Motors, 252-253
Genzyme Biosurgery, 253
Gillette Company, 253
Hannaford Brothers, 218, 253
Harris Corporation, 253
Hartford Life, 216, 253
Houston's Restaurants, Inc., 253-254
Internal Revenue Service, 215, 254
JCPenney, Inc., 254
Johnson & Johnson, 254
JP Morgan Chase, 254

L-P
Lexmark International, 254-255
M&T Bank Corporation, 255

NBA, 255
Nokia Inc., 255
Northrop Grumman IT, 255
Northwestern Mutual Financial Network, 255-256
Nova Group USA, 256
Owens Corning, 256
Peace Corps, 256
Pitney Bowes Mailing Systems, 256
PricewaterhouseCoopers LLP, 256-257

R-S
RadioShack, 257
Rolls-Royce North America, Inc., 257
SBC Communications, Inc., 257
Seagate Technology, 257
Siemens-Westinghouse Power Corporation, 216-217, 257-258
Staples, Inc., 215-216, 258
State Farm Insurance, 258

T-Y
Toyota Motor Sales, Inc., 258
U.S. Air Force – Civilian Careers, 218-219, 258
U.S. Army (MWR), 214, 258-259
U.S. Customs Service, 259
U.S. Secret Service, 259
Walt Disney World®, 218, 259
Wells Fargo Financial, 259

Subjects

A
Academic departments, 20
Accomplishments:
    statements, 42-43
    talking about, 34, 179
Achievements (see Accomplishments)

Approach letters (see Letters)
Assessment:
    books, 49-51
    centers, 25-26
    computerized, 48, 62
    online, 48-49, 62
    resources, 47-51
    tests, 57
Assistance:
    professional, 18-27
    resume writing, 26-27
    website, 20-21
Associations, 26, 91, 166

B
Behavior:
    changing, 212-213
    patterns, 8
    questions about, 181-182
    volatile, 14
Benefits, 35, 70, 206
Briefcase, 186

C
CampusCareerCenter.com, 8, 29-30,
    249-259
Career:
    advisors, 22
    check-up, 221-222
    conferences, 23
    fairs, 23
    planning, 5
Career services, 21-27
Classified ads, 101, 123-125
College:
    career centers, 18, 21-22
    experience, 1
Communities, 94-97
Contact information, 104
Cover letters:
    closing, 106-107
    handwritten, 107
    purpose of, 107
    sending, 106
Credentials file, 197

D
Dreams, 69

E
Education, 102
Employer profiles, 249-259
Employers:
    goals of, 70
    language of, 69-70
    letters to, 212
    needs of, 4, 35, 66-67
    network of, 249-259
Employment services, 24-25
Excuses, 13
Executive search firms, 24-25

Experience:
    accomplishments as, 37
    stating, 37

F
Federal government, 228-233
Fit, 8
Focus, 5, 84
Follow up:
    effective, 124
    methods, 109, 196
    resume, 108-109

G
Generations, 10-11
Goals:
    defining, 64
    employer-centered, 66-67
    manageable, 67-68
    setting, 72-82
Government:
    jobs, 227-233
    resources, 229-233

H
Habits, 8
Headhunters (see Executive search
    firms)
Hiring I.Q., 6–8, 92-93
Homepages, 111
Honesty, 157-158

I
Images, 99-100
Informational interviews (see Interviews)
Interests, 53-57
International:
    jobs, 239-248
    resources, 240-248
Internet:
    resources, 128-130, 165-167
    using, 97
Internships:
    acquiring, 27-29
    experiences, 28
    websites, 29
Interview:
    closing, 195-196
    communication, 183
    I.Q., 170-173
    job, 182-197
    knockouts, 173-181
    preparation, 184
    questions, 184-187
    stress, 169-170
Interviewing:
    mistakes, 173-181
    resources, 198-199
Interviews:
    closing, 179, 195-196
    conducting, 160-163

informational, 80, 149-151, 158-163
job, 169-199
resumes for, 100-101

J
Job:
    advancement, 222-225
    fairs, 23
    first, 11
    fit, 8, 11
    frustrations, 60
    keeping, 222-225
    leads, 163-164
    listings, 123, 126
    loss, 5
    revitalization, 225-226
Job markets:
    advertised, 145-146
    hidden, 123, 145-146, 150
Job search:
    assistance, 18-27
    clubs, 167
    failure, 13
    outdated, 11-12
    plan, 17-19
    proactive, 11-12
    quick, 5-6
    sequence, 14
    skills for, 4
    steps. 14-17
    support groups, 167
    updated, 12
Job seekers:
    mistakes of, 13-14
    self-centered, 70
Jobs:
    alternative, 87-89
    changing, 220-221, 225
    finding, 10
    government, 227-233
    hot, 65
    international, 239-248
    nonprofit, 233-239

L
Law enforcement jobs, 228-232
Letters:
    approach, 121-122, 159-160
    cover, 106-107
    distributing, 108
    examples of, 136-144
    importance of, 107
    job search, 107, 119-123
    reference, 197
    "T," 119-120
    thank-you, 122, 212
    types of, 121-122
    writing, 120-121
Likability, 194-195
Listening, 180
Locators, 167
Luck, 102

M
Marketing services, 25-26
Mailing lists, 166
Military locators, 167
Motivated skills and abilities, 34-52
Motivators, 35, 63

N
Negatives, 187-190
Networking:
    advice, 166
    books, 164-165
    importance of, 213
    Internet, 165-168
    relationships, 153
    savvy, 145-168
Networks:
    alumni, 167
    building, 152-154, 212
    linking, 155
    nurturing, 212
    women's, 166-167
Newspapers, 96
Nonprofit:
    jobs, 233-239
    resources, 233-239

O
Objections, 187-190
Objective:
    employer-centered, 66-67, 82-84
    formulating, 63-86
    future as, 62
    realistic, 67
    refining, 67
Office politics, 221

P
Performance:
    focus on, 36
Placement offices, 21-22
Procrastination, 4-5
Professional:
    assistance, 21-27
    associations, 26, 91
    certified career, 27
    resume writers, 26-27
Promotions, 224
Prospecting, 150,154-155
Public employment services, 23-24

Q
Qualifications, 125
Questions:
    answering, 184-192
    asking, 11, 92-94, 179-180, 193-194
    behavior-based, 191-192
    illegal, 193

R
Raises, 224

Recessions, 208
Recommendations (see References)
References, 197
Rejections, 156-157
Relocation, 96
Renegotiation, 206-207
Research:
   community-based, 94-97
   conducting, 87-98
   individuals, 91-93
   library, 79-80
   online, 78-79
   organizations, 89-91
Resources:
   career alternative, 87-89
   goal setting, 84-86
   government, 229-233
   international, 240-248
   interviewing, 198-199
   networking, 164-168
   nonprofit, 233-239
   online, 8
   resume, 126-131
   salary, 209-210
Resume:
   assistance, 129-130
   blasting, 130-131
   books, 126-129
   chronological, 115, 132
   combination, 115-116
   content, 102-104, 116-117
   copies, 105-106
   databases, 110
   distribution, 130-131
   do's, 118
   drafts, 117
   electronic, 126, 128
   evaluating, 118
   examples, 132-135
   functional, 115
   length, 103
   letters, 116
   mistakes, 111-114
   myths, 101-111
   objective on, 103
   paper, 119
   production, 104-106, 118-119
   rules, 117-118
   salary on, 103-104
   software, 128-129
   types, 114-116
   writers, 129-130
Resumes:
   defining, 100
   distributing, 108, 123, 130-131
   electronic, 109-110
   following up, 108-109
   printing, 118-119
   video, 110-111
   writing, 11, 99-118

S
Salary:
   dealing with, 180-181
   expectations, 103-104, 125, 208
   give-backs, 208
   negotiations, 200-210
   questions, 201-206
   resources, 209-210
   value, 208
Screening, 181-182
Self-transformation, 84-86
Skills:
   identifying, 37-49
   job search, 4
   motivated, 53
   transferable, 38-41
   work-content, 38
Storytelling, 35, 192-193, 213-220
Strangers, 34-35
Strengths, 53, 71-72
Students:
   assistance for, 3
   in transition, 2, 211
   job options for, 2
   skills of, 2, 4
Success:
   achieving, 10
   cramming for, 9
   prerequisites for, 30-33

T
Telephone, 125-126
Testing and assessment centers, 26
Tests, 38-39, 57, 73, 181-182
Timing, 207-208
Transition, 1-2

U
Usenet newsgroups, 165-166

V
Values, 57-62

W
Weaknesses, 188
Websites:
   business, 78-79, 90-91
   employment, 126
   government, 230-233
   international, 242-248
   interviewing, 199
   job search, 8-9
   nonprofit,
   salary, 210
   services of, 20-21
Women's centers, 23
Work experiences, 213-220

The Authors

FOR MORE THAN TWO DECADES RON AND CARYL KRAN-nich have pursued a passion – assisting hundreds of thousands of individuals, from students, the unemployed, and ex-offenders to military personnel, international job seekers, and CEOs, in making critical job and career transitions. Focusing on key job search skills, career changes, and employment fields, their impressive body of work has helped shape career thinking and behavior both in the United States and abroad. Their sound advice has changed numerous lives, including their own!

Ron and Caryl are two of America's leading career and travel writers who have authored more than 60 books. A former Peace Corps Volunteer and Fulbright Scholar, Ron received his Ph.D. in Political Science from Northern Illinois University. Caryl received her Ph.D. in Speech Communication from Penn State University. Together they operate Development Concepts Incorporated, a training, consulting, and publishing firm in Virginia.

The Krannichs are both former university professors, high school teachers, management trainers, and consultants. As trainers and consultants, they have completed numerous projects on management, career development, local government, population planning, and rural development in the United States and abroad. Their career books focus on key job search skills, military and civilian career transitions, government and international careers, travel jobs, and nonprofit organizations and include such classics as *High Impact Resumes and Letters*, *Interview for Success*, and *Change Your Job, Change Your Life*.

Their books represent one of today's most comprehensive collections of career writing. With over 2 million copies in print, their publications are widely available in bookstores, libraries, and career centers. No strangers to the world of Internet employment, they have written *America's Top Internet Job Sites* and *The Directory of Websites for International Jobs* and published several Internet recruitment and job search books. Ron served as the first Work Abroad Advisor to Monster.com. They also have developed several career-related websites: impactpublications.com, winningthejob.com, content forcareers.com, and veteransworld.com. Many of their career tips appear on such major websites as campuscareercenter.com, monster.com, careerbuilder. com, and employmentguide.com.

Ron and Caryl live a double life with travel being their best kept *"do what you love"* career secret. Authors of 19 travel-shopping guidebooks on various destinations around the world, they continue to pursue their international and travel interests through their innovative *Treasures and Pleasures of . . . Best of the Best* travel-shopping series and related websites: ishoparoundthe world.com and contentfortravel.com. When not found at their home and business in Virginia, they are probably somewhere in Europe, Asia, Africa, the Middle East, the South Pacific, or the Caribbean and South America following their other passion – researching and writing about quality arts and antiques as well as following the advice of their other Internet-related volume designed for road warriors and other travel types: *Travel Planning on the Internet: The Click and Easy™ Guide*. *"We follow the same career and life-changing advice we give to others – pursue a passion that enables you to do what you really love to do,"* say the Krannichs. Their passion is best represented on ishoparoundtheworld.com.

As both career and travel experts, the Krannichs' work is frequently featured in major newspapers, magazines, and newsletters as well as on radio, television, and the Internet. Available for interviews, consultation, and presentations, they can be contacted as follows:

Ron and Caryl Krannich
krannich@impactpublications.com

Career Resources

THE FOLLOWING CAREER RESOURCES ARE AVAILABLE directly from Impact Publications. Full descriptions of each title as well as nine downloadable catalogs, videos, and software can be found on our website: www.impactpublications.com. Complete the following form or list the titles, include shipping (see formula at the end), enclose payment, and send your order to:

IMPACT PUBLICATIONS
9104 Manassas Drive, Suite N
Manassas Park, VA 20111-5211 USA
1-800-361-1055 (orders only)
Tel. 703-361-7300 or Fax 703-335-9486
Email address: info@impactpublications.com
Quick & easy online ordering: www.impactpublications.com

Orders from individuals must be prepaid by check, money order, or major credit card. We accept telephone, fax, and email orders.

Qty.	TITLES	Price	TOTAL

Featured Title

Qty.	TITLES	Price	TOTAL
____	The Job Hunting Guide	$14.95	_____

College-to-Career Resources

Qty.	TITLES	Price	TOTAL
____	101 Best Resumes for Grads	11.95	_____
____	200 Best Jobs for College Graduates	16.95	_____
____	America's Top Jobs for College Graduates	15.95	_____
____	Best Jobs for the 21st Century for College Graduates	19.95	_____
____	Best Resumes for College Students and New Grads	12.95	_____
____	College Grad Job Hunter	14.95	_____
____	College Major Handbook	21.95	_____
____	College Majors and Careers	16.95	_____
____	College Majors Handbook	24.95	_____

_____ Complete Resume and Job Search Book for
College Students   12.95 _____
_____ Great Careers in Two Years   19.95 _____
_____ A Fork in the Road: A Career Planning Guide
for Young Adults   14.95 _____
_____ Gallery of Best Resumes for 2-Year Degree Graduates 18.95 _____
_____ Quick Guide to College Majors and Careers   16.95 _____
_____ Resumes for College Students and Recent Graduates 10.95 _____
_____ Ten Things I Wish I Knew Before Going Out
in the Real World   19.95 _____

Testing and Assessment

_____ Career Interests to Job Chart   19.95 _____
_____ Career Tests   12.95 _____
_____ Discover the Best Jobs for You   15.95 _____
_____ Discover What You're Best At   14.00 _____
_____ Do What You Are   18.95 _____
_____ Finding Your Perfect Work   16.95 _____
_____ Gifts Differing   16.95 _____
_____ I Could Do Anything If Only I Knew What It Was   13.95 _____
_____ I'm Not Crazy, I'm Just Not You   16.95 _____
_____ Making Vocational Choices   29.95 _____
_____ Now, Discover Your Strengths   27.00 _____
_____ Pathfinder   15.00 _____
_____ Please Understand Me II   15.95 _____
_____ TalentSort: The Career Decision Card Sort   29.95 _____
_____ What Type Am I?   14.95 _____
_____ What's Your Type of Career?   17.95 _____

Attitude and Motivation

_____ 100 Ways to Motivate Yourself   18.99 _____
_____ Change Your Attitude   15.99 _____
_____ Reinventing Yourself   18.99 _____

Inspiration and Empowerment

_____ 101 Secrets of Highly Effective Speakers   15.95 _____
_____ Do What You Love for the Rest of Your Life   24.95 _____
_____ Do What You Love, the Money Will Follow   13.95 _____
_____ Doing Work You Love   14.95 _____
_____ Eat That Frog!   19.95 _____
_____ Habit-Busting   13.00 _____
_____ Life Strategies   13.95 _____
_____ Maximum Success   24.95 _____
_____ Power of Purpose   20.00 _____
_____ Practical Dreamer's Handbook   13.95 _____
_____ Right Words at the Right Time   25.00 _____
_____ Self Matters   26.00 _____
_____ Seven Habits of Highly Effective People   14.00 _____
_____ Who Moved My Cheese?   19.95 _____

Career Exploration and Job Strategies

_____	25 Jobs That Have It All	12.95 _____
_____	50 Cutting Edge Jobs	15.95 _____
_____	95 Mistakes Job Seekers Make	13.95 _____
_____	100 Great Jobs and How to Get Them	17.95 _____
_____	101 Careers	16.95 _____
_____	101 Ways to Recession-Proof Your Career	14.95 _____
_____	Adams Jobs Almanac	16.95 _____
_____	Age Advantage	12.95 _____
_____	American Almanac of Jobs and Salaries	20.00 _____
_____	America's Top Jobs for People Without a Four-Year Degree	15.95 _____
_____	Back Door Guide to Short-Term Job Opportunities	21.95 _____
_____	Best Computer Jobs in America	18.95 _____
_____	Best Jobs for the 21st Century	19.95 _____
_____	Best Keywords for Resumes, Cover Letters, Interviews	17.95 _____
_____	Break the Rules	15.00 _____
_____	Career Change	14.95 _____
_____	Career Guide to Environmental Careers	17.95 _____
_____	Career Guide to Industries	16.95 _____
_____	Career Intelligence	15.95 _____
_____	Careers in Criminology	16.95 _____
_____	Change Your Job, Change Your Life (8th Edition)	17.95 _____
_____	Complete Idiot's Guide to Changing Careers	17.95 _____
_____	Cool Careers for Dummies	19.99 _____
_____	Dancing Naked	17.95 _____
_____	Directory of Executive Recruiters	47.95 _____
_____	Directory of Holland Occupational Codes	54.00 _____
_____	Enhanced Guide for Occupational Exploration	34.95 _____
_____	Enhanced Occupational Outlook Handbook	37.95 _____
_____	Five Secrets to Finding a Job	12.95 _____
_____	Health-Care Careers for the 21st Century	24.95 _____
_____	Help! Was That a Career Limiting Move?	10.95 _____
_____	High-Tech Careers for Low-Tech People	14.95 _____
_____	How to Be a Permanent Temp	12.95 _____
_____	How to Be a Star at Work	12.00 _____
_____	How to Get a Job and Keep It	16.95 _____
_____	How to Succeed Without a Career Path	13.95 _____
_____	Insider's Guide to Finding the Perfect Job	14.95 _____
_____	Internships	26.95 _____
_____	Is It Too Late to Run Away and Join the Circus?	16.95 _____
_____	Job Search Handbook for People With Disabilities	16.95 _____
_____	Job Smarts	16.95 _____
_____	JobBank Guide to Computer and High-Tech Jobs	17.95 _____
_____	Knock 'Em Dead	12.95 _____
_____	Me, Myself, and I, Inc.	17.95 _____
_____	No One Is Unemployable	29.95 _____
_____	No One Will Hire Me!	13.95 _____
_____	Occupational Outlook Handbook	16.95 _____
_____	O*NET Dictionary of Occupational Titles	39.95 _____
_____	The Portable Executive	12.00 _____

____	The Professional's Job Finder	18.95	____
____	Quit Your Job and Grow Some Hair	15.95	____
____	Rites of Passage at $100,000 to $1 Million+	29.95	____
____	Sunshine Jobs	16.95	____
____	Switching Careers	17.95	____
____	What Color Is Your Parachute?	17.95	____

Internet Job Search

____	100 Top Internet Job Sites	12.95	____
____	Adams Internet Job Search Almanac	10.95	____
____	America's Top Internet Job Sites	19.95	____
____	CareerXroads (annual)	26.95	____
____	Career Exploration On the Internet	24.95	____
____	Cyberspace Job Search Kit	18.95	____
____	Directory of Websites for International Jobs	19.95	____
____	e-Resumes	11.95	____
____	Electronic Resumes and Online Networking	13.99	____
____	Everything Online Job Search Book	12.95	____
____	Guide to Internet Job Searching	14.95	____
____	Haldane's Best Employment Websites for Professionals	15.95	____
____	Job-Hunting On the Internet	9.95	____
____	Job Search Online for Dummies (with CD-ROM)	24.99	____

Resumes and Letters

____	101 Best .Com Resumes and Letters	11.95	____
____	101 Best Cover Letters	11.95	____
____	101 Best Resumes	10.95	____
____	101 Great Resumes	9.99	____
____	101 More Best Resumes	11.95	____
____	101 Great Tips for a Dynamite Resume	13.95	____
____	175 High-Impact Cover Letters	14.95	____
____	175 High-Impact Resumes	14.95	____
____	201 Dynamite Job Search Letters	19.95	____
____	201 Killer Cover Letters	16.95	____
____	$100,000 Resumes	16.95	____
____	Adams Resume Almanac, with Disk	19.95	____
____	America's Top Resumes for America's Top Jobs	19.95	____
____	Asher's Bible of Executive Resumes	29.95	____
____	Best Resumes and CVs for International Jobs	24.95	____
____	Best Resumes for $100,000+ Jobs	24.95	____
____	Best Resumes for $75,000+ Executive Jobs	15.95	____
____	Best Cover Letters for $100,000+ Jobs	24.95	____
____	Big Red Book of Resumes	16.95	____
____	Building a Great Resume	15.00	____
____	Building Your Career Portfolio	13.99	____
____	Cover Letter Magic	16.95	____
____	Cover Letters for Dummies	16.99	____
____	Cover Letters That Knock 'Em Dead	10.95	____
____	Cyberspace Resume Kit	18.95	____

_____	Dynamite Cover Letters	14.95 _____
_____	Dynamite Resumes	14.95 _____
_____	e-Resumes	11.95 _____
_____	Electronic Resumes and Online Networking	13.99 _____
_____	Everything Cover Letter Book	12.95 _____
_____	Everything Resume Book	12.95 _____
_____	Expert Resumes for Computer and Web Jobs	16.95 _____
_____	Federal Resume Guidebook	21.95 _____
_____	Gallery of Best Cover Letters	18.95 _____
_____	Gallery of Best Resumes	18.95 _____
_____	Global Resume and CV Guide	17.95 _____
_____	Haldane's Best Cover Letters for Professionals	15.95 _____
_____	Haldane's Best Resumes for Professionals	15.95 _____
_____	High Impact Resumes and Letters (8th Edition)	19.95 _____
_____	Insider's Guide to Writing the Perfect Resume	14.95 _____
_____	Internet Resumes	14.95 _____
_____	Military Resumes and Cover Letters	19.95 _____
_____	Overnight Resume	12.95 _____
_____	Power Resumes	12.95 _____
_____	Professional Resumes for Executives, Managers, & Other Administrators	19.95 _____
_____	Professional Resumes for Accounting, Tax, Finance, and Law	19.95 _____
_____	Proven Resumes	19.95 _____
_____	Resume Catalog	15.95 _____
_____	Resume Kit	14.95 _____
_____	Resume Magic	18.95 _____
_____	Resume Shortcuts	14.95 _____
_____	Resumes for Dummies	16.99 _____
_____	Resumes for the Health Care Professional	14.95 _____
_____	Resumes in Cyberspace	14.95 _____
_____	Resumes That Knock 'Em Dead	12.95 _____
_____	The Savvy Resume Writer	12.95 _____
_____	Sure-Hire Resumes	14.95 _____

Networking

_____	Connecting With Success	20.95 _____
_____	Dynamite Telesearch	12.95 _____
_____	A Foot in the Door	14.95 _____
_____	Golden Rule of Schmoozing	12.95 _____
_____	Great Connections	11.95 _____
_____	How to Work a Room	14.00 _____
_____	Make Your Contacts Count	14.95 _____
_____	Masters of Networking	16.95 _____
_____	Networking for Everyone	16.95 _____
_____	Networking Smart	22.95 _____
_____	Power Networking	14.95 _____
_____	Power Schmoozing	12.95 _____
_____	Power to Get In	14.95 _____
_____	The Savvy Networker	13.95 _____
_____	The Secrets of Savvy Networking	13.99 _____

Dress, Image, and Etiquette

____ Dressing Smart for Men	14.95	_____
____ Dressing Smart for Women	14.95	_____
____ Dressing Smart for the New Millennium	15.95	_____
____ First Five Minutes	14.95	_____
____ New Professional Image	12.95	_____
____ New Women's Dress for Success	13.99	_____
____ Power Etiquette	15.95	_____
____ Professional Impressions	14.95	_____

Interviews

____ 101 Dynamite Answers to Interview Questions	12.95	_____
____ 101 Dynamite Questions to Ask At Your Job Interview	13.95	_____
____ 101 Great Answers to the Toughest Interview Questions	11.99	_____
____ Behavior-Based Interviewing	12.95	_____
____ Best Answers to the 201 Most Frequently Asked Questions	11.95	_____
____ Great Interview	12.95	_____
____ Haldane's Best Answers to Tough Interview Questions	15.95	_____
____ Interview for Success (8th Edition)	15.95	_____
____ Interview Power	14.95	_____
____ Interview Rehearsal Book	12.00	_____
____ Job Interviews for Dummies	16.99	_____
____ Power Interviews	15.95	_____
____ The Savvy Interviewer	10.95	_____
____ Sweaty Palms	12.95	_____
____ Winning Interviews for $100,000+ Jobs	17.95	_____

Salary Negotiations

____ 101 Salary Secrets	12.95	_____
____ Better Than Money	18.95	_____
____ Dynamite Salary Negotiations	15.95	_____
____ Get a Raise in 7 Days	14.95	_____
____ Get More Money On Your Next Job	17.95	_____
____ Get Paid More and Promoted Faster	19.95	_____
____ Haldane's Best Salary Tips for Professionals	15.95	_____
____ Negotiating Your Salary	12.95	_____

Government and Nonprofit Jobs

____ Complete Guide to Public Employment	19.95	_____
____ Directory of Federal Jobs and Employers	21.95	_____
____ Education Job Finder	18.95	_____
____ Federal Applications That Get Results	23.95	_____
____ Federal Employment From A to Z	14.50	_____
____ Federal Jobs in Law Enforcement	14.95	_____
____ FBI Careers	18.95	_____

_____ Find a Federal Job Fast!	15.95	_____
_____ From Making a Profit to Making a Difference	16.95	_____
_____ Government Job Finder	18.95	_____
_____ Jobs and Careers With Nonprofit Organizations	17.95	_____
_____ Nonprofits Job Finder	18.95	_____
_____ Ten Steps to a Federal Job	39.95	_____

International and Travel Jobs

_____ Back Door Guide to Short-Term Job Adventures	21.95	_____
_____ Best Resumes and CVs for International Jobs	24.95	_____
_____ Careers in International Affairs	17.95	_____
_____ Careers in Travel, Tourism, and Hospitality	19.95	_____
_____ Career Opportunities in Travel and Tourism	18.95	_____
_____ Directory of Jobs and Careers Abroad	16.95	_____
_____ Directory of Websites for International Jobs	19.95	_____
_____ Flight Attendant Job Finder and Career Guide	16.95	_____
_____ Global Citizen	16.95	_____
_____ Global Resume and CV Guide	17.95	_____
_____ How to Get a Job in Europe	21.95	_____
_____ How to Get a Job With a Cruise Line	16.95	_____
_____ How to Live Your Dream of Volunteering Overseas	17.00	_____
_____ Inside Secrets to Finding a Career in Travel	14.95	_____
_____ International Jobs	18.00	_____
_____ International Job Finder	19.95	_____
_____ Jobs for Travel Lovers	17.95	_____
_____ Living, Studying, and Working in Italy	17.00	_____
_____ Overseas Summer Jobs	17.95	_____
_____ So, You Want to Join the Peace Corps	12.95	_____
_____ Study Abroad	29.95	_____
_____ Summer Study Abroad	15.95	_____
_____ Teaching English Abroad	15.95	_____
_____ Teaching English Overseas	19.95	_____
_____ Work Abroad	15.95	_____
_____ Working Abroad	14.95	_____
_____ Work Your Way Around the World	17.95	_____

Career Counselors

_____ Career Counselor's Handbook	17.95	_____
_____ Handbook of Career Counseling Theory	69.95	_____

Directories

_____ Almanac of American Employers	199.99	_____
_____ Almanac of American Employers Mid-Sized Firms	179.99	_____
_____ American Salaries and Wages Survey	175.00	_____
_____ Career Guide to Industries	16.95	_____
_____ Directory of Executive Recruiters	47.95	_____
_____ Directory of Holland Occupational Codes	54.00	_____
_____ Encyclopedia of Associations	575.00	_____
_____ Enhanced Guide for Occupational Exploration	34.95	_____

_____	Enhanced Occupational Outlook Handbook	37.95 _____
_____	Headquarters USA	175.00 _____
_____	Job Hunter's Sourcebook	115.00 _____
_____	National Job Bank	450.00 _____
_____	Occupational Outlook Handbook	16.95 _____
_____	O*NET Directory of Occupational Titles	39.95 _____
_____	Professional Careers Sourcebook	125.00 _____
_____	Scholarships, Fellowships, and Loans	199.00 _____
_____	Vocational Careers Sourcebook	115.00 _____
_____	Worldwide College Scholarship Directory	23.99 _____
_____	Worldwide Graduate Scholarship Directory	26.99 _____

SUBTOTAL _____

Virginia residents add 4½% sales tax _____

POSTAGE/HANDLING ($5 for first
product and 8% of SUBTOTAL) $5.00

8% of SUBTOTAL -- _____

TOTAL ENCLOSED ------------------------- _____

SHIP TO:

NAME _____

ADDRESS _____

_____

_____

PAYMENT METHOD:

❑ I enclose check/money order for $ _____ made payable to
    IMPACT PUBLICATIONS.

❑ Please charge $ _____ to my credit card:
    ❑ Visa   ❑ MasterCard   ❑ American Express   ❑ Discover

    Card # _____ Expiration date: _____/_____

    Signature _____